Children, Childhood, and Everyday Life

Children's Perspectives

Children, Childhood, and Everyday Life

Children's Perspectives

edited by

Mariane Hedegaard
Copenhagen University

Karin Aronsson
Stockholm University

Charlotte Højholt
Roskilde University

Oddbjørg Skjær Ulvik
Oslo and Akershus University College

INFORMATION AGE PUBLISHING, INC.
Charlotte, NC • www.infoagepub.com

Library of Congress Cataloging-in-Publication Data

Children, childhood, and everyday life : children's perspective / edited by
Mariane Hedegaard ... [et al.].
    p. cm.
Includes bibliographical references.
ISBN 978-1-61735-734-3 (pbk.) – ISBN 978-1-61735-735-0 (hardcover) –
ISBN 978-1-61735-736-7 (ebook)
1. Child development. 2. Perception in children. 3. Socialization. I.
Hedegaard, Mariane.
HQ767.9.C4497 2012
305.231–dc23

                                                                      2011052453

CONTENTS

SECTION I

DEVELOPMENT, CHANGE, AND CHILDREN'S PERSPECTIVES ON SOCIAL LIFE

SECTION II

FAMILY LIFE PRACTICES AS AN ARENA FOR NEGOTIATIONS AND INFORMAL LEARNING

SECTION III

SCHOOLS AS SOCIAL ARENAS

INTRODUCTION

Mariane Hedegaard, Karin Aronsson, Charlotte Højholt and Oddbjørg Skjær Ulvik

Children live their lives, learn, and develop through participation in various social settings, including homes, kindergartens, schools, and different kinds of institutions. Children live their lives across very different places and take part in activities in social communities like families, peer groups, classrooms, and day care institutions.

But developmental psychology at large has presented decontextualized models of child development, featuring an ahistorical and "general" child (Burman, 2008; James, Jenks, & Prout, 1997). One of today's research challenges is to present empirical studies of child development that involve studies of children and children's development, situated across different social settings and activities. Our aim with the different studies in this book is to present a broad view of children's life trajectories and development as they participate in everyday activities, but also as a process that includes biological, cultural and historical transformations. This includes the child's positions in everyday institutional practices (family, child care, school) and the child's motives and how he or she experiences social demands in different situations.

This collection illustrates different ways of dealing with varying social contexts and focuses on questions about children's world-making, anchored in children's daily lives that are lived together with other persons in different societal arrangements for the upbringing of children. Moreover, it explicitly focuses on children's own perspectives.

Inspired by Vygotsky's (1998) theory of development, as well as childhood sociology and discursive analyses, we see such an approach as both an empirical and theoretical approach to the study of *children, childhood, and everyday life*. One of our aims is to problematize *time, change, continuity, developmental trajectories,* and *transitions* in order to identify novel ways of discussing different trajectories through childhood and youth, that is "development." The relation between social demands and the child's motives constitutes an important dynamic factor leading to psychological changes. In line with Vygotsky's work and the cultural-historical tradition of psychology, the child's development has to be seen as trajectories through institutional practices that at every point can be localized in relation to the child's social situation (Elkonin, 1999; Hedegaard, 2009; Rogoff, 2003; Valsiner, 1997; Vygotsky, 1998). This implies a perspective of development that offers possibilities to investigate children's agency, that is, how children meet demands and engage in activities, and how they thereby also contribute to their own development and life courses.

The authors of this book share these theoretical as well as analytical ambitions in their work on children's social participation in institutional practices. Our shared interest in the lives of children and children's social settings can be seen as a way of working with situated analyses of children as active agents in their own lives in specific social contexts, e.g., home, school, and "special" homes, such as foster homes. Within theories on childhood and childhood sociology, there has been a focus on children's agency (Corsaro, 2005; James et al., 1997; Prout, 2005). As yet, though, there has not appeared much work that empirically shows in what ways children are actors in their own lives, and there is a need for empirical work that show in what ways children are actors in their own lives. Recent work on everyday negotiations shows some ways in which children and adults engage in negotiations that at times involve elements of *mutual apprenticeship* (Aronsson & Cekaite, 2011; Aronsson & Gottzén, 2011; Kousholt, 2008; Pontecorvo, Fasulo, & Sterponi, 2001; Rogoff, 2003). Such analyses are in turn related to contemporary theorising on participation (Goodwin, 2006; Hedegaard, 2002; Højholt, 1999; Lave & Wenger, 1991; Rogoff, 1990). Participation is a central issue in several of these chapters, and it is, in its turn, related to participants' positionings of themselves and others (Aronsson & Gottzén, 2011; Bourdieu, 1984; Davies & Harré, 1990; Goffman, 1981), with respect to, for instance, social age.

One of the basic ambitions of this volume is to transcend the dichotomy between what is labeled the "common" and the "uncommon," or the "ordinary" and the "extraordinary." Social practices for children that are defined as "different," "extraordinary," or "special" in one or another respect may serve as analytical points of departure for discerning developmental conditions and children's perspectives.

CONTENT

In their research, the authors of this book have all been engaged in situated studies of *children's perspectives*, anchored in everyday activities and social settings, as the core in research on children's social lives and development. Children's perspectives involve *children's experiences*. When the notion of children's perspectives is used in this way, an important goal is to explore individual children's life-worlds and subjective meaning-making (Bruner, 1990). The empirical source of knowledge creation would then be the children themselves, and the documentation of children's experiences and their understanding of the interaction in which they are involved in their social life worlds. Children's perspectives may also involve exploration and analyses of children's life conditions, and children's social participation under different social conditions (Hedegaard & Fleer, 2008). This means that empirical sources do not have to be limited to the children themselves but could also include the perspectives of peers and adults with whom the children in question interact. Moreover, children's perspectives can be identified as *participants' perspectives*, that is, through the ways that children take part in social activities, as seen through how they orient to their co-participants (cf. Edwards, 1997; Goodwin, 2006; Potter, 1996), and how the co-participants orient to them. One aspect of such participation is, of course, to what extent children can be seen to engage with adults in negotiations that concern their own interests (Beck, 1997).

A theoretical focus on children's perspectives and situated practices obviously has implications for the methodological choices. Developmental narratives, video ethnographies, participatory observations, life mode interviews, and other novel methods for analyzing children's life trajectories form part of the methods used for exploring children's lives.

Within medical research, case study presentations have traditionally been important in tracing the roots of both illness and recovery trajectories. This volume offers a number of *case studies* of children's life experiences, beyond the normative restrictions of a clinical gaze or clinical analyses. The present authors all strive toward capturing *emic* perspectives on children's life stories, that is, the participants' own conceptualizations of what are fortunate or misfortunate life experiences. However, the authors contributing to this book work within different disciplinary fields of child research, and with different methodological approaches.

Observations across a series of settings in children's daily lives have drawn our attention to children's involvement in each others' lives and how their attention is recurrently oriented to classmates and towards being part of shared communities. Learning and cognition cannot be isolated from affective and social alignments. As discussed by Charlotte Højholt (in our final chapter; see also 2008) communities of learning always involve *commu-*

nities of learners. In institutional settings, children recurrently get engaged in social dilemmas as they seek to participate in relevant communities and to be acknowledged there. More than anything, our efforts to explore children's perspectives have turned our attention toward children's participation in communities of learners. Everyday learning practices routinely involve persons-in-practices, and phenomena such as inclusion/excluson, local hierarchies, and identity work.

The collection tries to integrate conceptions of child development and childhood with cultural-historical and discursive approaches to research on children's perspectives. Although it contributes to theoretical analyses, it also offers rich, empirically based descriptions, so that its broader usefulness will be immediately apparent to those who are tackling practical problems or are preparing to do so in child development courses, childhood studies, and similar courses. The analyses draw on empirical data from diverse social contexts in their problem formulations, and therefore the book may be of interest to a broad range of professionals as well as research students.

DISPOSITION

The book is organized into three sections. The first section focuses on children's perspectives on development, change, and social life. The second section focuses on family life as an arena for negotiations and informal learning. A third section focuses on schools as social arenas: Everyday life practices in "ordinary" and special school settings.

The authors of the chapters in Section I ("Development, Change, and Children's Perspectives on Social Life") are concerned with children's own conceptualizations of the process of growing up. On the basis of children's participation in everyday life activities, these chapters document children's own perspectives, analyzing how children learn and contribute to the conditions of their own development. It is argued that children's social interactions influence their life-worlds and social identities. An overall aim is to firmly situate children's learning and development within their daily life activities, anchoring these in cultural and historical events. In Chapter 1, Liv Mette Guldbrandsen (see also 2003) analyzes the process of children's development as children's active meaning-making and characterizes this as a pendulum movement where the past and present, as well as the children's projected future prospects, are included in continuous and ongoing processes of interpretation and reinterpretation within different social arenas in everyday life. At any moment past, present, and anticipated experiences are processed into stories, creating spaces for self-and-other constructions. In Chapter 2, Ruth Toverud problematizes individualism, collectivities, and young persons' meaning making of themselves in relation to their appropriation of norms for being of use and being oneself. Pernille Hviid, in Chapter 3, discusses concepts of time, change, and place on the basis of a young girl's own experience of her development over time.

In Section II ("Family Life Practices as an Arena for Negotiations and Formal Learning), the chapters focus on family life. Children, as well as parents, are analyzed as active agents, with developmental goals and strategies in everyday life practices. Children are thus seen as partners in negotiating generational relationships. Their active contributions to their families' care practice and family politics are highlighted in analyses, where the focus is on everyday practices and ways in which such practices are culturally situated in relation to, for instance, conflicting demands from school and work, available time, and contemporary consumption patterns. In Chapter 4, Mariane Hedegaard focuses on the different types of demands that both children and parents put on each other, and on how children's creative modeling of conflict resolutions is central in their learning and development within family life. In Chapter 5, Karin Aronsson analyzes time negotiations, and more specifically how time is situated and co-construed within family life micropolitics, illuminating how parents' and children's divergent take on time regulates various activities and family life spheres. In Chapter 6, Lucas Gottzén problematizes responsible consumption in his analyses of children's consumption patterns, showing how children and parents alike might be seen as consumers "in becoming."

In Chapter 7, Oddbjørg Skjær Ulvik analyzes narratives, drawing on everyday life practices in foster families, discussing constructions of a modern, autonomous, and "culturally adequate child." Moreover, she shows ways in which foster parents adopt corrective practices in order to attain such an overarching developmental goal. In Chapter 8, Dorte Kousholt addresses dilemmas in monitoring professional assistance to families who are defined as having special problems. In a problematization of the normal/special divide, she invokes material factors and knowledge about general dilemmas in children's and families' everyday lives.

The chapters in Section III ("Schools as Social Arenas") focus on everyday school practices and children's engagements in communities of children inside and outside of classroom contexts. Again, both "ordinary" and special settings are discussed. Within the school as a social arena, inclusion and exclusion may take place both informally among classmates and formally by authorities removing a child. A large number of children are, for different reasons, taken out of school for various periods of their school life, and this has inspired a focus on strategies for promoting inclusion in school settings. Still, the paradox of inclusion seems to be that children are excluded with the ultimate purpose of becoming included. Some children are offered fairly comprehensive professional arrangements for supporting children who are encountering difficulties; this may include intellectual, behavioral, or neuro-developmental disorders.

In Chapter 9, Maja Røn Larsen focuses on children in the transition between public schools and special education systems, spelling out para-doxical exclusion practices, that is, the apparent contradiction between ambitions of inclusion and practices of exclusion in special education. In Chapter 10, Louise Bøttcher invokes the theoretical perspective of cogni-tion in practice in order to understand children with disabilities and how their learning and development is situated in relation to both situational and individual factors. As part of her analyses, she criticizes "impaired prac-tices" for children with communicative impairment.

Children's friendships from their own perspectives are the theme of Ditte Winther-Lindqvist's contribution in Chapter 11. This chapter analyzes the identity work that children engage in during their school transition be-tween 6th and 7th grade. The children are shown to struggle to become ac-cepted in a hierarchical classroom context, structured around a popularity axis from high to low, in order not to risk exclusion by their classmates, and friendship formation is foregrounded as a crucial aspect of classroom life.

One of the ambitions of this volume is to illuminate learning as a lived enterprise. In Chapter 12, Charlotte Højholt (see also 2008) points out that children should be seen as central for each other's learning in the classroom. Her research shows that at school, children are not only ori-ented to school tasks, but to each other. Children are concerned about each other, and they jointly enter novel learning tasks and seem concerned about where to belong or not to belong. Communities of learning (Lave & Wenger, 1991) in school settings in fact also involve *communities of learners,* that is, persons with social goals and agendas. Yet, at large, professional support almost exclusively focuses on special, individual, and isolated func-tions and overlooks the crucial social challenges in children's everyday lives where they live together with each other across different social settings.

REFERENCES

Aronsson, K., & Cekaite, A. (2011). Activity contracts and directives in everyday fam-ily politics. *Discourse & Society, 22,* 137–154.

Aronsson, K., & Gottzén, L. (2011). Generational positions at family dinner: Food morality and social order. *Language in Society, 40,* 1–22.

Beck, U. (1997). Democratization of the family. *Childhood, 4,* 151–166

Bourdieu, P. (1984). *Distinction: A social critique of the judgment of taste* (R. Nice, Trans.). Cambridge, MA: Harvard University Press. (Original work published 1979).

Bruner, J. (1990). *Acts of meaning.* Cambridge, MA: Harvard University Press.

Burman, E. (2008). *Deconstructing developmental psychology.* London: Routledge. (First published 1994)

Corsaro, W. (2005). *The sociology of childhood.* Thousand Oakes, CA: Pin Forge Press.

Davies, B., & Harré, R. (1990). Positioning: The discursive production of selves. *Journal for the Theory of Social Behavior, 20,* 43–63.

Edwards, D. (1997). *Discourse and cognition.* London, UK: Sage.

Elkonin, D. B. (1999). Towards the problem of stages in the mental development of children. *Journal of Russian and East European psychology, 37,* 11–29

Goffman, E. (1981). *Forms of talk.* Oxford: Blackwell.

Goodwin, M. H. (2006). Participation, affect, and trajectory in family directive/response sequences. *Text & Talk, 26,* 515–544.

Guldbrandsen, M. (2003). Peer relations as arenas for gender constructions among young teenagers. *Pedagogy, Culture and Society, 11,* 113–132.

Hedegaard, M. (2002). *Learning and child development.* Aarhus, Denmark: Aarhus University Press.

Hedegaard, M., & Fleer, M. (2008). *Studying children: A cultural-historical approach.* New York, NY: Open University Press.

Højholt, C. (1999). Child development in trajectories of social practice. In W. Maiers, B. Bayer, & E. B. Duarte (Eds.), *Challenges to theoretical psychology.* North York, UK: Captus Press.

Højholt, C. (2008). Participation in communities: Living and learning across different contexts. *Australian Research in Early Childhood Education. 15,* 1–12.

James, A., Jenks, C., & Prout, A. (1999). *Theorizing childhood.* Cambridge, UK: Polity Press.

Lave, J., & E. Wenger (1991). *Situated learning: Legitimate peripheral participation.* New York, NY: Cambridge University Press.

Pontecorvo, C., Fasulo, A., & Sterponi, L. (2001). Mutual apprentices: The making of parenthood and childhood in family dinner conversations. *Human Development 44,* 340–361.

Potter, J. (1996). *Representing reality: Discourse, rhetoric and social construction.* London, UK. Sage:

Prout, J. (2005). *The future of childhood: Toward the interdisciplinary study of children.* London, UK: Routledge Falmer

Rogoff, B. (1990). *Apprenticeship in thinking: Cognitive development in social context.* Oxford: Oxford University Press.

Rogoff, B. (2003). *The cultural nature of human development.* Oxford: Oxford University Press.

Valsiner, J. (1997). *Culture and the development of children's actions.* Hoboken, NJ: John Wiley.

Vygotsky, L. S. (1998). *The collected works of L.S. Vygotsky. Volume 5. Child psychology.* New York, NY: Plenum Press.

SECTION I

DEVELOPMENT, CHANGE, AND CHILDREN'S
PERSPECTIVES ON SOCIAL LIFE

CHAPTER 1

BEING A CHILD, COMING OF AGE

Exploring Processes of Growing Up

Liv Mette Gulbrandsen

INTRODUCTION

As a developing person, the child attends in various ways to processes of continuity and change in her self- and other-making efforts.[1] Based on a longitudinal study of a group of children during their early teenage years[2] (Gulbrandsen, 2003; Haavind, 2007; Hauge, 2009), this chapter explores aspects of what we might call children's self- and other-constructing processes. These processes are both constituted by and constitute in themselves the actions and interactions of everyday life. The idea that "self- and other-constructing processes" make a significant contribution to psychological development is a working premise in a range of theories commonly subsumed under the umbrella of cultural psychology (Bronfenbrenner 1979, 2005; Bruner, 1990; Cole, 1996; Mead, 1934; Rogoff, 2003; Wertsch, 1991). It has guided the methodological formulation of the project presented here, and it also dominates the analyses in this chapter.

Children, Childhood, and Everyday Life, pages 3–19
Copyright © 2012 by Information Age Publishing
All rights of reproduction in any form reserved.

Studying children in a late modern society as developing persons one needs to consider an adequate methodology. Methodology concerns the interrelations between the various levels of a scientific enterprise; how do (meta-) theoretical levels guide the ways of constructing the research questions, and thus the choices of relevant methodical procedures for production as well as for analyses of data? And how are *results* connected with both the initial assumptions *and* the involved research practices?

A short theoretical opening will be followed by the chapter's methodological oriented main section. Two empirical cases will be used to exemplify crucial methodological points and methodical procedures.

THE THEORETICAL POINT OF ENTRY

> The construction of basic knowledge in the social sciences does not depend upon the sophistication of the analytic *techniques* in the treatment of the phenomena. Rather it depends on the *general strategies* for *where to look, which comparisons to make,* and *what to assume* about the phenomena *before* actual analytic techniques are put into use. (Valsiner, 2007, p. 363)

Valsiner (2007) points to the researcher's "basic axiomatic understanding of the world" (p. 364) as well as her or his theoretical platform as the foundation that directs the analytic attention and makes specific analytical strategies fruitful. The theoretical understanding underpinning the study that offers the empirical examples in this chapter will be shortly presented guiding the reader "where to look."

Psychological theories of development constitute one aspect of (late-) modern, Western cultural ideas concerning a child's coming of age. Over the course of time, theoretical currents fertilize folk theories of development (and vice versa), and both adults and children appropriate ways of understanding themselves and each other that derive from social sciences such as psychology, pedagogy, and sociology. We are all part of a folk psychological community of meaning consumers and makers (Bruner, 1990). This does not mean that psychology holds a hegemonic, cultural position, but that mainstream psychological logic essentially concurs with widespread Western ideas of growing up in our time.

Mainstream theories concerning psychological development have usually viewed the concept as a kind of inner, stable core that functions as a personal "engine" with a built-in GPS system indicating the correct route to maturity. Although this description may be overly brief and, perhaps, biased, there are good reasons why critical psychologists reject the notion of development altogether (Burman, 2008; Morss, 1996; Walkerdine, 1993). This critique also forms one of the constitutive elements of the contemporary tradition of sociology of childhood, with its insistence on childhood (and the persons populating this phase of life) as interesting and worth researching in itself (Jenks, 1982; James, Jenks, & Prout, 1998). Traditional developmental psychologies are seen as more focused on children as *becoming* than on children as *being*. The being/becoming distinction does, however, carry crucial challenges—among others that it may derive the child's (or any other person's) present being from its past experiences as well as from its future anticipations.

Like most scholars who identify with traditions categorized under the umbrella of cultural psychology, this author finds it problematic and restricting to treat children and childhood as phenomena isolated from any past or future existence. Every phase of life is embedded in—and gains meaning from—both past events and anticipated events in the future. Longitudinal studies have the advantage of following persons—including children—through some moments of the "here-and-now," which in the next interview are transformed into moments of "there-and-then." Through a series of interviews the child may also be encouraged to reflect on her or his future prospects (Jansen & Andenæs, 2011), whether "the future" is defined as next week or as a point in time five years ahead.

Development, however, is about more than the mere passage of time. A more important consideration is *how* an individual passes through time. How does she *create meaning* in and about her passage through time? And how does this meaning-making contribute to what we understand as developmental processes? Inspired by Valsiner's foregrounding of the *processes* of development, I will prioritize these considerations at the expense of developmental *results* (Valsiner, 2007).

How we distinguish "developmental" changes from other changes that occur during an individual's life course is primarily a theoretical issue. Traditionally, developmental changes have been defined as changes that lead to a "point of no return"—that is, to qualitative jumps in the way a person thinks, feels, or acts and interacts that will forever change these functions. Within contemporary theories of development, the ability of an individual to fluctuate between contextually anchored ways of *being* or *doing* is, however, commonly recognized, and there have been calls to expand the concept of development (Thorngate, 2006).

The process of constructing normative trajectories of growth is part of the general social production of *culture*. Constructions of age, favored trajectories through the course of life, ideas of "maturity" or of "adultness," ways of growing from infancy through childhood into youth, and so on, are all aspects of the cultural images of what it is to be a human being. These cultural images are available for children as well as for their parents, teachers, relatives, and neighbors. The child has to explore the range of opportunities accessible to her at any moment of the process of the growing up. In so doing, she acts as an organizing and synthesizing subject at the intersection of her past self-constructing efforts *and* her future possibilities. Past experiences, the present being, and the anticipated future are infused with the prevailing ideas of growing up as a girl or boy in the various contexts of a certain child.

The theoretical platform sketched above is meant to answer the question "Where to look?" It directs our empirical interest towards the child's ways of growing up: How does she *do* it? How does she *understand* the events she is involved in? And how is this understanding made relevant in the next moment of acting in the world? The platform does, however, also direct our attention to the cultural and social contexts in which the child is participating: What kind of cultural ideas, local as well as more general, are circulated in the family, the neighborhood, the school-class, or the mosque? *Who* are the social participants in these processes of circulation and *how do they negotiate* systems of meaning and personal opportunities in the social field established through their joint activities of everyday life?

METHODOLOGICAL CONSIDERATIONS AND CHOICES

The phenomenon to be studied is thus the-child-in-her-contexts throughout a period of time. In the study to be presented, the main methodical approach is interviews with the children. A certain space for talking is established in the meeting between the child and the researcher, and both contribute to the stories told even if the researcher's ambition first and foremost has been to invite the child to talk about her life. From the perspective of cultural psychology, we should draw attention to at least two layers of sociality within which research into children's experiences is embedded. The child's act of narrating as well as the stories told should be analyzed as an inter-activity between the child and the researcher as well as between the two of them on the one hand and persons outside the interview setting on the other. Seeing children, or any other persons, as embedded in fluctuating webs of meaning and meaning-making processes compels us to address the experiences of "the child-in-context" rather than those of "the Child."

On the basis of the theoretical platform established so far, this section highlights three methodological considerations. Firstly, I argue that interviewing is crucial for an exploration of the experiences of the child-in-context. Interviewing may of course be fruitfully *combined with* field observations, various creative methods, and quantitatively based data. Research interviews do, however, provide a certain amount of space for storying and reflecting upon experiences and plans, and may thus support the research ambition of exploring children's, as well as others', meaning making processes. Secondly, I highlight the methodological approach of interviewing persons who are linked through their shared institutional settings and regular interactions in their everyday lives. This approach may provide insights into the spaces for actions, interactions and meaning-making which participants in a social field create for themselves *and* for each other. And thirdly, I emphasize the fruitfulness of a longitudinal research design when development is a main focus for the study. By *following* children we get the stories of ongoing events as well as their reflections on those events at later points along the axis of time.

Design

The study providing the examples to be presented includes 33 girls and boys attending a publicly funded school in Oslo, Norway. The population of the area surrounding the school was socially, culturally, and ethnically mixed. The children were individually interviewed 6 to 10 times at school between the age of 12 and 16. The interviewers were a group of researchers and psychology students, and the same interviewer followed each child throughout the research period.

Life-mode Interviewing

Life-mode interviewing (Haavind, 1987) comprises research conversations that take everyday life activities as their point of departure. A classic life-mode interview starts with an open question about the previous day: "Can you tell me about yesterday—what happened from the moment you woke up until you went to bed/fell asleep?" This initial question prompts stories about the activities, places, interactions, and relationships of "yesterday." Interviewees are also invited to share their reflections on the events they relate. The use of temporality as an organizing principle in the research conversation frequently leads to the initial activation of a well-known narrative pattern. The interviewee has initial control over the story—its setting, content, plot, and characters. None of these elements are initially introduced by the interviewer, who nonetheless bears them in mind and allows them to guide her or his careful prompting during the course of the interview. Some of the subsequent questions are designed to follow up the interviewee's stories by eliciting more details and making the narrative more concrete, while others explore the interviewee's view of connections between the storied events and other events, experiences, and systems of meaning. On the one hand, how are the events of yesterday linked to former experiences? On the other hand, how are they incorporated into, or how do they shape, ideas of the future?

Like all qualitative forms of interviews, life-mode interviews are conversations where the patterns and the contents of the accounts are co-constructed in the interaction between the interviewer and the interviewee. Whether the interviewee is an adult or a child, she will story her experiences in a certain dialogical context that contributes to the way the accounts are formed (Gubrium & Holstein, 2009). What is recorded is not the "pure voice" of the interviewee, but rather the joint efforts of the interviewer and interviewee to negotiate a relevant story for this occasion. The form and content of the narrative will be affected by considerations such as the interview setting, the sensitivity of the interviewer towards the child's way of telling, and the reasons for the study and the specific interview.

In the case of follow-up studies, interviewers and interviewees also co-create conversational rules and routines throughout the series of interviews. And when—as in this study—the interviewees know each other, it often becomes obvious that the interview themes are actually discussed among the interviewees. Children in the study periodically asked if someone else had related a certain incident and would at times take the initiative to correct what they believed to be another child's story, and so on.

In this project, seven to ten interviews with each child focused on their everyday activities throughout the study period. When talking about their yesterdays, close attention was paid to trivial routines, unexpected events, minor details, and bigger issues. Intervals between interviews were also partially covered by conversations that followed up the content of the previous interview. "You talked about some quarrels with your best friend Sitin last time we met. How are the two of you getting along now?"

This methodological approach involved empirical material covering each child's histories concerning her/his activities, relationships, reflections, plans, hopes, as well as her or his interactions with adults and peers who were also included as informants in the study. Hence we also learned about some aspects of an individual child's social participation from other children (as well as from teachers and some parents). Taken as a whole, the children's stories about themselves and each other may be read as a collective story of a social field of which they were all co-constructors. In following these children over several years, their stories came to form both actual and historical accounts of events and moves within their social fields.

PRODUCING AND ANALYZING CHILDREN'S ACCOUNTS: TWO EMPIRICAL CASES

The aim of the empirical study presented here is to explore *how* (a group of) children create, negotiate, and change images of self and others in their social activities of everyday life during the teenage years. The *knowledge pro-*

posals produced by the study are, however, part of the methodological process. When deciding "where to look," the researcher also facilitates some sorts of knowledge proposals at the expense of others. To enlighten methodological considerations throughout the research process is therefore a crucial contribution to knowledge production.

This section illustrates methodological considerations that emerged as important during various phases of the research process. The cases focus our attention on the processes of both data production and analysis, with the latter process involving analyses made by both children and the researcher(s). The pseudonyms Magnhild and Maryam refer to the two girls whose accounts will be presented and analyzed.

Magnhild: The Process of Storying Crucial Events

The case of Magnhild sheds light on an act of narrating that comprises both the construction of the account and the process of communicating it. In cooperation with the interviewer, Magnhild singled out and linked episodes and reflections into a presentation of social processes that were of great significance to her. In so doing, she created a perspective that both fitted the occasion of the interview and seemed to clarify her own feelings about a complex social process.

The eighth interview with Magnhild took place when she was nearly 16 years of age. She had moved to a different school a year and a half ago and had got to know her new classmates and teachers. The interview took place in an office at her new school, and I started by asking her about the process of settling in. This question introduced a retrospective perspective and Magnhild followed this up by telling me about past events: how she got to know Anne and Beate and their shared interests and activities, a friendship that had thrived throughout her time in ninth grade. After exploring this phase of their friendship for a while, I brought up the "the now"—the current situation between the three girls. Were Magnhild, Anne, and Beate still close as they approached the end of tenth grade?

Magnhild hesitated slightly before saying

> Now it is . . . . . .[3] It got like—there was a lot of fuss with Anne, because . . . . .Well, it was—at least it was . . . .*I don't think I have to go into details about this* . . . .
> (No . . . . . .)
> *Because it's rather complex* . . . .
> (Mm . . . . .)

> But........ but...... we—Anne and I and Beate were kind of a
>   threesome
> (Mm......)
> And................ it went very well. It is—it was very good. We
>   were very happy together for several months, but then Anne was
>   very...... she became very—like...intense after a while, be-
>   cause....Well, there are some persons who have a tendency to get
>   like that...... they...they...... you're friends and then..........
>   In a way they swallow you whole......... because they want to *pos-*
>   *sess* you.
> (Mm)
> And it became very...like....I got....I got five texts every day
>   saying "I'm so incredibly fond of you and you and Beate are the
>   most important people in my life and"......... Eh, things like
>   that. And then......... that we should be together every day
>   and........ if I didn't call her for a couple of days, it was like
>   "Oh, are you angry with me? What is it? What's going on?" She
>   became almost paranoid.
> (Mm).
> —Magnhild, eighth interview, tenth grade

Magnhild had been invited to participate in a form of conversation that she was very familiar with from previous interviews. Initially her attitude was enthusiastic and reflective, but she became hesitant when asked about the current relationship between the three girls. Magnhild started to say that she did not want to go into details: the matter was too complex. Nevertheless, she continued her story—although with some hesitation—about the crumbling of the trio's friendship. She had to search for words in order to connect the events in ways that could explain the present situation. With just some minimal verbal support on my part, she gave an account (running to several pages in the interview transcript) of how the trio had fallen apart, of her attempts to handle this, of her experiences of the process at the time, of conversations she had with the other two girls, of *their* experiences of the process, and of the situation at the time of the interview: Magnhild and Beate were still best friends, but Anne was no longer included in their close friendship.

There are several ways to interpret Magnhild's hesitation during this part of the interview. A sensitizing concept to guide the analytic approach could be *narrative work*, which highlights the situated "interactional activity through which narratives are constructed, communicated, and sustained or reconfigured" (Gubrium & Holstein, 2009, p. xvii). The concept of narrative work focuses our attention on the wider context of which the act of storytelling forms part. The axis of time is of importance, as the interview is embedded within processes that extend both before and after the tape-recorded accounts. When Magnhild's eighth interview was finished and the tape recorder had been turned off, Magnhild (successfully) asked for a copy of the tape. She explained that she had been struggling to understand what had happened between Anne, Beate, and herself. She had not been able to connect the various incidents before, but when given space to relate them in the interview setting, she had managed to formulate them into a meaningful story. Now she was able to understand the process, and she wanted a copy of the tape so that she would be able to listen to her own story again and make even clearer sense of the course of events and their meanings.

Consideration of several aspects of the narrative practice used here highlights *the process of constructing the story*. Magnhild did not present a story that was ready to be told: She had to work through her experiences, analyzing them as she went and making them intelligible on this specific narrative occasion. The interviewer too played an active part by posing questions and waiting for the answers in an interested but relaxed way. The interviewer also, of course, provided the technical equipment that enabled the conversation to be recorded.

Magnhild used the interview to give meaning to past events. By constructing a story that fashioned the events into a sequence, she became able to talk about them. The series of troublesome events between the three girls were no longer isolated episodes, but evolved into a meaningful story that she was able to voice. Through a present (i.e., at the time of the interview) reinterpretation of past events, Magnhild shaped this phase of life in a particular way, making her "here and now" relevant for her "there and then." She did not, however, conclude at this point: She moved "forward" by letting her present understanding of past events form the basis of further reflections. Thus she allowed for the possibility of future reinterpretations of her present understanding of past events. Magnhild could be seen to create a room for reflexivity wherein she can continue her self-and-other-constructing processes by forming stories about what happened and why.

During the interview, I saw Magnhild as presenting herself as a constructing, synthesizing, and organizing subject. By asking for the tape, she exposed her ability to make her "self" into an object of analysis: she would then be in a position to explore how this story sounded at any point in the future, as well as how it affected her and the significance of her part in the story. To adopt the language of George Herbert Mead (1934), one could say that she furnished the me-aspect of her self with an analytic device by asking for the tape. By making her self an object of analysis, she may—as a subject—make additional reflections on the possible meanings of the events and even reconfigure her analysis in the future. Magnhild is actively engaged in her self-making process as well as in the process of understanding and constructing others. Her way of turning the events between the three girls into a story contributes to the space of possibilities within which they all are fashioning their selves. Magnhild's account of the processes of present configuration of past events and of adaptation for future reinterpretation exemplifies how meaning-making is continuing along the axis of time, as both retrospective and prospective processes. All the time, other voices are contributing through the co-establishment of spaces for storying experiences, as well as through the provision of viewpoints and perspectives.

Magnhild's continuous work in making sense of processes in a particular area of her everyday life illustrates the social bases used when forming a personal perspective. Magnhild had discussed the events with Beate and Anne as they went along. She took advantage of the interview situation to further her understanding, and she prepared for future reinterpretations by asking for the tape. Magnhild had told us in a previous interview that her mother had suggested that she should record her own stories if she was struggling with something in her everyday life. Magnhild had done so throughout secondary school and felt that this process sometimes helped her sort out her thoughts. Magnhild's mother had pointed out a tool for self-reflective efforts and thereby also offered her daughter one route into a general culture of active meaning making.

The above presentation of Magnhild's efforts to story her experiences has highlighted her *act of telling a story*. Let this section be closed, however, by focusing on a significant aspect of *what was told*, namely the way Magnhild explained the process between the three girls. In the extract quoted here, as well as in the rest of this particular account, she mostly attributes the group's troubles to Anne. Magnhild draws on a psychological discourse that favors an individual character as the main causative force in the dissolution of social relationships. By using terms like "very intense," "swallow you whole," "want to possess you," "almost paranoid" to describe personal properties of Anne, Magnhild tends to put the burden of the relational breakdown on her. There are few signs in Magnhild's account of a more interactional analysis of the conflicts. Even if psychology provides both individualistic and interactional discourses in an attempt to explain interpersonal difficulties, the former are probably more prominent within the forms of folk psychology (Bruner, 1990) most prevalent in our own times. Once more the presence of multiple voices appears in Magnhild's presentation of her experiences.

In presenting Magnhild's account, I have highlighted the narrative work, that is, the situated act of producing and telling a story that guides the continuous creation of "self" and "others." An ambition derived from my theoretical point of entry has also been to point out a series of interactive aspects involving participants outside the interview dyad. To answer the question of "where to look," actual here-and-now interactions as well as the ongoing processes of making them meaningful along the axis of time should be emphasized.

In the next section, which presents interviews with Maryam, the focus will be on the analytical work.

On Analyzing Stories of and About Maryam

Maryam is a girl from a North African background who has spent most of her life in Norway. In the series of interviews, Maryam told *her* stories about her daily life. Like Magnhild and the other children involved, Maryam *positioned* (Davies & Harré, 1990) herself and others through her way of storying the events she highlighted in her interviews. At the same time, she also told how she saw herself positioned *by* others. Meanwhile, other children were telling stories about the same events. Through these stories the children could be seen to position themselves, as well as Maryam and the other participants in the activities in question. Davies and Harré use *positioning* as "the discursive process whereby people are located in conversations as observably and subjectively coherent participants in jointly produced storylines" (Davies & Harré, 1990, p. 48). The discursive processes may, however, be marked by contrasts and contradictions that emphasize the aspects of negotiation connected with the concept of *positioning*.

Throughout the early years of the interviewing process, Maryam spoke much about the difficulties of becoming included with the "Norwegians," in particular with the circle of girls who were seen as the in crowd in her class at school. While most of these girls were "Norwegians," a couple of "foreigners" were also associated with the group and had adopted "Westernized" styles of dress and behavior. The children generally made a distinction between the Norwegians on the one hand and the foreigners on the other. The girls categorized as foreigners tended to have their family roots in Asia or Africa, while children from various Nordic or other European backgrounds more easily passed as Norwegians. Although she used the word herself, Maryam complained about the common use of the word "foreigner." She pointed out the word's negative connotations in phrases such as "damned foreigners" and so on. However, she did not think that she had any influence on the way of establishing and of phrasing this categorization. Power seemed to be an integral element in this distinction: opportunities for social positioning, and cultural definitions were unevenly distributed in the social field of the peers as well as on a societal level.

The members of the in crowd, a loosely knit circle of five to seven girls, were trendsetters when it came to clothes, make-up, boys, activities, and ideas about becoming teenagers and young women. In their stories the "ordinary" (their word) girls often positioned themselves in relation to the in crowd either by actively dissociating themselves from or by explicitly adopting their views. The girls in the in crowd could hardly be ignored, and this reinforced their social influence.

When analyzing the first interviews, I was struck by the various ways in which most of the girls, at the ages of 12 to14, highlighted their efforts to "be themselves." Their reflections upon being "oneself" were commonly linked to stories about various kinds of preferences: their choices of friends, films, music, clothes, activities, and so on, were presented as the result of genuine interest (e.g., an expensive brand of jeans was preferred not because it was fashionable, but because the jeans were extremely well cut, etc.). The girls stressed their individual choices; the researcher, however, will rather explore how appropriation of the idea of "being themselves" is actually what eases their inclusion into the peer group. What is recognized as "being oneself" is continually negotiated, and among the girls in the in crowd it is stressed as the primary criterion for participation in the group. "Being oneself" is frequently contrasted with being "childish." "Independence" was accordingly cited as a more "mature" personal quality.

One way in which the girls highlighted their efforts to be "independent" was to tell stories about opposing their parents, teachers, or other adults. From time to time, this opposition was even played out with some kind of tacit agreement on the part of the parents, who saw their daughters as progressing towards autonomy during their early teenage years. One girl, for example, who had been awarded a very high test score, explained how she had persuaded her mother to agree to her playing truant from a gym class in order to escape being positioned as the teacher's pet. Being seen as the teacher's pet could have threatened her position of independence. A general discourse based on statements such as "it's her age" or "she's a teenager" seemed to position the young persons as rebels. This rebellion was, however, considered to constitute a proper and necessary stage on the course to the autonomy attributed to an adult person in this historical and cultural context. Accordingly, the parents and teachers, as well as the children, knew that this opposition was both sound and future-oriented.

When talking about themselves, most of the girls positioned themselves as independent in having *their own reasons* for their likes and dislikes: They asserted that they made their own choices and decisions in everyday life. They did, however, often dispute the independence of other girls, who were characterized as "childish," "wannabees," "fashion victims," or "repressed." When analyzing the interactional patterns whereby the girls *positioned* themselves and others, as well as *being positioned by* others, the social hierarchy favoring the in crowd re-emerged.

It was within the social and discursive field outlined above that Maryam worked on both her self-construction as well as her other-constructions throughout her early teenage years. Again and again, she told stories about her struggles to be accepted as an "independent" person—as a girl who, like her peers, saw herself as a person following her own preferences and making her own decisions. However, as a girl from a Muslim family, she often found that the "Norwegian" girls mistrusted her independence. When Maryam didn't want to join her class on a school trip, this was not accepted as *her* choice, but as a decision made by her parents. Maryam, for her part, explained to her interviewer how she felt that she *disappeared* when she was in the company of the in crowd. To avoid this feeling of disappearance as a person, Maryam preferred to stay at home, even though she realized that this decision would merely reinforce the prevailing view of her as a dependent, or even repressed, Muslim girl.

Maryam told several stories about how Norwegian girls passed on ideas about Muslim girls as dependent or repressed. When Maryam did not participate in activities, there were often insinuations that this was because her parents had forbidden it. By challenging Maryam's potential to make her own decisions, other girls denied her the opportunity to be "herself." Maryam fought against this by explaining her point of view, by shouting and scolding, by fighting and by withdrawing and playing truant.

In the interviews, Maryam, like most other children in the study, also talked about conflicts with her parents: conflicts about where she could go on her own (the city center was generally off limits for these children at the ages of 12–14); at what time she had to return home in the afternoon/evening (a common source of disagreement referred to by most of the girls), standards of school/homework (also a fairly common source of disagreement); and how to dress (a frequent topic of controversy between girls in their early teenage years and their parents, even if the question of the Hijab was restricted to the Muslim families), to mention just some of the themes Maryam brought up in her early interviews. Even though Maryam related quite fiery discussions that mainly concerned the same issues that were discussed by other girls of her age, the trendsetters did not accord her a position of "independence." Maryam's understanding of her position within her peer group was that no matter what she said or did, it was impossible for her to gain acceptance as an "independent" person in the eyes of the socially dominant girls.

The discourse of the "dependent," or even the "repressed," Muslim girl or woman did not, of course, originate among a group of girls aged 12–14 in a schoolyard in Oslo. A series of discourses that position girls and women in Muslim milieus as "repressed" flourish in formal as well as informal discourses at higher social levels. The teenage girls in this study took up the ideas prevailing in society around them and invoked them, in various ways, in their social interactions with their peers.

In my reading of the interviews with Maryam, I saw her as a girl who was fighting to position herself *within* the discourse of "being herself," as well as to achieve a common acceptance of this positioning among the other girls. In my analyses of the interviews, I chose to foreground Maryam's stated efforts to act as "herself" and how these efforts seemed to correspond to strong, general trends among the young teenage girls. My analytic ambition has been to challenge some of the processes of social categorization that the empirical material seemed to reveal. By enlightening Maryam's teenage quarrels at home and her ambition to "be herself" among her peers, it has been possible to understand Maryam as *one of the teenage girls* as many of them, including the in crowd, storied their experiences.

Some years later, talking to the 17-year-old Maryam, I heard new stories about conflicts at home, mainly concerning her present agency and her choices for the future. Her parents assumed she would follow a traditional, female path of life, with marriage being the only way out of the parental home and education being rather unnecessary. Maryam's priorities were the opposite, and this caused further conflicts and quarrels at home.

Regarding the conflicts at home, Maryam said, "I didn't tell you much about this in the interviews when I was younger; I've been wondering why." I have also wondered how to understand this statement. One conceivable interpretation is that in former interviews she downplayed the extent of the conflicts and the ways in which they were handled.

But when reviewing the early interviews with Maryam, I saw that in fact she *did* talk quite a lot about quarrels at home. She related them as part of her stories of daily life, although she did not combine them under a thematic heading into a particular story—that is, a story about growing up with strict and traditional, perhaps even fundamentalist, parents. *This* story seemed to be created later as the conflicts continued and Maryam's concerns about her *future* prospects increased. It is possible to understand the reformulation of the accounts from the past in the light of *present* experiences. Scanning the presently available discourses, Maryam will easily come to know the repertoire of interpretations dominating the media and public sphere. This time she did not set out to challenge the prevailing discourses; instead she seemed to appropriate them as encompassing her personal experiences.

According to *my* analysis, both the earlier and later stories and interpretations are of interest and they challenge simplistic ways of understanding development as a series of straight lines from one point to another. When working with children over a period of several years, both the children's and the researcher's frames of reference will change. At any particular of time, as Magnhild's account illustrated, there are many loose ends and unfinished stories. As time goes by, some of these loose ends become organized into coherent stories that make sense of some of the experiences. Others, however, are left out as irrelevant or uninteresting. *The continuous work* of including and excluding elements in self-and other-creating stories can be seen as processes of development, that is, processes of change that take up as well as challenge the practices and meanings offered and negotiated in certain contexts.

In Maryam's early stories, I saw the same kinds of conflicts as in the "Norwegian" homes. The quarrels and opposition could be understood as processes through which independence was being negotiated between parents and their teenage daughters. Aged 17, however, Maryam produced a new analysis, which was one she had not previously communicated to the research team, even though she had related the relevant episodes several years previously. Both these "truths" about Maryam's conflicts with her parents and her understanding of her self are important components in the *researcher's* analysis of Maryam's process of self-construction.

A relevant question is whether the initial analyses, both Maryam's and mine, were "wrong." Did the Norwegian girls actually interpret her position correctly? They may be seen to have done so if we draw a causal arrow from a stereotyped representation of Maryam's Muslim family background to her stories at the age of 17. If, however, we look more closely into the storied experiences of everyday life throughout the teenage years of these girls, we may glimpse a myriad of parallel as well as contradictory processes making up a causal field (Ford & Lerner, 1992), rather than an unambiguous causal arrow. Part of this involves processes conceptualized by Michael Cole as *prolepsis* (Cole, 1996). Cole's concept of prolepsis implies acting today as if anticipated future events are already present. Thereby the anticipated events may become part of a causal field of significance for developmental processes. For Maryam it seemed difficult to gain recognition as a person by being "herself" at the age of 13–14 when a culturally stereotyped image of a repressed, Muslim woman served to shape the understanding of her among her peers. Some years later, however, she positioned herself within a concurrent discourse and thereby seemed to reorganize her former experiences into a culturally dominant storyline. This is probably not the last repositioning in Maryam's developmental moves. The future processes are dependent on her social experiences, her meaning-making efforts as well as the discursive practices and structural frames offered her as participant in future contexts.

CONCLUDING REMARKS

In this chapter the process of development, which here refers to active meaning-making and self-and-other-creating efforts, is seen as a spiral trajectory where the past and present, as well as future prospects, are included in continuous and ongoing processes of interpretation and reinterpretation in social fields of everyday life. At any moment past, present, and anticipated experiences are processed into stories creating spaces for self-and-other-constructions. To shape oneself in a certain way do also produce conditions for self-making efforts of others.

As mentioned at the beginning of the chapter, Valsiner underscores the significance of "the general strategies for where to look "in order to construct "basic knowledge in the social sciences" (Valsiner, 2007). The general strategies for "where to look" are anchored in the initial constitution of the phenomenon of interest and they direct the research practices to be employed. The *results* of the research should answer the research questions elaborated on the base of the initial understanding. *Results* may, however, also comprise elaborated ways of understanding and specifying the initial assumptions.

In the presentation of empirical cases in this chapter, it is the *dynamic character* of the young girls' efforts to make sense of social experiences that has come out strongly. The voices of the girls' interactional partners are prominent in these processes, and power relations seem to be embedded in the discursive practices the children take up and negotiate. In order to constitute a fruitful concept of development, further attention should be directed towards the intertwinement of the individual child's dynamic understandings of self *and* others, joint activities and meaning-making in the child's various social contexts, and the prevailing discursive practices at a social and political level. Following children and young persons through years with qualitative interviews emphasizing their various social participations in everyday life contexts provides data suited for these kinds of developmental analyses.

NOTES

1. In this chapter two girls provide us with empirical material. To escape the awkward s/he or his/her formulations throughout the paper, the child will always be referred to as she. This does not mean that the principal points of the chapter are restricted to girls only.
2. The paper is based on a study funded by the Norwegian Research Council and originally based at the Department of Psychology, University of Oslo, Norway.
3. The dots indicate (short) pauses of various duration in the process of telling.

REFERENCES

Bronfenbrenner, U. (1979). *The ecology of human development. Experiments by nature and design.* Cambridge, MA: Harvard University Press.
Bronfenbrenner, U. (Ed.). (2005). *Making human beings human.* Thousand Oaks, CA: Sage.

Bruner, J. (1990). *Acts of meaning*. Cambridge, MA: Harvard University Press.

Burman, E. (2008). *Deconstructing developmental psychology*. London, UK: Routledge.

Cole, M. (1996). *Cultural psychology. A once and future discipline*. Cambridge, MA: Harvard University Press.

Davies, B., & Harré, R. (1990). Positioning: The discursive production of selves. *Journal for the Theory of Social Behaviour, 20*(1), 43–63.

Ford, D. H., & Lerner, R. M. (1992). *Developmental systems theory: An integrative approach*. Thousand Oaks, CA: Sage.

Gubrium, J. F., & Holstein, J. A. (2009). *Analyzing narrative reality*. Thousand Oakes, CA: Sage.

Gulbrandsen, M. (2003). Peer relations as arenas for gender constructions among young teenagers. *Pedagogy, Culture and Society, 11*(1), 113–132.

Haavind, H. (1987). *Liten og Stor. Mødres omsorg og barns utviklingsmuligheter.* [*The big and the little one. Maternal care and the developmental possibilities for children*]. Oslo, Norway: Universitetsforlaget.

Haavind, H. (2007). Accountability in persons. What is in the telling to others about yourself. In D. Staunæs & J. Kofoed (Eds.), *Magtballader (Ballads of power)*. København, Denmark: Danmarks Pædagogiske Universitets Forlag.

Hauge, M. I. (2009). *Doing, being and becoming: Young people's processes of subjectivation between categories of age*. Oslo, Norway: Unipub.

James, A., Jenks, C., & Prout, A. (1998). *Theorizing childhood*. Cambridge: Polity Press.

Jansen, A., & Andenæs, A. (2011). "Heading for Japan"—Prospective narratives among youth living in residential care. *Qualitative Social Work*. DOI: 10.1177/1473325011423588

Jenks, C. (Ed.). (1982). *The sociology of childhood: Essential readings*. London, UK: Batsford.

Mead, G. H. (1934). *Mind, self and society*. Chicago, IL: University of Chicago Press.

Morss, J. R. (1996). *Growing critical. Alternatives to developmental psychology*. London, UK: Routledge.

Rogoff, B. (2003). *The cultural nature of human development*. New York, NY: Oxford University Press.

Thorngate, W. (2006). The seductive danger of visual methaphors: It's about time. *Culture & Psychology, 12*(2), 215–219.

Valsiner, J. (2007). *Culture in minds and societies. Foundations of cultural psychology*. Los Angeles: Sage

Walkerdine, V. (1993). Beyond developmentalism? *Theory and Psychology, 3*, 451–469

Wertsch, J. (1991). *Voices of the mind. A sociocultural approach to mediated action*. London, UK: Harvester Wheatsheaf.

CHAPTER 2

"BEING ONESELF" AND "BEING OF USE"

On Children's Appropriation of Values

Ruth E. Toverud

INTRODUCTION

Children's appropriation of moral and cultural values is explored in this chapter. As an aspect of development, this issue involves complex and changing intergenerational practices and activities. Earlier, this theme was often seen in the light of the dichotomized analytical "looking glasses" of individualism versus collectivism—a perspective that, for instance, has made us see pursuing of individual goals in opposition to making oneself useful to others. Here, I address how individual and collective values and goals are not necessarily opposites, but rather interdependent, and balanced in the practice of everyday life. This enables us to look at how children combine "self-making" with actively growing into their surroundings as social, responsible, and interacting participants. How, for example, do children combine caring for others with pursuing their own ambitions and interests? How might autonomy and independence be an essential part of acquiring cultural values, and thereby imply being loyal and obedient to them? How

Children, Childhood, and Everyday Life, pages 21–36
Copyright © 2012 by Information Age Publishing

do contradictions in the culturally preferred goals for development "work out" for parents when they try to assure optimal developmental conditions for their children to "find themselves" and at the same time assure that they become culturally adequate and useful citizens?

The aim is to reveal both children's agency as well as their developmental dependence on their surroundings. According to Bruner (1985), all forms of development and knowledge acquisition depend on support systems in the environment and an acquisition process in the learner. In the case of the complex and contradictory nature of cultural and moral values, these are probably more learned than taught, depending on active appropriation from the child more than on purposeful and willed teaching from the child's supporters. Valsiner (2007) goes further and discards the concept of learning as too passive since every transfer of knowledge from one generation to the next must involve recreation and novel elements.

Perspectives on Intergenerational Interaction and Values

In several comparative cultural studies of parenting styles and developmental goals for children performed in the last decades of the twentieth century, growing up in "modern,"[1] technologically advanced societies has been contrasted to "traditional" societies. Notions such as caring, obedience, and responsibility have been associated with collectivism and traditionalism, while ambition, autonomy, and self-promotion have been associated with individualism and modern societies (Hundeide, 2003; Kagitcibasi, 1996; LeVine & White, 1986). The distinction of collectivism versus individualism has been the most influential framework for conceptualizing cultural variation in parental practices and developmental goals for children (Oyserman, Coon, & Kemmelmeier, 2002; Tamis-LeMonda, Way, Hughes, Yoshikawa, Kalman, & Niwa, 2007).

The contrast between individualism and collectivism has been used in the analysis of cultural changes in Norwegian society by the anthropologist Marianne Gullestad (1997), who compared "classic modernity" in the first part of the twentieth century with the subsequent "transformed modernity" by analyzing autobiographies. According to Gullestad, there was a change in Norwegian society from a collectivistic towards a more individualistic emphasis. New priorities between different cultural and moral values, different developmental goals as well as intergenerational styles of interaction, are part of these changes. Parenting practice turned from demands of obedience towards complex negotiation and persuasion. Gullestad connects this to a change from a rhetoric emphasis on "being of use" to an emphasis on "being oneself."[2]

Both Gullestad (1997) and Hundeide (2003) have emphasized changes towards more complex and indirect interaction between generations. They find that parents' roles have become more indistinct and difficult to figure out and want more research on what actually happens in a Norwegian context. Gullestad concludes with an awareness "of the complex and often contradictory nature of value-transmission" (Gullestad, 1997, p. 217). She suspects that the influence of older generations may not be less than before, but rather more difficult to observe, and emphasizes the need to address "how the past lives on in the present" (Gullestad, 1997, p. 217). Hundeide argues that children contribute to goals and priorities of their development to a larger extent than previously. He calls for more theorizing and research on the intergenerational interactions.

On Individualism and Collectivism as Analytical Dimensions

There has been a growing recognition of the shortcoming of individualism versus collectivism as a dichotomous framework for analyzing developmental goals, parenting, and children's acquisition of values. Several authors see this framework as theoretically and empirically limiting, and a much too simplistic approach to extremely complex topics (Kagitcibasi, 2005). To describe societies in terms of the unitary traits of individualism versus collectivism has, according to Valsiner and Van der Veer (2000), led to the construction of cultures as "ontological" entities, and to the use of culture as an over-generalizing label, assuming both qualitative homogeneity among members and a temporal stability (Valsiner, 2007). During different historical periods, however, the "*we* versus *they*" has become exaggerated "precisely through an emphasis of the individual's active looking after him or herself in accordance with the collectivist emphasis" (Valsiner & Van der Veer, 2000, p. 180). Besides, individualistic ethos in one activity domain such as commerce may be paralleled by an ethos that accepts collectivism in other domains—for instance, family life, according to these same authors. One could add that other academic disciplines see a variety of developmental goals in connection to culturally normative differentiation attached to gender, class, or ethnic divisions. Societies based exclusively on values connected to individualism or collectivism may seem unthinkable. Diversity in patterns of differentiation towards groups or individuals across societies and times is, on the other hand, well known. The polarized understanding of differences in cultures and societies produced by the dichotomous perspectives above functions, as I see it, in an often seemingly self-derogatory way, precisely as creating an instance of "*we* versus *they*."

According to Valsiner and Van der Veer (2000), to look at the *unity* of collectivism and individualism may be a productive theoretical strategy as it is the form of *interdependence* between the ethos that varies between societies, groups, and times. Tamis-LeMonda et al. (2007) argue that cultural value systems must be seen in light of *dynamic coexistence* of individualism and collectivism. This seems to be a good starting point for exploring "values of everyday life" in some contemporary Norwegian families.

METHODOLOGY AND METHODS

The intention here is to explore how we may attain knowledge on the matter of children's acquisition of values through studying what they and their caregivers actually do in daily life, and how they think about what they do. How they make use of, and transform values in self-making is an important aspect of the issue of interest. The aim is at the same time to make practices, personal meaning-making, and cultural context the object of study. The versions of childhood marked by the Norwegian kind of welfare state and the specific Nordic child-centeredness (Kristjansson, 2006) are, in a wider context, assumed to hold analytic potential contained both in its particularities and in its likeness with similar environments for growing up. I draw on analyses of interviews with 10- to 11-year-old girls and boys and their mothers in contemporary local communities in central eastern Norway about daily life practices. Forty interviews with dyads of twenty mothers, 10 girls and 10 boys, were performed in local communities in central eastern Norway in 2002–2003. Children and mothers were interviewed at home, in separate rooms, simultaneously by me and my colleague.[3] Following the principles of life mode interviews (Andenæs, 1991), the interviewer and interviewee together explored the events of the preceding day. The prime focus of life mode interview is on the rhythm and organization of everyday-life practices. This is, however, only to be seen as a point of departure as the procedures are shaped in accordance with the focus of interest in each project. The shared purpose is to obtain knowledge of the interviewed persons' construction and understanding of themselves and their life.

In this chapter I use elements from the narratives from five of the children and four of their mothers. These persons were chosen because they illustrate well the focus of the chapter. In some respects their stories also represent more common tendencies in several of the interviews. The intention, however, is mainly to inspire reflections on conceptual and methodological issues.

INTERVIEWS AND ANALYSIS

The interviews gave rich material on how children and mothers positioned themselves within cultural discourses on age and gender as well as on their ambitions and plans, hopes, or fears for the future. How individual aims and collective aspects were balanced in contemporary day-to-day life of children of this age, in their friendships and family roles, were some of the themes that we reflected upon between and after the interviews. Our attention was set on thought-provoking patterns of differences between how children and their mothers positioned themselves towards, and reflected in values and developmental goals.

Being Oneself and Being of Use—Ola

First I will introduce Ola,[4] a boy who, like many other Norwegian children, has lived through his parents' divorce. My colleague and I interviewed Ola and his mother, in different rooms, when Ola was nearly eleven years old.

When they described the organization and rhythm of their daily life, both Ola and his mother talked about the period after the parent's separation. Ola's family, a lower-middle-class family living in the outskirts of an urban area, had chosen the officially recommended solution in case of parents' separation: the children stayed one week with each of the parents. Ola and his mother each told their versions of what may be interpreted as *vacancies*[5] emerging when the mother moved out and the children started to live every second week with the father, and the other weeks with mother in her new apartment.

In contrast to his siblings, not reported to be engaged in these aspects of daily life at all, Ola strongly disliked the diminishing of household standards that occurred when his mother moved out. His father had never been particularly oriented towards such activities and now worked hard to manage the mortgage repayments on the house alone, besides being an active father when it came to follow up sport activities. After a while Ola started to make up for his mother's absence; he took on several household tasks such as ironing, cooking, and baking, and often called his mother for advice and instructions which on the whole, she willingly gave him.

By setting out to make daily life more to his liking, Ola surely influenced the life in his family as well as the systems of social relations involved, but also in a wider context, as he set off far-reaching interactions and reflections among the persons surrounding him. Ola formed his own position as an apprentice in a way that was quite unusual in his community. He made some of his mother's skills and interests his own and went about learning with eagerness. Even if uninvited, this was not exactly unwanted.

In spite of being concerned, Ola's mother decided that this was a manifestation of the "true nature" of her son, whom she looked upon as a resourceful and special boy. She described several acts on her own part. Besides guiding him in certain household tasks, often by telephone at a distance, she also took part in negotiations with Ola, sometimes characterized by intense conflict, on what kind of tasks he was supposed to take up both in her house and that of his father. She also negotiated with her former husband about this issue and finally discovered that she had to fight with other relatives and friends. They were worried about Ola being too untypical, too little "boy-like." His mother took up the fight for Ola's right to be special and not very typical. She was more than willing to take on this fight; it rather became like a principled task for her.

In other words, movement and positioning in cultural discourses both on age and gender were set in motion in various perspectives on Ola's choice of activities. Ola himself, however, seemed to be actively combining individual goals with making himself useful to his family. Besides, he and his mother show how intergenerational practice may find new forms in contemporary family situations. The mother's possibilities for shaping support systems around Ola's different projects and plans were restricted simply by her being in control of the immediate conditions of his daily life only half of the time, but also that he was becoming older and through his strong interests and opinions. We may think that she was in danger of being assigned responsibilities both by herself and others in areas where she was not in control. If Ola, according both to her description and his own, had not always been a fairly clever student at school, and had he not had friends and interests outside of household tasks, this would probably have been even more difficult.

Independence and Loyalty—Linda and Espen

Compared to Ola's situation, eleven-year-old Linda's plans of taking on household tasks appeared to be given a much less provocative and difficult meaning. Also Linda occupied herself with the possibilities of taking up *vacant functions.* Her story of daily life was characterized by many plans and projects, for the present and the future. Linda was intertwining her aim of making herself useful with her wish of pursuing interests and goals that she explained as being important. Her family lived in a slightly more rural area than Ola, close to several other relatives. Her grandmother had always kept Linda and her brother company when the parents worked long hours. Together with her grandmother she had often done creative activities, which she loved.

At the time of the interview, Linda was occupied with several projects and was a little dissatisfied with the availability of handicraft equipment at home. Besides, she was more interested in clothes than she had been before and would have liked more freedom of action in this respect. Linda could, in other words, use more money than she thought that her parents could spare, and had a plan of how she would handle this:

> You see, my parents are often short of money, but that's OK. We have enough for food, and sometimes clothes. But I plan to do some cleaning for grandma. . . . She smokes cigarettes, and it smells somewhat in her house. I want her to stop smoking, and I want to clean for her. Then it will be fresher there, and I may earn some money for things I need.

Nothing told us that her plans to expand possibilities of usefulness and self-making caused worries or conflicts among the adults. Linda's mother did not comment on these specific plans, and it is not clear to us how much she knew about them. What is common to Linda's and Ola's stories is that they seem to understand their plans and projects on being of use as closely associated to their own comprehension of what characterizes just them as special beings.

Linda's plans might not necessarily have been shared with her parents. At the age of eleven, she not only moves between different social settings, but the parents are no longer necessarily the coordinators of her activities across different settings. There are now open time spaces, "empty" or vacant places, and children of this age make several decisions autonomously. Negotiation of age now goes on in partly *hidden* ways (Solberg, 1997). During the 40 interviews that we had with mothers and children in this age group, we got several versions of how children in their daily schedules negotiated time and various tasks. We also heard several versions of how the control gradually was transferred to the children. In varying degrees and in various ways, parents were also beginning to face the fact that theirs sons' and daughters' interests, opinions, and ambitions would, sooner or later, be decisive for how they would use their time in the future.

Espen, an eleven-year-old boy, illustrates a way of using the open space, out of adult control, to find his own way of taking a stance towards his parents' display of values. Espen's mother, a well-educated middle-class woman, was telling me about the importance she attached to opening the house for her son and his friends after school before she and her husband came home—an open time-space they tried to make as short as possible. After homework was done, the parents allowed video games or watching films, but ruled out certain kinds of games they considered too aggressive and war-like.

Espen, who was being interviewed in another room nearby, told my colleague how he had watched and tried out exactly the same films and games in a friend's house in the neighborhood. He also told her how highly surprised he was that this friend's younger brother was allowed access, something he volunteered that he thought very unwise.

In other words, Espen broke the parents' rules. At least he sidestepped them in another house than his own. He agreed with his parents' conclusion, apparently, at least for children younger than him. A ban by Espen's parents may of course have heightened his interest. Indirectly, he seems to tell us that he actively works on taking a stance on his parents' value-oriented rules, but is craving to look into the premises of their decisions. His loyalty and submission is in no way unconditional, it seems.

Serious Chores—Jorun

Some contradictions in contemporary views on children may become particularly salient when children take up serious chores. Do their activities really matter? Is it a violation of cultural codes if children are assigned important, difficult, or time-consuming tasks? In our part of the world, the ethos of taking children's participation and contribution seriously is paralleled by, and perhaps interdependent on, children being separated from most of the important adult activity areas. Adults are no longer dependent on children for handling daily challenges in work or family life. Nor, in the contemporary Scandinavian welfare-state setting, do children represent parents' economic security in old age, at least not personally, on a one-to-one basis. Also in a wider setting, the importance of children for economic security in old age is reduced in modern societies, and instead exchanged for their *emotional* importance (Kagitcibasi, 1996). Often the weight is put on *parents'* emotions evoked or met by the child, which may be seen in accordance with the still often predominant emphasis on children as objects (Greene & Hill, 2005). But there is also increasing focus, especially in sociocultural research, towards what is going on *between children*, and on how they contribute in important ways to developmental conditions for each other.

Ten-year-old Jorun told me how she and her best friend had often previously been frightened and bullied by older boys on their way to school. This went on in spite of her family's efforts to intervene until these boys advanced to secondary school. In this period, Jorun often had stomach-ache before leaving for school in the morning. Now, she is one of the pupils selected to sit on a kind of a *conflict resolution board* initiated by the school just to get to terms with bullying and conflicts between students. She is proud of this honorable appointment. Having been bullied herself, she has some special knowledge about fairness and about acceptable and unacceptable conduct among schoolmates.

Jorun's mother also mentioned the appointment to the conflict resolution board. She engaged in lovingly describing her oldest child as she appeared just now, in the midst of both being a child and approaching adolescence, and the funny episodes, abrupt shifts, and peculiar variations in conduct and interests that followed. What concerned her for the time being was that Jorun occasionally seemed too engaged in what the mother saw as "grown up" kinds of worries, for instance about the parents' happiness or health. Sometimes she just wanted to tell her, "You should just be a child, Jorun, and leave the rest to me."

In this, Jorun's mother illustrates a pattern in several of the interviews. Mothers were anxious that their daughters took too much responsibility or were too considerate of other people's feelings or well-being. The school's involvement of children in conflict resolution boards, on the other hand, represents an innovative contemporary way of involving children in taking responsibility for the good of the community. At the same time, this practice seems to implicate an awareness of children's competence and adult dependency upon them to come to terms with problems, conflicts, and eventual harassment in children's relationships to others. In other words, the values coloring the children's communities must be "owned" by themselves.

Critical Reflections on Inconsistency—Henrik

Henrik, ten years old, was also involved in taking up important tasks for the community of which he is part. He was engaged in improving relationships among pals at school, and apart from reflecting critically on his own achievement, he was less than impressed with the contributions from adults.

According to Henrik, school subjects were easy for him; his plans were quite ambitious and he had just told that he sometimes was called "*skolelys*" (or "whiz kid")— a somewhat derogatory Norwegian expression that children may use against pals doing well at school. "I don't mind so much, being called '*skolelys,*' but it is not very nice," he said. This does not mean, however, that Henrik was bullied or lonely. According to himself and his mother, he had several good friends besides taking much responsibility as a friend and a class-mate.

> I: Is anyone else in your class bullied?
> H: Yes; a girl called "xxx," she is bullied a lot.
> I: How do the rest of you handle it; can you do something?
> H: We try, but it is difficult. When I take her side, the teach-
> ers . . . in a way they go against it . . . saying she has to handle
> it herself. And then, the next moment they say we should
> come to them if somebody is bullied. It is simply not good
> enough, I think . . .

A little later, Henrik and the interviewer were talking about how the classmates usually handled disputes between themselves. He seldom had quarrels with other children himself, he said, but often observed quarrels between others.

> **I:** So you do not get involved in their quarrels?
> **H:** Yes, sometimes, when I have an opinion, I involve myself, but I cannot when I don't know who is right . . .
> **I:** What do you usually do then?
> **H:** . . . for instance, when one of my friends quarrels with someone else, and I am not sure that I can support my friend, then it is very difficult . . . I usually support my friends, but I think I ought not . . . because the other part may be right . . .

Henrik critically scrutinizes his own contributions as well as those of others, both fellow pupils and teachers. He combines care for others with ambitions as well as self-assurance. Flaws and inconsistencies in ideals and practices are mercilessly pointed out. His expectations and demands are high, which is not without social costs and risk-taking. He seems to balance between being a moral challenger, or "guardian," and a pal and friend among his friends. His indignation is more easily directed, I think, towards adults than other children. He is undoubtedly deeply absorbed in taking in, and perhaps reshaping, the values of his community, and making them his own. Conflicts and inconsistencies seem to play an important role in this work.

DISCUSSION

Conflicts, Mutuality and Power

As Espen illustrated, children may oppose parents at one level, but at the same time remain loyal to parents' opinions and goals on another. They may also be loyal to what they comprehend as the *generic meaning* of values displayed by adults on an explicit, normative level but still, like Henrik, critically devaluate the actual adult practice. And just these conflicting aspects of what Henrik observed seem central to his process of appropriation of values.

It can be productive to look for what role tensions, resistance, conflicts, or even crises play in children's appropriation of values. According to Wertsch (1998), in the attempts to extend some of Vygotsky's ideas of "zone of proximal development," researchers may be in danger of missing some essential aspects of interaction and change, namely that discrepancy and differences in opinions play important roles in cognitive development. "some of the most important developmental landmarks for children may arise through conflict rather than consensus" (Wertsch, 1998, pp. 118–119). Similarly, Davies (2003), based on her own childhood, exemplifies how children, through parents exercising power over them, may conceive themselves as persons capable of being in opposition and thereby discover themselves as agents, even if they temporarily have to yield to adult power.

Conflicts and heated discussions were not so unusual in the narratives we were told during the interviews. A negotiating atmosphere was conveyed to us most of the time. Examples of parenting practice marked by repressive authority were rare. This picture may obscure the authority and power involved in parent–child relationships. In the most "culturally correct" interaction, there may be instances when a parent puts a foot down and demands obedience. Besides, if we focus too one-sidedly on the immediate interaction and communication between generations, it may be easy to forget how parents' decisive power has other important expressions. They have, for instance, the possibility to determine children's activities and who they spend time with, to restrict or enhance mobility; in sum to determine the *scenario* of children's participation and experience. This is an aspect that has a great influence on their social world (Rogoff, 1990). Of course, parents do not decide independently, given that material and cultural forces structure families' lives (Solberg, 1997). The diversity of scenarios made available—or not—for children's participation still has far-reaching consequences, sometimes intended and sometimes not.

Contradictions in Cultural Messages

Thought-provoking tensions seem to be built into the intricate messages in contemporary discourses on age, gender and childhood. In contemporary Western societies parents surely get the message now that children of both genders should not have too much responsibility in the daily organization of the household and family life. To be ambitious in school and education, and to be socially and physically active, are the culturally prescribed main assignments for children. Those discourses are filled with stern messages concerning developmental goals, not easy for all parents to fulfil, at least not if the family, temporarily or lasting, has limited resources or lives through crises and upheavals. Besides, it is a challenging task in the negotiating climate of contemporary Norwegian families to combine children's possibilities to make choices on several occasions daily with school ambitions and tight schedules. The emphasis on negotiating with children and including them in choices, securing their opportunities of finding and developing unique characteristics and possibilities, may clearly come into conflict with the educational ambitions marking the education-oriented Norwegian society.

Further, there is a cultural message that children should be included as participants and be taken seriously. There are tensions between this and the possibilities of children being "put aside" in relation to much of the parent's daily activity and duties, also inside a family. Several of the children we interviewed seemed somewhat more prone to seek out situations where they could be of use, and motivated to take up more important tasks than the mothers wanted them to. As exemplified in this chapter, *open spaces* and *vacant functions* may occur when the child has reached the age of ten or eleven years, giving them the opportunity of forming possibilities in ways that they did not have previously.

The contradictions in discourses on gender interact with those of age. The general public places a heavy, but also a kind of ambiguous weight on similar opportunities for boys and girls. Boys *not* being typical boys may cause concern, and girls *being* typical girls may do the same. These stories in themselves tell their contradictory tales both about changes and about how the past lives on in the present. New forms of boundary-crossing and fluidity between the "old" binary categories of male and female seem at the same time both welcomed, and highly controversial and disturbing. The worries that were provoked by Ola's reactions to changes in his family were probably increased by his activities not being boy-like. It is my guess that Linda's plans, on the other hand, would sound like a sweet little story in many people's ears, quite typical of girls her age, and not one that should cause worry. Her story may remind us of a very appealing picture in one of Rogoff's books, of a girl slightly younger, already an expert in following recipes and using household utensils, seeking guidance from her grand-mother on the right consistency of whipped cream. It might cause worry in some families if a girl made much out of plans like Linda's. Jorun, being a considerate and emphatic girl, a trait easily understood as typically girlish, aroused concern as well. More than one of the mothers of unproblematic and well-adapted girls told us they were somewhat concerned that their daughters were a "little too considerate and caring," and they were careful to avoid tasks that would strengthen these tendencies. The balance between following individual goals and becoming part of community seemed gendered in new ways, and the tendency points in more than one direction.

The Introduction of Heterogeneity...

The children and mothers we interviewed comprised only ethnic Norwegians. The reason for this is that they were mainly selected from a longitudinal study that already had been going on for several years. However, Norway is moving rapidly towards a more ethnically heterogeneous society. The contemporary discourse of gender in Norwegian general debate is therefore colored by new contrasts actualized by a growing minority population. New forms of "*we* versus *they*" emerge partly based on a—sometimes surprising—loyalty to an agenda of gender equality from new groups within ethnic Norwegian population.

There is a tendency in all parts of the "developed" world that girls do better at school than boys (Burman, 2008). This may be understood as girls being more conscientious and continuous workers, and more willing to subordinate to educational demands than boys. This is also so in Norway, both in the majority and in the minority populations (Bakken, 2009). Until now it has been usual to look at the interplay or intersections between gender, class, and ethnicity in order to understand differences in school results (Bakken, 2008). Against a background of assumed heavier demands on many immigrant girls when it comes to responsibility, caring, loyalty, and obedience, it would be interesting to look further into how these intersections color what Hundeide (2005) calls *opportunity structures* for young people in Norwegian society today.

CONCLUDING REMARKS

Appropriation of cultural values is a complex endeavor, and children's ways of actively going about it are often equally advanced. The children I have described and quoted are actively engaged in exploring the values of their communities, and they also criticize, shape, and transform them and eventually make them their own. They may enjoy this or be troubled by it, as their care-takers also may do. A one-sided picture of how the expert helps the novice is clearly limiting when we try to understand how children acquire knowledge and practice related to contradictory and complex cultural values. It seems important to be aware of possible unwanted meanings of discursive uni-direction that may follow when, for instance, we use the metaphor of apprenticeship that Rogoff (1990) introduced in the understanding of children's development.

It is in the interaction between the child and others that change and novelty in a child's activity and orientation happens, also called "the dynamic edge of development" (Hickmann, 1985). Children take part in intricate webs of interaction. Looking for the interdependence and dynamic coexistence of individualism and collectivism has highlighted some interesting tendencies in such webs. One of these is that the balance and unity between individual and common goals is gendered in new ways.

It was an intention to see individual development as embedded and interacting with development and change on the socio-cultural level as is important in an activity-oriented analysis. To look at how children take part in interactional webs is in itself only the inner figure in the "Russian set of dolls" that characterizes the ecological environment of development (Bronfenbrenner, 1979; Rogoff, 1990).

I have used analytic perspectives that make visible contradictory and conflicting messages in cultural and moral values. Children aged ten to eleven years are reflective about contradictions in the messages they receive. This is probably of importance in their active appropriation and reshaping of values. Conflicts and inconsistencies can play important parts. At this age children's possibilities of finding their own ways of acting, in the open spaces without adult surveillance, is rapidly expanding. In the cases I have studied, their appropriation of values was marked by both loyalty and opposition, both continuity and novelty.

A main purpose of this chapter was to examine how individual goals and personal identity work on the one hand, and becoming a useful member of community on the other, are connected in children's appropriation of values. My interpretation is that this is promising perspective to get away from a polarizing picture of what happens in this matter. There is still, and probably always has been, considerable variation connected to, for instance, the intersections of gender, age, and class. These variations form different possibilities for children, both for being a useful member of their surroundings, and for finding, strengthening, and developing unique characteristics, talents, and interests and making the best out of it. For now, I will conclude with the impression that "being oneself" and "being of use" seem closely intertwined for children, surely in ways that will vary with cultural context, and in ways we do not fully understand.

NOTES

1. "Modern societies" are usually understood as European countries, North America, and also Western-style educated enclaves in other countries.
2. The title of this chapter is a light paraphrasing of Gullestad's title of her chapter (1997): *From "being of use" to "finding oneself": Dilemmas of value transmission between generations in Norway.*
3. Thanks to Kristin Schelderup Mathiesen for us to plan, travel around and carry out interviews together, and for making it all feasible by getting informants from her longitudinal study, still going on.
4. All names are pseudonyms.
5. Solberg (1997) is occupied with emerging *vacancies* for children this age. Children are, for instance, coming home to vacant instead of empty houses.

REFERENCES

Andenæs, A. (1991). Fra forskningsobjekt til medforsker? Livsformsintervju med 4-5-åringer. [From investigated object to co-researcher? Way of life interviews with four to five year old children]. *Nordisk Psykologi, 43*, 274–292.

Bakken, A. (2009). Nye tall om ungdom: Tidlig skolestart og skoleprestasjoner for språklige minoritetselever [New figures about youths: Early start and school results for language minority pupils]. *Tidsskrift for ungdomsforskning, 9*(1), 79–89.

Bakken, A. (2008). Nye tall om ungdom: Er kjønnsforskjeller i skoleprestasjoner avhengig av klassebakgrunn og minoritetsstatus? [New figures about youths: Is gender differences in school results dependent on class and minority status?]. *Tidsskrift for ungdomsforskning, 8*(1), 85–93.

Bronfenbrenner, U. (1979). *The ecology of human development.* Cambridge, MA: Harvard University Press.

Bruner, J. (1985). Vygotsky: A historical and conceptual perspective. In J. V. Wertsch (Ed.), *Culture, communication and cognition: Vygotskian perspectives* (pp. 21–34). Cambridge, UK: Cambridge University Press.

Burman, E. (2008). *Deconstructing developmental psychology* (2nd ed.). London, UK: Routledge.

Davies, B. (2003). *Shards of glass: Children reading and writing beyond gendered identities.* Cresskill, NJ: Hampton Press.

Greene, S., & Hill, M. (2005). Researching children's experience: Methods and methodological issues. In S. Greene & D. Hogan (Eds.). *Researching children's experience: Approaches and methods* (pp. 1–21). London, UK: Sage.

Gullestad, M. (1997). From "being of use" to "finding oneself": Dilemmas of value transmission between generations in Norway. In M. Gullestad & M. Segalen (Eds.), *Family and kinship in Europe* (pp. 202–219). London, England: Pinter.

Hickmann, M. E. (1985). Discourse skills and developmental theory. In J. V. Wertsch (Ed.), *Culture, communication and cognition: Vygotskian perspectives* (pp. 236–257). Cambridge, UK: Cambridge University Press.

Hundeide, K. (2003). *Barns livsverden: Sociokulturelle rammer for barns utvikling.* [Childrens world of life: Socio-cultural frames for children's development]. Oslo, Norway: Cappelen.

Hundeide, K. (2005). Socio-cultural tracks of development, opportunity situations and access skills. *Culture and Psychology, 11*, 241–261.

Kagitcibasi, C. (1996). *Family and human development across cultures.* Mahwah, NJ: Lawrence Erlbaum.

Kagitcibasi, C. (2005). Autonomy and relatedness in cultural context: Implications for self and family. *Journal of Cross-Cultural Psychology, 36*, 403–422.

Kristjansson, B. (2006). The making of Nordic childhoods. In J. Einarsdottir & J.Wagner (Eds.), *Nordic childhoods and early education: Philosophy, research, policy and practice in Denmark, Finland, Iceland, Norway and Sweden* (pp. 13–42). Greenwich, CT: Information Age Publishing.

LeVine, A., & White, M. I. (1986). *Human conditions: The cultural basis of educational development.* London, UK: Routledge & Kegan Paul.

Oyserman, D., Coon, H., & Kemmelmeier, M. (2002). Rethinking individualism and collectivism: Evaluation of theoretical assumptions and meta-analysis. *Psychological Bulletin, 128*, 3–72.

Rogoff, B. (1990). *Apprenticeship in thinking: Cognitive development in social context.* Oxford, UK: Oxford University Press.

Solberg, A. (1997). Negotiating childhood: Changing constructions of age for Norwegian children. In A. James & A. Prout (Eds.), *Constructing and reconstructing childhood: Contemporary issues in the sociological study of childhood* (pp. 126–144). London, UK: Routledge Falmer.

Tamis-LeMonda, C. S., Way, N., Hughes, D.,Yoshikawa, H., Kalman, R. K., & Niwa, E. Y. (2008). Parents' goals for children: The dynamic coexistence of individualism and collectivism in cultures and individuals. *Social Development, 17,* 183–209.

Valsiner, J., & Van der Veer, I. (2000). *The social mind: Construction of the idea.* Cambridge, UK: Cambridge University Press

Valsiner, J. (2007). *Culture in minds and societies: foundations of cultural psychology.* New Dehli, India: Sage.

Wertsch, J. V. (1998). *Mind as action.* New York, NY: Oxford University Press.

CHAPTER 3

"REMAINING THE SAME" AND CHILDREN'S EXPERIENCE OF DEVELOPMENT

Pernille Hviid

INTRODUCTION

Among major thinkers in developmental theory, from Baldwin (1895), Piaget (1970) and Vygotsky (1998), to modern developmental scientist such as Cairns, Elder, and Costello (1996), Lerner, Perkins, and Jacobsen (1993), and Valsiner (1993), there seems to be a general agreement that developmental processes take place at a different pace and show different degrees of strength during ontogenesis, although the criteria and explanations for what constitute change or stability differ radically in the different theoretical orientations. In the following I will investigate developmental processes, not as either periods of change or stability, but rather as a processes of *changing configurations* of the remaining present and the emerging novelties. This is done with a special interest in understanding the processes during seemingly stable periods, when no big novelties occur. In doing so, I draw mostly on cultural historical contributions, and mainly the work of Vygotsky (e.g., 1998).

Children, Childhood, and Everyday Life, pages 37–52
Copyright © 2012 by Information Age Publishing

37

In modern developmental psychology, development implies some kind of interaction between novel and remaining aspects in the developing system (Valsiner & Connolly, 2003). These interactional processes are here examined through Vygotsky's analysis of critical and stable periods during ontogenesis, where either conservatism or new evolving aspects dominate the developmental picture, and thus make development go either "slow and smooth" or "revolutionary and chaotic" (Vygotsky, 1998, p. 191). Despite describing stable periods as smooth and slow, Vygotsky nevertheless noticed "great alterations" in development during these periods: therefore, what is happening, what can account for these great alterations, when nothing great or novel is occurring?

Drawing on Vygotsky's notion of development and Bergson's (1915) notion of the experience of time, I suggest to study novelties and remaining in a very fluid sense, in the light of each other. This means that the precise developmental implication of novelties can only be understood in their functional dialogue with the already evolved aspects. Different patterns of these functional dialogues between the novel aspects and the already evolved aspects are hypothesized and examined through an analysis of a 12-year-old girl's narrative of her own developmental processes. It will be shown that stability in development is indeed a highly active process, and by no means a period in time where nothing happens. On the contrary, many novelties occur, but they function predominantly in the service of what has already developed. This stability is deliberate and sought for by the girl herself, on the basis of her personal will and active selection of contexts, where she can re-experience what she considers to be important in her life. It is done in a reflected dialogue with the plenitude of alternative offers to a girl in a late-modern capital.

THE CONFIGURATION OF THE NOVEL AND THE REMAINING IN DEVELOPMENTAL SYSTEMS: A QUESTION OF DEVELOPMENTAL STRENGTH AND PACE

The changing configurations of change and stability in development imply that novel aspects appear and dominate some periods of the child's life, whereas already given aspects seem to dominate other periods of life and thus keep the system more stable. Vygotsky dealt with these configurations in detail in his analysis of *critical periods* in ontogenesis (Vygotsky, 1998). During some periods, and, chronologically speaking, during most of childhood, Vygotsky writes that "development is marked by slow, evolutionally or lytic flow", with "unremarkable internal changes in the child's personality, changes that are accomplished by insignificant 'molecular' attainments" (Vygotsky, 1998. p.190). In these smooth and frequent periods, "development occurs mainly through microscopic changes in the child's personality that accumulate to a certain limit and then appear spasmodically in the form of some kind of neoformation of the age level" (Vygotsky, 1998, p. 191). Critical periods are, on the other hand,

> characterised by traits which are the opposite of the firm or stable age levels. During these periods abrupt and major shifts and displacements, changes and discontinuities in the child's personality are concentrated in a relatively short time.... Development takes on a stormy, impetuous and sometimes catastrophic character that resembles a revolutionary course of events in both range of the changes that are occurring and in the sense of the alterations that are made. (ibid., p. 191)

Through his conceptualization of stable and critical periods, Vygotsky created a periodic developmental system for analysing crucial novelty and different developmental periods in ontogenesis. Although Vygotsky's main focus concerned the critical periods of ontogenesis, he nevertheless noted that "great alterations in his personality are evident if a child is compared at the beginning and at the end of a stable period" (1998, p. 191). What Vygotsky seems to claim is that a period dominated by stability may nevertheless produce great alterations. The dynamics of these periods, their stability, their slowness, their orderliness, and yet, the "great alterations" in development, are the conceptual challenges of this chapter. What is happening when nothing novel and great seems to happen?

Drawing on general developmental theory, it makes sense to anticipate such a high degree of maintenance in children's developmental paths, as Vygotsky did, since a developing system logically would transform and become another system, and thus lose its identity, if only composed by changes (Valsiner, 1997). Rather, in general theory it would be anticipated that the forces towards the creation of novelty would be matched with some corresponding degree of maintaining the developing system; if not, it would break down or constitute an ongoing developmental crisis, as Vygotsky described in cultural-historical terms.

METHODOLOGICAL CONSIDERATIONS IN DEVELOPMENTAL STUDIES: A STUDY OF DEVELOPMENTAL EXPERIENCE

In the following, a child's experience of her developmental path will be presented in order to present and discuss the conceptual challenge. Before that, however, some methodological considerations will be briefly presented regarding developmental research. This is done in order to explain how children's accounts of their *personal experiences of living and developing* can be considered as useful data for studying developmental processes.

Vygotsky (1998) considered *experience* to be the basic unit from which the interdependent developing relationship between the child's personality and environment could be studied: "experience is the unity of the personality and the environment as it is represented in development" (Vygotsky, 1998, p.294). As a developmental concept, experience is a very broad and complex concept, not only including present perception, cognitive performance or understanding of the situation, but also being flavored by emotions and engagements, interests and more macro-oriented motives of the subject; and all of this subsisting in a temporal fashion. "[E]xperience is affected by the extent to which all my properties, and how they came about in the course in development, participate here at a given moment" (Vygotsky, 1998, p. 294).

Vygotsky underlined the child's active participation in restructuring her relationship with the environment, thereby co-creating conditions and experiences for her development. Children's experiences of their situations— be they long (as with life) or short (as in an experiment)—are therefore not merely built into present developmental psychology for democratic reasons (e.g., "Let the children be heard!"), but are on the contrary considered as central features of the very developmental process to be studied, and must therefore be taken into account in methodology. "[I]t [experience] 'informs' people what their relationship to their environment is and correspondingly orients their behaviour to act" (Bozhovich, 2009, p. 74). Therefore, an insight into children's experiences is essential for our understanding of how children and their environments mutually benefit each other's development.

Temporal experiences are in the core of the question to be investigated, since it takes time to remain the same, and it takes time for something or somebody to become a novel form. Therefore, the conceptual use of time in developmental psychology and especially the subjective experience of time will be briefly introduced.

Developmental psychology often posits a double conception of time. In a cultural-historical framework, the "objective clock-time dimension" usually includes not only the ages of the children studied, but also the historical time the children are part of (Elder, 2001), as well as the timing of, for instance, different socio-cultural childhood arrangements in the children's lives (Rogoff, Sellers, Pirrotta, Fox, & White, 1975; Schousboe, 2000). But how do people experience time? Here, developmental psychology often posits a fluid concept of temporality, inspired by Bergson's (1915) notion of *la durée.* In this conception of time, the subjective past, present, and future fluidly interpenetrate each other and form an entangled experience that is very different from orderly clock-time and much closer to the experience of, for instance, listening to a piece of music. When listening to music, one (usually) does not hear music as single notes; rather, music is experienced in its temporal progression of novel and recurrent themes. Likewise, in the subjective experience of time, the past, present, and future are intertwined in the temporal composition of life, as in Vygotsky's notion of experience.

According to the Bergsonian view of time, novelty preserves, and preservations generate the novel (Bergson, 1915), which points to some kind of interaction between the two aspects in the course of life and development. This functional "dialogue" between novelty and already evolved is given analytic attention.

When can the novelties in children's development be considered to be "genuine" novelties, in the sense that they present themselves as *co-existing complements* to the remaining present? Co-existing complements are considered to be a kind of novelties, which do not appear to be due to any strong dialogue with the remaining present life. When do the novelties function to *overrule* the remaining present and diminish its importance, and when are the possible novelties overruled or dismissed by the remaining present? When can novelties be considered as *serving* the remaining present? This would take place when novel inspirations lead to further explorations of the remaining present—perhaps in new directions, or with a changed motivation. But novelties could also serve the remaining present in creating *a distance from or a distraction from* the remaining present—precisely by aid of the novel.

"Personal experience" is a challenging empirical unit of analysis, and this concerns the "immediate given-ness," and, later in a child's life, the "mine-ness" of personal experiences (Zahavi, 2007). A researcher can neither assume that she experiences situations the way the research participant does, and thus know the identical experience first hand, herself, nor can she assume that words, descriptions, or narratives, put into use in order to present or explain certain experiences, mirror the actual experiences in an identical way.

Nevertheless, and however complex and intriguing the work on experience is, it is assumed here that one can 'track' needs, interests, motives, tensions, conflicts, and so on—"a child's motivational sphere" (Bozhovich, 2009, p. 71)—and the configuration of remaining and novel at work behind the experiences expressed.

AN INVESTIGATION OF CHILDREN'S EXPERIENCE OF THEIR DEVELOPMENT

In this section, data from interviews with a 12-year-old girl (Maria) will be presented, preceded by a short introduction to the research agenda in which Maria took part. The interviews with her and five other 12-year-old children were conducted in order to gain some insight into children's experiences of developing (Hviid, 2008a, 2008b). During three 2-hour-long interviews, the children drew "life-maps" on big pieces of paper, representing *places* of importance to their lives (such as the kindergarten and the swimming pool); made roads or motorways, representing the *connections* between different socio-cultural arrangements, such as school and afterschool and home; and wrote *names* or made *drawings* of people, animals, symbols, and arrangements (e.g., a circus Maria attended) referring to something or somebody they themselves considered very important in their lives. During the life-mapping interviews, the children described novel experiences and novel situations as well as recurring themes. They described the guidance that they had received, the choices they had made, together with obstacles and boundaries for their activities, and the conflicts that had arisen, as well as their more or less satisfying resolutions.

In the following description of Maria's narratives, and in excerpts from them, the reader will notice many 'first time appearances', as well as recurring themes. At the present time of the experience, the precise function of the novel or the maintained cannot be determined, but can only be understood over time; in relation to past and future movements. It is the aim here to look into the dynamics between these novel and remaining aspects of importance to Maria's experience of her life.

Data are presented in a spatial–temporal fashion, close to Bronfenbrenner's concepts of space in micro-, meso- and chrono-systems (Bronfenbrenner, 1993). This has been done in order to get the fullest impression of the diversity of settings Maria lived in and by, at different periods in her ontogenesis. This periodicity is organized according to major organizational changes in Maria's life. Danish society organizes childhood in more or less optional stays and transitions from family care to nursery care, then kindergarten, school and after-school arrangements, and later youth clubs. Other arrangements were chosen by the family and Maria, such as horse riding in her spare time. We may speak of changing meso-systems over time and notice that the complexity of these meso-systems grows with her age.

The first meso-unit to be presented here contains Maria's family, her kindergarten, and her leisure time spaces, whereas the second meso-unit from which she gained her developmental experiences contained her family, school, afterschool center, and her leisure time activities, such as horse riding and cat breeding. The third meso-level contains school, youth club, friends, horse riding, circus, and her pets. Although the data thus follow an objective societal time-scale, Maria's experiences about her becoming are much less tied up with chronological time; they seem to be fluid and changing shapes of something persistent.

First Chrono-system: Maria's Family Context, Kindergarten, and Leisure Time as a Preschooler

Maria grew up with her mother, grandmother, and her older sister. Her father left the family even before she was born. Shortly after her birth, her grandmother came to live with her in Copenhagen. Maria had always felt very close to her grandmother. At the point of the interview, she described her as "the finest person in the world." She got along fine with her mother, but she and her sister had problems in getting along with each other. They were, on both sides, very critical about each other's behavior.

During her time in kindergarten, Maria and her little family moved out of Copenhagen to live closer to nature, and she came to "love nature." She remembers herself as having been a little bit sad to have left the kindergarten and the friends she had made there, but also that she soon made new friends in the new kindergarten. She liked the pedagogues too, and the food, especially strawberry pudding. She became very happy with the move: the nature and the beach she lived near to. Around her fourth year of age the family got two dogs (Siberian Huskies). She was very fond of those dogs, and remembered many small lively episodes together with them. When her mother chose to move back to Copenhagen a couple of years later, it was decided that life in the capital was too unfit for that breed of dogs. Since Maria's grandmother stayed in the countryside, their two dogs stayed with her, which meant that Maria could still visit them. She considered that to be a fine solution. Also, while living in the countryside, Maria began riding horses. This became one of her great and longstanding interests; as a 12-year-old, she still rode a couple of days a week.

In this first chrono-system, we remark both issues that remained important in Maria's life, as well as new appearances. Maria's family was extremely important to her, especially her mother, but maybe even more so her grandmother, to whom she got more and more attached over the years. The novel elements experienced in this period can be considered as *co-existing complements* to the remaining, to what Maria was already engaged in: She became fond of playmates in kindergarten, she developed love for nature and affection for dogs, and she became a rather skilled horse rider in a relatively short time.

Second Chrono-system: School Start, Leisure Time Activity Center, Horse-Riding and Family-Life

Starting school went fine for Maria. She soon made new friends in both school and after-school institutions. She was interested in school work and worked effectively. Her favorite subject became biology. Her time in the leisure time activity center was not attractive to her. She felt bored there, and she felt "forced into excursions" of little relevance to her, which to her contradicted the very term "leisure time." She was happy to leave the center by the end of third grade. Perhaps because of the quality of the activity center, or possibly because of her engagements with horses, she kept on riding horses in the afternoons, three days a week. She also made friends with many of the other horse-riding girls there.

In addition, Maria engaged in a shared family interest (her sister was an exception to that): cat breeding. Her mother began breeding Norwegian Forest cats upon returning to Copenhagen at her sixth year of age. Maria didn't know where that interest came from, but at approximately nine years of age, they had 20 cats and kittens in their flat in the center of the city. Maria's grandmother got interested in cat breeding as well, and together they went to cat exhibitions and competitions, which went very well for them in terms of success in cat championships. A few years later, Maria's mother got tired of cat breeding and started to sell them, and one of the hardest times in Maria's life was the day she discovered that her mother had secretly sold a cat that belonged to her. She missed her cat, and she lost respect for her mother in her having behaved in the way that she did.

During this period of time, Maria both maintained parts of her life while also meeting or creating novelties. She remained close to her family while still opposing her sister's "alternative" activities, or criticizing her sister's lack of attention towards shared family projects. She started school, and participated in instruction and learning activities, which can be considered as a *co-existing complement* to the aspects she maintained. Schooling did not, as a novelty, compromise earlier developed orientations. But when looking at the novel aspects in this period of her life, they were predominantly *in the service* of the remaining present or *overruled* by what had already evolved. Maria overruled the activities of the leisure-time activity center and instead preferred spending afternoons in horse riding. But her interest in biology stood *in the service* of the remaining present, since she "loved nature," and so did her intense engagement in Norwegian Forest cats. Animals of many sorts occupied Maria's life and deepened her engagement in what she later called "being personal with animals."

Third Chrono-time: Family, School, Youth Club, Parties, Circus, Horse Riding, and Dogs

At the time of interviewing, in 7th grade, Maria still judged herself to be doing acceptably in relation to school, and also that teachers and her mother were content with her school performance. She worked hard, and got good marks. Her favorite subject was still biology, but she also strived hard in maths.

Maria spent some weekly afternoons in a youth club; there she liked to sew, play theatre, and chat with her friends. She appreciated the pedagogues too, although she voiced some critical remarks about their unbalanced attention towards the younger children in the youth club. Almost once a week, she visited her grandmother. She liked to just be there, as well as the surrounding nature and the coziness in her grandmother's house. An important leisure-time activity was the circus that Maria visited, together with some other girls from the club. A provincial circus toured around Denmark and stopped in Copenhagen every year between June and August on the edge of the park just opposite Maria's school. Maria became friendly with some of the artists and with the owner of the circus. She ran errands for the staff, and took care of the horses, elephants, and the children (mentioned in that order). Maria loved the circus community, the intense feeling of group spirit and belonging, as well as the animals. The circus manager had offered her to join the circus for a year, after the obligatory nine years of schooling, and her mother had accepted the idea. The day of the first interview with Maria, she was about to get a puppy, a little curly, black poodle puppy—a gift from the circus. Maria's excitement and joy was overwhelming. Meanwhile, Maria rode horses "only" twice a week, since she had promised her mother to balance horse riding and taking care of the new dog.

Maria's life with her sister never ceased to pose problems and give rise to conflicts. As Maria explained, her sister did everything she did not want to do, and was everything she did not want to be. She sang in a choir, she danced and had parties with friends and older youngsters. Maria's sister became her alter-ego and, possibly, vice versa. Nevertheless, their mutual hostility started to pose Maria new problems, since her older sister successfully blocked her possibilities of attending parties with the eighth graders, as Maria's classmates did. Since her sister insisted: "It is me or her!" to her classmates, Maria was not invited as a newcomer seventh grader at the eighth graders' parties. Maria found that strategy annoying and low, but felt she could do nothing about it.

In this third chrono-period, Maria maintained closeness to her family, engagement in schoolwork, and horse riding. She also maintained a problematic relationship with her sister, which started to pose her problems elsewhere in her youth life, and thus blocked a novel engagement (parties) from developing. Although this constraint annoyed her deeply, it did not make her reconsider her strongly maintained conflict with her sister. Some of the novel engagements in her life can be considered as *co-existing complements* to what she maintained. This concerns her enjoyment in sewing and theatre playing at the youth club. Other novelties can be seen as *serving* what Maria already maintained. The circus life gave her new contacts with animals, and people who were engaged in animals, while at the same time leading on to a novel *co-existing complement* (at least to the researcher): She announced she "loved the community and group spirit in the circus."

MARIA'S REMAINING ENGAGEMENTS IN THE WORLD

Looking at Maria's engagements, she was able to transform many arenas into the activities she was most fond of: being with animals. There were intelligent horses she loved riding, cute dogs she cared for and trained, beautiful canary birds she listened to, world champion cats she went to competitions with, and fantastic elephants she fed and watched being trained. In biology, she combined schoolwork with pure pleasure; in math, she aimed at entry to veterinarian university. She spent hours, days, and weeks with animals in her youth club time and in leisure time at the riding school, and her family life was a community of professional cat-breeders. Her mother supported her interest in animals by allowing her to get a dog of her own, and accepted the idea of her touring with the circus when the school years were over. Looking across the contexts of Maria's everyday life, the multiplicity of activities with animals is striking.

This engagement might be thought of as a replacement for absent or hostile relationships with human beings. That was not the case. Rather, Maria's social networks seemed to function in a satisfying manner to her: at school, in her riding club, with other cat fans, and at youth club. She made friends with other kids, some of whom shared her interest in animals, circus, cat-breeding, and riding—others did not. Her relationships with adults, such as pedagogues and teachers, seemed also to be rather sound and unproblematic. Her narratives about her childhood and early young life portrayed a harmonious and happy life, except for her continual quarrels with her older sister.

Maria's thoughts of the future
    Maria: I know what I want to become.
Interviewer: Oh?
    Maria: Yes. A vet!
Interviewer: Of course!
    Maria: I want to work with animals.
Interviewer: Yes.
    Maria: I love animals.
Interviewer: Yes.
    Maria: It's simply; if I can work with animals, I am happy. Vet! But I am worried about the marks needed. I really have to work very, very hard, but I would so much like to become a vet.

Interviewer: When did you decide that? It is a thought that projects far into the future.

Maria: Three years ago, I think. My friends—many wanted to be actors, but now two of them want to be architects. But I want to stick with it. I will do all I can to stick with it. I need high marks in biology and math but of course I love biology, nature. I love nature.

It was of no surprise to the interviewer that Maria wanted to become a vet. Before that she had thought of becoming a horse-whisperer, but had rejected the idea. Nevertheless, Maria was concerned with her own developmental path. She feared that her dreams and aspirations would change, as they had already done with so many other children she knew. Realizing that risk in development, she had made a promise to herself not to change. She would, she said, *do all she could*, to stick and stay with her plan for her future, and fight her own tendencies to change, should she ever feel inclined to do so. Maria wanted to remain the same, to be true to her professional goals. In these reflections we may notice how the dominant aspects of the remaining present are in *the service of* the anticipated future and vice versa.

One and a Half Years Later...

Maria met for an interview one and a half years later, since data revealed more questions to be asked, and she was willing to help. She was now fourteen years old. A sentence in a former interview was still puzzling. She had said: "You know, children don't like changes," and she said it in a way that presented it as self-evident: that sentence was the theme of the meeting. The upcoming meeting had inspired her to think of her life, and of how many new things had happened in her life since we had met last time. "I have got yet another dog, and a job and some new friends," she said. When we came to talk about the puzzling sentence, she gave the following example:

Maria: I think most children are happy with what they have got: the things they have.

Interviewer: That might be true...

Maria: Yes. And I believe that that is why many children have difficulties with death and that sort of thing, right? If an animal dies. They don't like the change. They like the way it is and this is how it should continue to be.

The general logic in the statement was, primarily—but not only—derived from her engagement with animals; she didn't like to lose them. Besides, Maria had been giving her future plans some serious thought, and had decided that she didn't want to become a vet after all. Therefore, her marks in maths did not have the same importance to her anymore, so she worked less intensely on the subject. Maria had after all changed. She did not want to be a vet, and explained:

> **Maria:** I do not have the same compassion for human beings as I have for animals. We (humans) have created the world. I know it is not the individual person who has done it; but still, humans have created the world, and we have done it in a stupid way, and now it doesn't go that well, with nature. But animals have only been here as an audience. They haven't been heard at all. That's why I feel much sorrier for animals. (...) And a vet, she is also engaged with the wishes of human beings. If a dog has a wart above the eye you can have it removed for purely cosmetic reasons. If a dog bites a human being, it is killed. It is never seen from the perspective of the dog. If it was chained up and afraid...
>
> **Interviewer:** I see...
>
> **Maria:** We are allowed to protect and defend ourselves when we are afraid, but when they do so, they are thought of as aggressive, and killed. And when people get bored with their animals, they are killed. I do not want to be a vet. As a vet I will not be in a personal relationship with animals. I want to save animals. I almost feel pain to know that animals are treated badly. I want to work in an NGO, like ANIMAL or SPA (Safe Place for Animals), or something like that. Because I feel they need our help.

Now, this is a good place to pause: a powerful "new appearance" has appeared in Maria's life that not only changes her perception of her future, but also changes her practical orientation in her everyday life in present time. The analytical question to be dealt with concerns whether novel goals (and refraining from becoming a vet and joining an NGO) are in the service of strengthening Maria's "remaining herself," or whether the novel disturbs how Maria remains herself, and thereby "becomes novel," in the *overruling* sense of the term. The excerpt contains a correction of the knowledge of what a vet does, and in the service of whom. Maria said in previous interview: "If I can work with animals, I am happy"; but she discovered later that other ways to work with animals offered her more satisfaction. In this way, the novel element marked by her interest working for an NGO in the future was, in another way, and on another level, her "coming home," with respect to who Maria regarded herself to be, and to what Maria considered to be worthwhile striving for. This novel goal is *in the service of* Maria's attempt to remain the same. Withdrawing her efforts in math shows how it served her first goal, becoming a vet, and how it lost importance in the light of her new long-term goal. Math is thereby *overruled* by her novel orientation towards remaining the same.

ON CHANGES AND STABILITY IN MARIA'S DEVELOPMENT AND LIFE

One the one hand, a plenitude of novelties in Maria's life springs to one's attention: Maria meets new people, goes to new places, develops new specific interests, participates in new activities, and changes future plans; and with these changed plans she also changes her present strivings in other fields (like math). Novelties are thus easy to notice in Maria's development. On the other hand, Maria's maintaining of herself is just as visible and active in her daily life. Throughout most of her life she has maintained, refined, and elaborated on a commitment, or multi-faceted project, which could be named "being close to animals," or, as she termed it: "I want to be *personal* with animals." Some characteristics of the remaining will be discussed in what follows.

First of all, the *active engagement* of remaining the same is worth highlighting. Remaining the same is not a neutral process, where "nothing to bring development forward is happening," and thus the developmental process can neither be considered to be "slow" nor "weak." Rather, a strong dedication works behind it, a will, a striving that is reflected upon when meeting opportunities for new activities. Stable periods may therefore be characterized not as periods where no novelties occur, but as periods where novelties are predominantly in the service of the remaining present, and may therefore be considered as some kind of generative conservatism.

Maria's remaining the same *cannot be explained by contextual chance.* The range of other possible activities and the plenitude of opportunities for the development of other engagements and interests, as a girl in the center of the capital city, are obvious. Her maintaining "being personal with animals" and not everything else is definitely not promoted by rich environmental affordances for an girl in a capital city in Europe. There are not that many elephants and horses or other animals in the center of Copenhagen. Behind the redundancy in her everyday engagements and practical life with animals is a dedication in selecting and creating experiences Maria finds worthwhile repeating or elaborating. As a theoretical comment on theories working with concepts of "situated learning" (e.g., Lave & Wenger, 1991), Maria's development *is* constrained by the situatedness of her life, but, on another level, the very situatedness is strongly composed by herself in order to re-experience, or experience anew, what she finds worthwhile experiencing.

With respect to the dynamics between many of the novelties and Maria's remaining herself, it is worth remarking that the changes Maria partici-pates in, in her concrete life, are *in the service of* her remaining herself on a macro-level, and not the other way around, although this was not always the case. Through concrete experiences with animals and in dialogue in school subjects as biology with other animal-interested people—especially her grandmother who also loved animals—and with knowledge of what her anticipated future occupation as a vet would contain, her long-term per-sonal project sharpened, which eventually made her change plans of her professional occupation as she realized that the occupation of a vet did not match her personal project. It was discharged together with math in school.

While Maria's project deepened, her attention towards her own direc-tionality sharpened. The self-regulatory principle that comes into play is described by Valsiner (1997) as "my own will":

> [T]he most general intrapsychological generator—"my own will"—can over-ride an elaborate set of external constraints upon conduct, and let the person resists canalization efforts, and to be psychologically distanced from the goal-directed efforts of the "social others". The emergence of this self-constraining system guarantees the person's dependent independence even in situations where the external actions of the person are maximally limited. (Valsiner, 1997, p. 309)

One might argue that there are no such "social others" in Maria's life who intend to lead Maria off her track, and channel her development in other directions. But late-modern society does. Late modern society is in general fast, fluid, and changing; life-long learning and development are the keywords for late modern life; a person's concrete daily encounters with "new opportunities" are numerous, as are invitations to change the orienta-tion of attention. Maria seems to have been aware of these societal calls for change at a very young age, and she actively resisted their invitations.

CONCLUSION

In this chapter, an attempt has been made to investigate development as dynamic and changing configurations of novel and maintained aspects of life, as they are experienced by the person in question. As the experience of life is fluid, intertwining the actual situation with past experiences and present orientations towards future, so are the maintained and novel as-pects intertwined, in the course of development. Some of these dynamics have been investigated, and certain novel aspects have been conceptualized as *complements* to the remained present, whereas others were considered as *overruling* or *serving* the maintained present. On the basis of the above empirical investigations of children's development, it emerges that novelties can maintain, and that the maintained can be precisely maintained by novelties, as was proposed by Bergson's (op. cit.) philosophy.

Looking closer at the dynamics of the maintained, remaining turns out to be a highly active process, a deliberate engaged choosing of opportunities to re-experience or experience from a new angle what seem important to be maintained in life and as oneself. Under the "smooth" surface of stable developmental periods, as Vygotsky described, occurs an enormous effort to repeat, elaborate, and refine.

In order to investigate these dynamics in greater depth, it is necessary to introduce a slower timescale along which changing configurations of novelty and remaining can be followed. Methodologically speaking, analyzing changing configurations of "remaining the same" and "the novel" takes a longer time to be studied than the plain appearances of novelties. Further investigations rely precisely on how children experience, make their lives, and make meaning of their lives, and will thus be obvious fields for future collaboration between children and researchers.

REFERENCES

Baldwin, J. M. (1895). *Mental development in the child and the race.* New York, NY: Macmillan.

Bergson, H. (1915). *Den skabende udvikling* [Creative development]. Copenhagen, Denmark: Gads Forlag.

Bozhovich, L. I. (2009). The social situation of the child. *Journal of Russian and East European Psychology, 47*(4), 59–86.

Bronfenbrenner, U. (1993). Ecological models of human development. In M. Gauvain & M. Cole (Eds.), *Readings on the development of children* (pp. 37–43). New York, NY: Freeman.

Cairns, R.B., Elder, G. E., & Costello, E. J. (Eds.). (1996). *Developmental science.* New York, NY: Cambridge University Press.

Elder, G.H. (2001). The life course paradigm: Social change and individual development. In P. Moen, G.H. Elder, & K. Lüsher (Eds.), *Examining lives in context—Perspectives on the ecology of human development* (pp. 101–141). Washington, DC: American Psychological Association.

Hviid, P. (2008a). Interviewing using a cultural-historical approach. In M. Hedegaard, M. Fleer, J. Bang, & P. Hviid (Eds.), *Studying Children. A cultural-historical approach,* (pp. 139–157). Maidenhead, UK: McGraw-Hill Education/Open University Press.

Hviid, P. (2008b). Next year we are small, right? Different times in children's development. *European Journal of Psychology of Education, 23*(2), 183–198.

Lave, J., & Wenger, E. (1991). *Situated learning: Legitimate peripheral participation.* New York, NY: Cambridge University Press.

Lerner, R.M., Perkins, D. F., & Jacobsen, L.P. (1993). Timing, process and the diversity of development in human life: A developmental perspective In G. Turkewitz & D. Devenny (Eds.), *Developmental time and timing* (pp. 41–61). Hillsdale, NJ: Lawrence Erlbaum Associates.

Piaget, J. (1970). *Genetic epistemology.* New York, NY: Colombia University Press.

Rogoff, B., Sellers, M.J., Pirrotta, S., Fox, N. & White, S.H. (1975). Age of assignment of roles and responsibilities to children: A cross-cultural survey. *Human Development, 18,* 353–369.

Schousboe, I. (2000). Udviklingspsykologi og børn i virkeligheden. [Developmental psychology and children in real life.]. In L. Reimer, I. Schousboe, & P. Thorborg (Eds.), *I nærheden. En antologi om børneperspektiver* [Close. An anthology on children's perspectives] (pp. 151–171). Copenhagen, Denmark: Hans Reitzels Forlag.

Valsiner, J. (1993). Making the future: Temporality and the constructive nature of human development. In G. Turkewitz & D. Devenny (Eds.), Developmental time and timing. (pp.13–41). Hillsdale, NJ: Lawrence Erlbaum Associates Inc.

Valsiner, J. (1997). *Culture and the development of children's actions.* New York, NY: John Wiley.

Valsiner, J. & Connelly, K. J. (2003). The nature of development: The continuing dialogue of processes and outcomes. In J. Valsiner & K.J. Connolly (Eds.), *Handbook of developmental psychology* (pp. ix–xix). London, UK: Sage Publications.

Vygotsky, L.S. (1998). *Collected works. Vol. V. Child psychology.* New York, NY: Kluwer Academic/Plenum Publishers.

Zahavi, D. (2007). Self and other: The limits of narrative understanding. In D.D. Hutto (Ed.), *Narrative and understanding persons* (pp. 179–201). Royal institute of philosophy supplement 60. Cambridge, UK: Cambridge University Press.

SECTION II

FAMILY LIFE PRACTICES AS AN ARENA
FOR NEGOTIATIONS AND INFORMAL LEARNING

CHAPTER 4

CHILDREN'S CREATIVE MODELING OF CONFLICT RESOLUTIONS IN EVERYDAY LIFE AS CENTRAL IN THEIR LEARNING AND DEVELOPMENT IN FAMILIES

Mariane Hedegaard

INTRODUCTION

Children appropriate motives and competencies through entering institutional practices and sharing activities with other people within activity settings (Hedegaard, 2012). This chapter will focus on the characteristics of children's learning through participating in home practices and how children's activities at home are influenced by other kinds of institutional practice. Children meet different types of demands in home activity settings but children also put demands on other participants in these activity settings especially on their parents. The aim in this chapter is to present a theoretical conceptualisation and discuss how children through imitating, modelling and constructing activities contribute to the solutions of conflicts between demands from parents and their own wants and motive orientations and thereby create conditions for their own learning and development.

The theoretical discussion is supported by the analyses of a case-study of a child's everyday life in a family's daily practice. The analyses will focus on a six-year-old boy, Emil, and his siblings' activities at home and how Emil's engagement in the activities at home also is influenced by practice in institutions outside home, especially school practice, where he has just entered the first grade in school—in Denmark called the kindergarten class.

In the cultural-historical activity tradition, a conception of children as actively contributing to their own learning and development conditions has become central (Bozhovich, 2007; Bruner, 1972, 1999; Elkonin, 1999; Hedegaard, 2002, 2009; Rogoff, 2003; Vygotsky, 1998). The theoretical conception of how children actually contribute to their own learning and development has has been vague and unexplored. Through analyzing a child's everyday activities, a more nuanced conception is intended of how children contribute to their family's everyday activity settings and thereby to their own social situation as conditions for their own learning and development.

Earlier research on children's learning at home has mostly been on how different family and community practices with literacy and math influence children's literacy and math learning in school (Goldman, 2005; Heath, 1983; Moll & Greenberg, 1990; Scribner & Cole, 1981; Tharp & Galimore, 1988). Another kind of reseach about children and families is how different home traditions, in different cultures and in different social classes, influence children's involvement in activities at home (Ochs & Izguierdo 2009; Rogoff, 2003; Tudge, 2008). Studies of family practices show a great diversity in terms of how much children are integrated in daily chores and work activities. Rogoff (2003), in several studies from Guatemala, shows how children become involved in household productions and how older siblings have to care for their younger siblings. In Ochs and Izguierdo's study (2009), children in Samoa and Matsigenka (Peruvian Amazon) from a very early age attain responsibilities for contributing to the daily practice of the family's work chores. Even though the discourse can be found to include the children in the daily chores, in Western societies, there is mostly not any responsibility for "serious" family chores distributed to them (Tudge, 2008). The demands on children's contributions to the families' household are much less demanding in late modern society where the different work, school, and home activities are no longer located in the family but are divided between different institutions. Since family households are not dependent on children's work, children's school activity and leisure activity have a more prominent place in the family's everyday activities; this is reflected in the Danish family study I draw upon.

Even though demands from other institutions are brought into the analyses of the study, the focus in this chapter will be on how children and parents relate to different demands in their interaction, either to accomplish them or oppose them, and how this influences and contributes to the complexity of children's learning activities at home. The analyses will draw on the concepts of demand, motive, conflict, imitation, and modeling.

In this chapter the focus is especially on the relation between demands that children meet and the demands children put on parents in their everyday activities and the conflict between parents' demands and children's motives. Parents' demands can be direct, as when a mother asks a child to do homework, or to postpone eating at the dinner table until all participants have food on their plates. These demands then gradually become indirect and become family traditions located in concrete activity settings. A setting then places demands on the participants, that is, as conduct for table manners. In the example presenting in the last part of the chapter, this can be seen when the focus child, Emil, tells his friend to wait at the dinner table when he grabs a pizza piece before everybody are seated at the table. Here we see a child directly put demands on his friend in the dinner setting to behave according to the family traditions he has learned. Traditions in a family are dependent both on the family practices as well as practice outside home (i.e., school and work) that put demands on a family for how the families structure their day and for activities that have to take place. Furthermore, the child's motives and inentions interact with these conditions and can take the form of demands on other participant in a setting.

CHILDREN LEARN AND DEVELOP THROUGH PARTICIPATING IN PRACTICE

From a cultural-historical activity perspective, children are seen as active participants also in educating themselves at home and in school by modeling other persons, thereby contributing to their own conditions for learning and development in their everyday practice (Hedegaard, 2002, 2009; Rogoff, 1990, 2003; Vygotsky, 1998). These theoretical conceptions imply that one has to make specific analyses that can include the child's perspective. In order to make the analyses of a person's activities more specific within the institutional practice, the concept of activity setting will be introduced.[1] An activity setting can be compared to a scene in a play, with a beginning and an end (i.e., the dinner setting, or morning setting before going to school). Activity settings are recurrent events located in practices based on traditions in a society's different institutions. Within such activity settings, the different participants activities takes place.

One can then differentiate between an institutional practice, which can contain several different activity settings where individuals participate, and a person's concrete activity within a specific activity setting and across activity settings in different institutions. The same activity is different in the various institutional settings, such as eating lunch at home and in school, or reading at home or in school settings. One can also follow a child in his different activity settings such as the morning setting with breakfast, walking to school, afternoon snack time, dinnertime, and bedtime. Seen from a specific person's perspective, an activity setting is a person's social situation. Different persons in the same activity setting can experience different social situations. In an activity setting, the traditions may be experienced as demands, as when Emil's friend has to wait until all participants are seated to grab a pizza slice. Tensions and conflicts between demands in the activity setting (with its traditions introduced by more competent participants) and children's motivated activities (from the perspective of their social situations) are the focus in the case study drawn upon. Children meet demands and put demands on others in their everyday activity settings. Their activities reflect how they integrate these demands.

It might be relevant to distinguish between the child's motives and the demands that a child put on other person's. A child's motives are related to what matters for the child—that is, what is meaningful and important for a child. In a specific situation, a child's motive can be seen as an orientation in the activity setting. A child's motive orientation is expressed in his intentional activities and his wishes. A child's demands can reflect both his or her need for care and the child's motive orientation. The child can put demands on his surrounding that are not only related to the child himself. Such a demand can be seen reflecting the caregiver's need to live up to expectations in a society for his or her responsibility as a caregiver. When a small child is tired and cries, or when a school child does not want to leave for school, then the parents are concerned to solve the problem not only because they perceive the child's need but also because of the expectations put on them as parents. A child's need for food and care to survive during the first years of life results in heavy demands on parents' caretaking. In these early years, a child's exploration of his environment leads to a motive orientation toward other aspects of everyday life; the child's demands thereby become more specific and sophisticated. A child's playfulness and modeling of other persons in his or her social situations lead to new motive orientations that surpass the basic needs for care. Supported by adults, these new orientations create new possibilities for a child's interaction, learning, and development.

Children's learning and development are anchored in their social situations through the demands they meet and the motives they express in the different activity settings in which they participate. To exemplify a child's activities in a social situation and the different demands put on him, I will draw on Emil's participation in the morning activity setting in his family:

> In this activity setting, the family is gathered around the kitchen table eating breakfast when the researchers enter. Grandmother is visiting. Emil is crying when we enter because he has to leave for school, which he does not want because Grandmother is there and his younger sister Kaisa is allowed to stay home from kindergarten. Mother and Grandmother are consoling Emil, and they find a compromise in that Emil does not have to go to the after-school daycare. In the same breakfast setting, Laura, his older sister, then tells about a play performance they are practicing in school and this catches Emil's interest.

Emil's social situation in this setting can then be seen thus: Emil wants to stay home with Grandmother and is unhappy and protests because of Mother's demand that Emil has to go to school. When Emil is consoled by Mother's and Grandmother's compromise, he becomes attentive to and interested in Laura's telling about her play performance in school and he forgets his unhappiness for a while.

The distinction between the activity setting and the child's social situation anchors the child's activity both within the conditions of a specific practice and the child's motivated orientation. In the morning setting it is the dynamic between Mother's demands that Emil has to go to school and Emil's wish to stay home that reflects his social situation. The solution to this conflict, when accepted, made Emil orient himself to new activities: attending to his sister's story about a school activity and getting ready to go to school. When following Emil over a span of time, we find that he later models this kind of compromise in difficult situations—for instance, with his friend Tom (as will be illustrated later in the chapter).

Conflicts can arise from the child not being able to handle a parent's demands, but also as a result of differences between parents' demands and the child's motive. In the breakfast example with Emil, where there was a conflict between the demand that Emil has to leave for school and his motive for staying home with Grandmother, it is obvious that this demand does not only come from the parents, but from a general societal demand that children have to attend school and be there on time. Institutional objectives as well as a person's motive function as different demands that are confronted in the activity settings.

The relation between different planes of analyses—from societal conditions, to institutional practices, activity settings, and the person's social situation and activity—can be seen in Table 4.1. To get a system that more clearly depicts the relations between the concepts, I distinguish between various entities where changes take place, the processes of change, and the dynamic within the changes. The society, the institution, the activity set-

TABLE 4.1   Planes of Analyses

Structure	Process	Dynamic
Society	Tradition	Societal conditions
Institution	Practice	Value motive/objectives
Activity setting	Social Situation	Motivation/engagement/demands
Person	Activity	Motives/intentions
Human biology	Neurophysiologic processes	Primary need/drives

Source: Modified from Hedegaard 2008)
Note: The different planes have to be understood as dialectically related.

ting, the person, the organism are conceptualized as entitities and should not be seen as fixed but changing, because they are related to each other and can not be seen in isolation (except in an analytical fixation). It is through processes that the entities are related and through analysing them we can follow how the changes take place in the organism, the person, the activity setting, the practice and the institution, because these entities define each other. The changes in the process is both initiated by as well as influence the dynamics therefore there is a dialectic between the structures that are always changing through the processes. But these changes do not take place the same way or at the same pace because the processes are nested into each other and initiated but also influencing by different dynamics both in the society but also as part of the person. The different entities, processes and dynamics have to be understood as dialectically related both between each other at the same level and between the different levels.

The concepts in Table 4.1 are central in the analyses of children learning in their social situation and participating in an activity setting. Analyzing the child's social situation, one has to take into account both the demands children are meeting when entering everyday activities in different institutions, and the demands that children put on others—that is, members of the family in their home practice through their need for care and the motives they express. An analysis can take form through the following questions:

- What kind of institutional practices do children in modern society participate in?
- What activity settings tend to dominate the institutional practices of modern society?
- What demands do these activity settings put on children?
- What possibilities for activities are generated in these settings and how do children act in relation to the activities the settings afford?
- What kind of demands do children put on the other participants especially the caregivers in these activity settings?

For the specific child, one has to focus on the conflicts that occur between caregivers' and key persons' demands and a child's motives and intentions.

Development Seen as Pathways Through Different Institutional Practices

Children's development has been described as directed forward by their participation in different types of trajectories or pathways (Dreier, 2008; Elder, 1998; Elkonin, 1999; Hedegaard, 2008; Hundeide, 1998, 2005; Riegel, 1975; Vygotsky, 1998). The main point in using the concept of trajectories or pathways in relation to conceptualizations of development is that society with its material and institutional conditions gives different possibilities for a person's psychological development through the access to participate in different institutional practices.

It is important to see the institutional practices as possibilities for children's trajectories in a society. At the same time, one has to conceptualize that at a given period in life each child participates in more than one institution and to conceptualize how this leads to shared or conflicting conditions for a child's learning and development; that is, when a child starts at school, the practice at school influences home practice through time scheduled for going to school, coming home, and children's homework. These structural influences can be seen as demands in a family when analyzing children's everyday life in a family.

LEARNING AND DEVELOPMENT CONNECTED TO DIFFERENT INSTITUTIONAL TRADITIONS

In different types of institutions, there are various traditions that dominate. The activity settings and the ways of interaction in a family practice are different from activity settings and the ways of interaction in school practice. How general traditions are actualized in a specific family or school differs even in the same society. The activies in the family and school influence each other; therefore, one can find recurring home/school tensions and dilemmas that both are connected to the traditions as well as how these are actualized in the specific school and home. At the personal plane, children participate in different activity settings in family and school, where they imitate and model other members' activities.

Imitation as a Learning Form

For infant children, neuropsychological conditions such as attention span, bodily competence, and movement capacity make both families and nurseries educate children through emotional relation of imitation that can also be found with toddlers. In this connection, I will point to Vygotsky's remark, that even when learning takes place as imitation, the child imitates with a meaningful understanding (Vygotsky, 1998, p. 202). This meaningful understanding, I interpret in relation to Stern's research as the infant's and young child's emotional relation to caregivers that create the conditions for imitation (Stern, 1985).

In infancy, the emotional relation for learning is the leading educational form; emotional learning does not disappear in later age periods but takes other forms than in infancy as the child's motives for being competent start to be visible. Forms of learning that are established in early age do not disappear but can be found in new versions. Imitation can be a very strong way of learning also in adult ages, especially when learning motor competences such as dancing, skiing, and so on. But this enactive learning has turned into another form than in infancy (Bruner, 1966).

Modeling as a Learning Form

Modeling is a more encompassing concept than imitation, because the person the child imitates has to be conceptualized as a person. Bronfenbrenner (1970), in his book *Two Worlds of Childhood*, discusses the importance of the emotional relation for a child to other persons, for learning by modeling. He points out that adults have to take an ethical responsibility in relation to children to give them the possibility through modeling to relate to their community and society. Adults' involvement as models for children will lead to children's growing involvement and responsibility on behalf of their own family, community, and society as well as to individual autonomy (Bronfenbrenner, 1970, pp. 165–166). Modeling as a part of learning has to be related to the moral concern of the adults and how they relate to the child. Bronfenbrenner used modeling as a process that goes further than imitation of actions and that involves relationships with other persons. In some sense also in Bronfenbrenner's conceptualization, the child just imitates (cf. Vygotsky, 1998, p. 202). By including the characteristic of the model that is imitated, as a caring or interesting person such as a child's parent, sibling, playmate, or other person who plays a prominent role in the child's everyday, life Bronfenbrenner foregrounds both the learning activity and the child's engagement in the model and social concerns in the activity.

The ways modeling is used as an educational device in early childhood change for kindergarten children when modeling through role play activities becomes the leading activity (Elkonin, 1978, 1999; Vygotsky, 1982). As Vygotsky puts it, education in preschool age has to follow the child's program, but around school age, education can relate also to the institutional tradition of using systematic teaching. In this chapter, the systematic education in school is only indirectly touched since it is a child's activities in the family home that will be followed. The child we follow in this chapter has just started in school. He orients himself to school and instruction, but at the same time the learning that takes place through home activities, except for children's homework, is dominated by children's imitation and modeling of parents and siblings and their own exploration.

A SITUATED STUDY OF A CHILD'S EVERYDAY ACTIVITIES IN FAMILY AND SCHOOL SETTINGS

The case drawn upon in this presentation is based on visits to a family home over a year containing 31 visits making participant observations, where the children were also followed from home into school, kindergarten, after school-day care and free-time activities. The observations were recorded by two observers writing on lap-tops. In this presentation, the focus will be on Emil and his activities at home

Everyday Practice in Emil's Family and the Conditions This Gives for Learning and Development

This is a middle-class family living in a middle-class neighborhood in Copenhagen, with six members; both father and mother work. The children are: Kaisa, the youngest, who is 4 years old; Emil, the only boy, 6 years old; Lulu, 8 years; and Laura, the oldest child, who is 10 years old. Emil's family lives in an apartment on the fifth floor in a block with several other families with children. The apartment is designed for life with four children.

Based on the general questions formulated in the first part of the chapter, I formulated the following categories to analyze the research protocols from the family project.

The Activity Settings Emil Participates In
The main activity settings of Emil's day are: morning activities, class hours, recess, after-school day care, coming home, afternoon activities (tea, playtime/homework), the evening meal, and going to bed—as the defining settings in his week days, they frame Emil's social situations and the activities that he engages in.

Emil's Social Situation
The categories for interpretation of Emil's social situations in different activity settings at home are:

- Emil's intentions and engagements
- Demands in the activity settings from parents
- Conflicts between Emil's engagements and demands from other persons
- Emil's imitation and modeling in conflict solutions

Analyses of Emil's Activities in His Everyday Activity Settings Over Two Days

The visits took place on Wednesday and the following Saturday as the 2nd and 3rd visit to this family.

Wednesday (from 4 p.m. to 8 p.m.)
Tom (6 years old), Emil's classmate, visits the family the whole afternoon and eats dinner with them.

Main activity settings:
Play in Emil's room
Drinking tea around the main table in the living room downstairs
Visit to the swim bath (not analyzed here)
Dinner upstairs

Playroom Activities
Robber play. Kaisa, Emil, and Tom are playing. The two boys are together as robbers. Kaisa is the victim. Emil and Tom are sitting in a small tent, the robbers' "house." Kaisa's home is on the top of the bunk beds. Emil is going to rob her and enters the bunk bed. Tom suggests to "kill" her. Emil does not like to pretend that Kaisa has to die and suggests that she should only faint. He then wants to rob some of her playthings, but Kaisa won't let him do this; he ends up saying that he only spies on her, and they negotiate that he will only take a few things that she accepts. Back at the robbers' "house," he shows the "treasures" to Tom.

The money activity. Tom is not interested; he has found Emil's purse and empties it out on the floor. Tom wants to take some money. Emil tries to stop him. Tom then turns the money activity into their robber play and suggests that they should hide the money as a treasure. Emil does not really want to accept the play with his money, but then accepts that they can hide the money. (See Table 4.2.)

Drinking Tea, Doing Homework Around the Main Table in the Living Room
The two older girls are doing their homework before the trip to the swim bath. The mother supports their work by being at the table and giving them

TABLE 4.2   Conflicts and Their Solutions in the Play

Emil's engagement and intention	Demands on Emil	Conflicts/ oppositions	Solutions
Engaged in the play and intents to keep the play going	To "kill" his sister in play	The consequences is too much for Emil	Emil goes into the 'planning sphere' in the play and says that she should only faint
Intention to keep the play going	The robber play means that Emil has to take something from Kaisa	Kaisa does not want Emil to take her things	They negotiate what he may take
Intention to keep the play going	Tom looses interest in the play and gets absorbed by Emil's purse and money	Emil tries to stop him. Tom keeps engaging in Emil's money	Tom then enters back into the play and suggest hiding the money for the enemy in the robbers house, that Emil accepts
Intention to keep a friendly relation to Tom – they stop playing	Tom then takes 10 Dkr of Emil's and says he wants to buy potato chips	Emil goes to his mother in the other room with this idea. She rejects this.	Mother feeds them since (she argues) they must be hungry when thinking at buying chips

attention when needed. The three children from the play room also gather around the table together with the two girls and Mother. Emil crawls unto his mother's lap, and suggests buying potato chips; she leaves the table to make sandwiches. In the 20 minutes between when mother goes away and when she comes back, Emil tries intentionally to create some conflicts.

Emil's activities to create conflicts and Mother's solutions:

- When entering the room Emil provokes Lulu because he suggests to Tom that they should erase her homework. Lulu talks to Mother and Mother solves this conflict by preventing this very quietly telling Emil that he should not say so.
- Play with Mother's purse. When Mother goes into the kitchen, Emil tries to provoke the observer Kasper by peeking into his Mother's purse and taking out money—the same thing that Tom did to him some minutes ago with Emil's purse. Mother comes back and says he must not take her money. Later, he is allowed to sit on her lap and take things out of her purse.

- Talks very loud. Nobody reacts, so he comments on it himself.
- Puts his legs on the table, but takes them down when asked by Mother

Mother's solutions to the conflicts are direct, but at the same time Emil is on her lap and she compromises so he is allowed to play with her purse (see Table 4.3).

Around the Dinner Table

The children get some of their favorite food, pizza; they all except for the guest child Tom wait to start to eat until everybody is at the table. Emil looks at him a little amazed, and then tells Tom to wait. At the table, the parents make conversation with the children about their activities in the school and kindergarten. Emil takes jalapenos, and Mother says they are "gruff." Emil then starts to talk about his mother sending each child to bed being gruff, imitating Mother's voice. Kaisa also imitates Mother by saying "now you have to go to bed, 'bebser'," in a high-pitched voice.

Tom wants Emil to hit the observer, Kasper, in his forehead (perhaps to get Emil's attention, and make him stop being attentive to Kasper and the computer). Father uses this as an introduction of a figure of speech "bash on the head." The word association can be seen as a way to take a conflict at its start and turn it into a language game, thereby turning the attention away from an unwanted activity. Later Emil creates another word game

TABLE 4.3   Conflicts and Their Solutions in the Homework Setting

Emil's engagement and intentions	Demands on Emil	Conflicts/ oppositions	Solutions
No engagement in the homework but intention to provoke his sister Lulu to get Tom's approval	To respect his sister's activity of doing homework	Provokes Lulu	Mother solves by telling Emil to quit
Engage in play with Mother's purse and the money	To respect that the money are Mother's	Provokes Mother	Allows to play with the money
Loud talking, wants Mother's attention	Tradition for good behaviour	Provokes Mother	Mother does not pay attention, so he corrects himself
Legs on table, wants Mother's attention	Tradition for good behaviour	Provokes Mother	Mother solves by telling Emil to quit

TABLE 4.4   Conflicts, Tensions, and Their Resolutions at the Dinner Table

Emil's engagement and intentions	Demands on Emil	Conflicts/ oppositions	Solutions
To keep table manner	To behave kindly to a guest	Emil stops Tom to start eating before everybody have sat down	Mother interferes
To object to Mother's authority	No demands	Emil and Kaisa imitate conflict with Mother of sending them to bed	Parents approve
To have contact with the Observer Kasper	Tom demands Emil's attention	Tom wants Emil to 'bash' Observer at the head	Father interferes with word game
To support Tom to follow demands	To keep adults demands	Tom does not want to leave for home	Emil interferes with word game

when Tom has to leave and does not want to go with his father, Emil then says that he will give him a "pizza hug." (See Table 4.4.)

Modeling Mother's Creation of Solutions

In solving the conflict with Kaisa and Tom in the play situation, Emil models Mother's way of arguing and finding alternative solutions. In the money situation, Emil solves the conflict with Tom by accepting his demands and seeking support from Mother.

These ways of solving problems we also found in our observations of Emil the same day at the dinner table. Here we saw how Father used a word game when Tom wanted Emil to do something that is not acceptable and how Emil later used this solution when Tom had to leave.

The Following Saturday (9:30 a.m. to 12:00 Noon)

Activity settings:

Mother is reading aloud to Laura (not analyzed here)

Watching television upstairs

Playing upstairs (not analyzed here)

Doing homework and playing in the living room downstairs

Watching Television Upstairs

This seems a relaxing activity as Lulu and Emil are covered by their duvets, while Kaisa puts her feet at the table. All three of the children are intensely engaged watching cartoons. The animated film generates several responses, especially from Emil and Kaisa. Emil and Kaisa both repeat phrases from the film, while Kaisa in particular gets very excited. Emil is not excited in the same way as Kaisa, and he overtly states that cartoons always have a happy ending. Mother yells to Kaisa, Emil, and Lulu from downstairs that they will have to turn off the television. Lulu replies that they should be allowed to watch until the cartoon ends. Mother walks upstairs to make sure that the cartoon will be ending shortly. Later Mother argues that the children have been watching TV since 8 o'clock. Therefore, they have to stop now. (See Table 4.5.)

Homework

Laura and Lulu have started homework. Mother is on the phone. After the TV is closed Emil enters and asks Mother whether he can play with some stickers. While talking on the phone, Mother accepts this. Emil goes into his room to get some extra stickers, but returns with a play cash register. Emil starts to make money by writing different numbers on small pieces of paper, while playing with the cash register. Mother watches and explains to Emil that there is a difference between writing 100 and 001. (See Table 4.6.)

Modeling Solutions

The older sister has obeyed her parents' demands, but Emil provokes both Mother and Lulu, and does not want to stop the TV. The conflict is

TABLE 4.5   Conflicts Watching TV

Emil's engagement and intentions	Demands on Emil	Conflicts/ oppositions	Solutions
Wants to watch TV	To turn off TV	Emil wants to continue watching TV	Mother allows the three children to finish watching the cartoon
Want to continue	Older sister demands TV turned off	Oppose and fight his sister, provoke mother	Mother closes TV

TABLE 4.6   The Homework Setting

Emil's engagement and intentions	Demands on Emil	Conflicts/ oppositions	Solutions
To join the activity at the table, engages in money and numbers	To do something that looks like homework	Mother finds a problem when Emil writes numbers in the wrong order	Mother supports his engagement and corrects his writing

first solved when mother makes a direct demand on Emil. At the homework table, Emil engages in an activity that looks like homework and thereby models his older sisters.

GENERAL DISCUSSION OF EMIL'S ACTIVITIES IN THE FAMILY SETTINGS AND HOW THIS CONTRIBUTES TO HIS LEARNING AND DEVELOPMENT

Typical settings in the family's everyday practice have been chosen to show the diversity in Emil's social situation, and how he relates to a friend, to siblings, and to parents, particularly his mother, since she is the main caretaker. In the concrete analyses presented here, the aim was to get a deeper insight into how a child's activities are framed by family practice, and how the child within this contributes to the shared activity settings and thereby creates conditions for his own learning and development. The activity settings in the family have to be seen in relation to demands from societal institutions (that influence the family). In the analyses, this has primarily been children's school and parents' work.

Societal Conditions Influence Home Practice

It is obvious that the formal practice of school and daycare attendance have shaped the everyday morning activity and the afternoon activity in this family. This also shaped bedtime in the family, so the children were sent to bed around the same time to be able to get up early to be in time for school. School, daycare, and work were coordinated so that Father had the responsibility for attending to school and daycare's demands in relation to children in the morning and Mother in the afternoon.

Parents and Children's Mutual Demands

In Emil's family, it is obvious that the routines of shared homework and shared dinner are demands that children just accept. Emil starts to join the homework setting in the beginning, sitting on his mother's lap when homework takes place. He thereby prepares himself for the homework activity. Through the homework activity, the two oldest children each create their own space with demands on the mother. Each of them seeks and competes for their mother's attention in the joint homework activity. Emil starts to enter into the competition by bringing activities into the shared situation that look like school activities as in the third visit by writing numbers on small paper money to put into the play cash register. This is both play and a transition to learning about numbers. With this activity, Emil is getting his mother to attend to what he is doing. In another homework situation, Emil asks his mother to play a word game with him where she names a letter, and he is then supposed to find a word that starts with this letter. The two older girls also attend to this game.

In the activity setting around the table with homework, Emil has some difficulty keeping his mother's attention since he does not yet have any real homework. At the Wednesday visit, he makes several provocations to try to get her attention by taking the money out of her purse, by talking loudly, and by putting his legs on the table. In relation to emptying her purse, Mother makes a compromise solution but mostly otherwise ignores his provocations. By and large, Mother takes his provocations in a rather relaxed manner and gives him some attention by letting him sit on her lap, while attending to the two girls who are doing homework.

Demands on the child can gradually turn into the child modelling the mothers demand so that the child put the same kind on demands on others (when resuming the roles of the adult). Emil takes the role of the adult when Tom empties his purse and demands that he quits. Tom suggests integrating the money in the play and this compromise is accepted by Emil. Emil also takes the adult role at the dinner table when he demands that his friend show table manners and wait until everybody has sat down at the table before he can take a pizza piece. At the Saturday visit, Lulu takes the adult role when they have to turn off the TV, but in this relation she does not get anywhere by arguing, so she physically tries to stop Emil without success.

In conflict situations, the parents in this family often use language and play with language to orient the children to other aspects than the conflict activity. Mother told Emil when he emptied her purse that he should not do so. Father used the word game "bash on the head" when Tom and Emil get too physical in relation to Kasper (observer). We can see the children modeling word game solutions when both Emil and Kaisa associate Mother's use of the word *gruff* for the jalapeños with the mother's keeping time when sending them to bed, and also when Emil uses language association in the same way as his parents to help Tom to accept to leave when he does not want this and Emil says that he will give him a pizza hug.

Besides solving conflicts verbally, what Emil thus learns in these settings around the table is also an orientation to school matters such as numbers, mathematics, and reading. Moreover, he also learns about money. This is a topic that fascinates him and that comes up several times in other visits.

CONCLUSION ABOUT LEARNING AND DEVELOPMENT

Both the formal societal conditions as well as material conditions influence the practice in the family. What was most obvious was how school demands influence the structure of the day at home. But it is in the analyses of children's activities in activity settings in the family practice that children's learning and development are revealed. The dinner time is in modern families mostly a shared setting. The demands in this setting are more or less formalized, as when Emil tells Tom to wait to take food until everybody has sat down. Aronsson and Gottzn (2010) view the dinner table in a family as a moral setting. This can be seen both directly in relation to how and what food the family eats and in their interactions with each other around the dinner table. In the case of Emil, the parent and children discuss with each other what has happened during the day and relate to it morally. In this setting, events from other settings are reflected upon.

It is also important to see that the child is active and creates activities in the settings and demands on the caregivers. We saw this in the breakfast setting with Grandmother, as in the money situation and in the TV situation. Emil with his motives put demands on mother, so much that she in the first example in the morning with Grandmother is late for work. In the second example, Mother fetches sandwiches for Emil and all the children, as a compromise to his demand of money to buy chips. Mother attends to Emil's activities when he plays with her purse and when he writes numbers for the cash register. These are activities that are important for the child's competence with numbers and for becoming a school child. The openness and compromise mother shows to Emil's motives, we see modeled in Emil's negotiation with his sister and Tom in the robber play. We also saw fierce opposition to his older sister's demands of turning off the TV even though she only acted as a mother substitute, reflecting Mother's demand. It is not the demand in itself, but the person together with the demand and the child's position in relation to this person that matters in relation to the demands. As Bronfenbrenner (1970) pointed out, the emotional relation to the caretakers—here, the mother—is important for the child's learning through modeling and appropriation of skills of and for compromising and interacting with other persons as well as for acquiring knowledge and novel motives.

In the analyses of Emil's everyday activities, the oppositions and conflicts he enters into or himself provokes have been central, not because conflicts dominate his day, but because they reveal exploration activities as well as modeling. When conflicts are seen, the way they are approached both by child or/and caregiver gives hints about the child's learning and development. Several conflicts in Emil's homework setting relate to getting attention. This could indicate that Emil is learning specific skills but also that he starts to position himself at the homework table and thereby develops an understanding of himself as starting to become a school boy. At the homework setting, he cannot get Mother's attention in the same way as his two older sisters, but in being part of this setting, his social situation actually changes.

Also at home, children learn in other ways than through imitation and modeling. For instance, they learn though explorations, both directly and by playing. They learn by being instructed, as when children in the family help with baking, and mother tells them what to do, or being instructed in the homework setting (Goodwin, 2007). In this chapter, the focus has been on learning through modeling other persons. Imitation has been seen as part of modeling. The focus in learning by modeling has been on conflict solutions. One could think that this is the only way modeling takes place: By focusing on conflicts one could also think that this is the dominant relation between parent and children—an impression one easily gets from Grieshaber's (2004) *Rethinking Parent and Child Conflict.* The focus in this book as well as in this chapter has been how children's behavior is regulated to follow particular norms characteristic of daily traditions. The aim in this chapter, though, is more to rethink the concept of conflict as a developmental concept having a positive role in the upbringing and education of children. By focusing on conflict, it is possible to follow more of the subtle way of bringing up children that takes places through the implicit and explicit demands put on children, as well as following children's own contribution to the conditions for their upbringing through the demands they put on their parents within everyday practices in families.

NOTE

1. Barker and Wright (1971) use the idea of behavioral settings in their description of children's life in a Midwestern town. Within the activity traditon this can be reformulated as activity settings (See also Tharp & Galimore, 1988).

REFERENCES

Aronsson, K., & Gottzén, L. (2011). Generational positions at a family dinner: Food morality and social order. *Language in Society, 40,* 1–22.

Barker, R. G., & Wright, H. F. (1971). *Midwestern and its children: The psychological ecology of an American Town.* North Haven, CT: Archon Books.

Bozhovich, L.I. (2009). The social situation of child development. *Journal of Russian and East European Psychology, 47,* 59–86.

Bronfenbrenner, U. (1970). *Two worlds of childhood. U.S. and U.S.S.R.* New York, NY: Simon & Schuster.

Bruner, J. (1972). *Processes of cognitive growth: Infancy.* Vol. 3, Heinz Werner Lecture Series. Wooster, MA: Clark University Press.

Bruner, J.S. (1986). *Actual minds, possible worlds.* Cambridge, MA: Harvard University Press.

Bruner, J.S. (1999). Infancy and culture: A story. In S. Chaiklin, M. Hedegaard, & U. J. Jensen (Eds.), *Activity theory and social practice* (pp. 225–234). Aarhus, Denmark: Aarhus University Press.

Dreier, O. (2008). *Psychotherapy in everyday life.* Cambridge, UK: Cambridge University Press.

Elder, G. H. (1998). The life course of developmental theory. *Child Development, 69,* 1–12.

Elkonin, D. (1978). *Legens psykologi.* Copenhagen, Denmark: Sputnik.

Elkonin, D.B. (1999). Toward the problem of stages in the mental development of children. *Journal of Russian and East European Psychology, 37*(6), 11–30.

Goldman, S. (2005). A new angle on families: Connecting the mathematics in daily life with school mathematics. In Z. Bekerman, N. Burbules, & D. Silberman-Keller (Eds.), *Learning in places: The informal education reader* (pp. 55–76). Bern, Switzerland: Peter Lang Publishing Group.

Goodwin, C. (2007). Particpation, stance and affect in the organization of activities. *Discourse & Society, 18,* 53–73.

Grieshaber, S. (2004). *Rethinking parent and child conflict.* New York, NY: Routledge Falmer.

Heath, S.B. (1983). *Ways with words. Language, life, and work in communities and classrooms.* Cambridge, UK: Cambridge University Press.

Hedegaard, M. (2002). *Children's learning and development.* Aarhus, Denmark: Aarhus University Press.

Hedegaard, M. (2008). Developing a dialectic approach to studying children's development. In M. Hedegaard & M. Fleer (Eds.), *Studying children. A cultural-historical approach* (pp. 10–30). New York, NY: Open University Press.

Hedegaard, M. (2009). Child development from a cultural-historical approach: Children's activity in everyday local settings as foundation for their development. *Mind Culture and Activity, 6,* 64–81.

Hedegaard, M. (2012). The dynamic aspects in children's learning and development. In M.Hedegaard, A. Edwards, & M. Fleer (Eds.), *Children's development of motives: A cultural-historical approach* (pp. 9–27). Cambridge, UK: Cambridge University Press.

Hundeide, K. (2005). Socio-cultural tracks of development, opportunity situations and access skills. *Culture & Psychology, 11,* 241–261.

Leontiev, A.N. (1978). *Activity, consciousness, and personality.* Englewood Cliffs, NJ: Prentice-Hall.

Moll, L. C., & Greenberg, J.B. (1990). Creating zones of possibilities: Combining social contexts for instruction. In L.C. Moll (Ed.), *Vygotsky and education. Instructional implications and applications of sociohistorical psychology* (pp. 319–348). New York, NY: Cambridge University Press.

Ochs, E., & Izguierdo, C. (2009). Responsibility in childhood: Three developmental trajectories. *Ethos, Journal of the Society for Psychological Anthropology. 37,* 391–413.

Riegel, K. F. (1975). Toward a dialectical theory of development. *Human Development, 18,* 50–64.

Rogoff, B (1990). *Apprenteship in thinking: Cognitive development in social context.* New York, NY: Oxford University Press.

Rogoff, B. (2003). *The cultural nature of human development.* Oxford: Oxford University Press.

Scribner, S., & Cole, M. (1981). *The psychology of literacy.* Cambridge, MA: Harvard University Press.

Stern, D. N. (1985). *The interpersonal world of the infant: A view from psychoanalysis and developmental psychology.* New York, NY: Basic Books

Tharp, R.G., & Galimore, R. (1988). *Rousing minds to life.* Cambridge, UK: Cambridge University Press.

Tudge, J. (2008). *The everyday lives of young children. Culture, class, and child rearing in diverse societies.* Cambridge, UK: Cambridge University Press.

Vygotsky, L. S. (1982). *Barnets psykiske udvikling.* Copenhagen, Denmark: Reitzel.

Vygotsky, L. S. (1998). *The collected works of L.S. Vygotsky.* Child Psychology, Vol. 5. New York, NY: Plenum Press.

CHAPTER 5

FAMILY LIFE ACTIVITIES AND EVERYDAY TIME POLITICS

Karin Aronsson

INTRODUCTION

In contemporary Western societies, authoritarian models of child-rearing have successively been abandonded in favor of so called child-oriented or non-authoritarian ways of shaping inter-generational encounters (Beck, 1997). Like the other Nordic countries, Swedish politics is child-oriented in many ways. In 1958, Sweden outlawed physical punishments in schools, and in 1979, physical punishment in homes. The first *Barneombud* (children's spokesman) was appointed in Norway in 1981 and in Sweden in 1993. Post-war Sweden has, in many ways, established itself as a child-oriented country, and it was one of the first countries to ratify the United Nation Children's Rights Convention (UNCNRC). In the childhood of late modernity, family life is marked by egalitarian values, free choice, and everyday democracy (Bauman, 2003; Beck, 1997; Giddens, 1992). Children are invited to contest authority, and Sweden is a prototypical such modern welfare society that celebrates intergenerational negotiations (Beck, 1997). On the basis of a large-scale video ethnography of family life in three cultural settings—Italy, Sweden and the United States—this chapter explores everyday negotiations in Swedish family life. One of our findings is that negotiations are

Children, Childhood, and Everyday Life, pages 75–90
Copyright © 2012 by Information Age Publishing
All rights of reproduction in any form reserved.

pervasive features of intergenerational encounters and that such negotiations recurrently concern time and time regulations.

In line with both Bourdieu (1991, 2003) and cultural psychology (Rogoff, 2003; Vygotsky, 1998; Wertsch, 1998), as well as language socialization theories (Heath, 1983; Ochs, 1992, 1993; Ochs & Schieffelin, 1984), the analytical units of this chapter are *social practices*. Prior work on mealtime discourse has, for instance, shown that children and parents at times adopt contrasting perspectives on mealtime protocol, where parents tend to set up various procedural rules for mealtime practices, whereas children may resist these very rules (Grieshaber, 1997; Ochs, Pontecorvo, & Fasulo, 1996).

When focusing on social practices (Bourdieu, 1991, 2003), generation is primarily analyzed as a social category, like class, where different generations engage in distinct activities that in turn shape ways of organizing time. In line with cultural psychology (Rogoff, 2003; Vygotsky, 1998; Wertsch, 1998), *cultural tools* are also seen as important elements in organizing the participants' world making. Language is such a tool, as are calendars, clock time, and other time notation systems. In this chapter, we will specifically explore families' local time charts.

Children's and parents' joint world making should thus be studied through the participants' own perspectives, as displayed in everyday conversations and practices (cf. discursive psychology and its focus on members' perspectives: Edwards, 1997; Potter, 1996). Family members' reflections on moral issues are to be primarily situated in immediate action, rather than in reconstructions of social events *in vacuo*. Such analyses of members' perspectives are also prominent features of detailed ethnographies of family life (e.g., Blum-Kulka, 1997; Capps & Ochs, 1995). As yet though, participants' divergent time perspectives in daily life have not been the primary focus of other work on everyday family practices.

One area of contested perspectives is that of play time versus work time. In Vygotsky's (1998) theorizing, there is no sharp divide between work and play (or between work time and play time). When at play, children can be seen to rise above themselves, and role play and other forms of social play may involve very complex forms of thinking (Vygotsky, 2004). Yet, contemporary discourse on children and childhood often involves implicit hierarchies between work and play (Prout, 2005), for instance:

Work	Play
Adult	Child
Mature	Immature
Being	Becoming

Play is construed in terms of emergent work, that is, not as something in its own worth, but as "work to be" as it were. Prout (2005) argues that children, those who are as yet only "becoming," are less valued than adult members of society. He does not specifically focus on time, but from his analysis, it can be deduced that "play time" is normally less valued than "work time."

As is shown in this chapter, many everyday conflicts in family life tend to concern what will here be called families' *time politics*, that is, in what way time is situated and co-construed within family life negotiations, sorting out rights and responsibilities concerning who has come of age, as well as negotiations about *when* or for *how long* a target activity is to take place. In line with phenomenological theorizing on time (Goffman, 1983; Luckman, 1983), the intersubjectivity of *inner time* is coordinated into *social time* through face-to-face encounters. A basic argument of this chapter is that family life encounters can be seen to involve the synchronization or co-ordination of family members' time. Families and other team formations involve the co-construction of *joint biographies* (Goffman, 1983). Work on childhood in different cultures reveals ways in which rites of passage and important points of life transition occur at quite different points of time in different cultures, and that childhood life trajectories may look quite varied in different cultural settings (James & Prout, 1990).

This chapter draws on both reported findings from the larger study in Italy, Sweden, and the U.S. (mentioned above), and on novel analyses of temporal aspects of everyday life from the same data set. It can be seen that conflicts recurrently concern time bargaining and time in a broad sense (Aarsand, 2007; Aarsand & Aronsson, 2009; Aronsson & Cekaite, 2011; Aronsson & Gottzén, 2011; Cekaite, 2010; Fasulo, Loyd, & Padiglione, 2007; Forsberg, 2007; 2008; Pontecorvo, Fasulo & Sterponi, 2001; Sirota, 2006).

This chapter discusses a series of ways in which parents orient to time: adults regulating and children negotiating about ways of spending their time, and ways in which everyday life practices entail competing notions of gaming time (Aarsand, 2007), homework time (Wingard & Forsberg, 2009), and cleaning time (Aronsson & Cekaite, 2011; Cekaite, 2010). Many of these negotiations concern parents' and children's distinct framings of play and nonplay—for instance, play time, computer gaming time, time to clean up, and bedtime. In brief, the analyses concern social time and time negotiations, rather than time as something fixed or given.

The present analyses focus on the precise ways in which children and parents construe and co-construe various time categories, such as play time, gaming time, and bedtime. It is shown that time is a feature of social order, and that time categories invoke various moral issues that have to do with children's accountabilities to parents and other elders.

DATA

The analyses primarily draw on a *video ethnography* (cf. Ochs et al., 2006) of everyday life negotiations in Swedish middle-class families, involving about 300 hours of video recordings and trackings of family life interactions, featuring eight children of 8 to 10 years of age, as well as their younger and elder siblings (in all, 25 children between 2 and 16) and their parents.[1] Activity logs, that is, codings of the family members' activities across time and home spaces, have been used for identifying episodes that involve social interaction that has a bearing on children's and parents' take on time. These episodes have then been played and replayed many times, in order to identify key episodes, where the participants (that is, the family members themselves) orient to and negotiate about time management (when? how long?). At what point in time is it appropriate to apply local family rules—for instance, about what is "in time," "too early," "too much time," or "timely."

SOCIAL ORDER AND FAMILIES' LOCAL TIME CHARTS

Social order was recurrently linked to the distinct family members' ways of categorizing time within family life. In our interviews, the parents would, for instance, present themselves as *involved parents*, persons who would not only invest time *for* their children, but also persons who would spend time *with* their children (Forsberg, 2009, 2010). The dual earner parents in the present families spent a lot of time on child care in a broad sense, including shopping, cleaning, and various duties in the home–school interface (e.g., school conferences, making cakes for school events, etc.), which required a lot of time. This differed from their own notions of ideal parents who would spend a lot more time *with* their children (Forsberg, 2010), and many of them complained that they often had a really bad conscience for not having more time available, contesting the timing and time allocation of different rights and obligations within family life.

One of our findings is that within Swedish middle-class families, where material objects are generally not contested in family life, time is still a restricted resource, and intersubjectivity in family life partly concerns the coordination and synchronization of time. On a moment-by-moment basis, revealed in our analyses of everyday life videos, both children and parents drew on a series of resources in contesting each others' versions of ideal time tables for undertaking or not undertaking specific activities, and contesting the other party's ideas of *when* to do things or for *how long* or at *what age*. The contrasting versions of time categorizations testify to inventiveness and creativity by members of both generations. Yet, by and large, the parents were the ones who regulated and formulated the time frames and

TABLE 5.1 Contested Time, Moral Order, and Generational Hierarchies

Time Arrangements: (and target practices in present examples)	Parent's Accounts:	Child's Accounts:
Procedural rules (at mealtime)	e.g., 'first proper food, then sweets'	'sweets now'
Adult's time regulations (in relation to homework)	'now' 'more time'	'later' 'less time'
Child's time bargaining (in relation to gaming)	'over' or 'later' ('after x') 'less time'	'now' 'more time'
Activity contracts (and cleaning practices)	Parent drafts & revises child's acountability	child accountable

time demands, and their children were the ones who bargained for time or who found novel ways of revising local time charts or ways of evading time restrictions (see Table 5.1).

The time negotiations concerned a series of practices such as mealtime events (Extract 1), homework events (Extract 2), computer gaming (Extract 3), and cleaning practices (Extract 4). Parents' and children's divergent accounts can be seen as different versions of representing time in everyday life. As can be seen, these versions are at times contested by the other party, which means that intergenerational disputes involve elements of family politics (e.g., Ochs & Taylor, 1992)—in this case, time politics.

MEALTIME PRACTICES AND PROCEDURAL RULES

Mealtime practices constitute one arena where the social and cultural order of family life is revealed in the ways in which family members engage and do not engage in adjusting their activities to the expectations of other family members (Blum-Kulka, 1997; Grieshaber, 1997; Ochs et al., 1996; Sterponi, 2009). In a pioneer paper on food morality and language socialization practices, drawing on Italian and U.S. ethnographic data, Ochs, Pontecorvo and Fasulo (1996) have shown that such practices are grounded in local cultural patterns. Italian and U.S. parents all orient to table manners and food protocols, but in different ways and to varying degrees. The U.S. mealtime practices are marked by intergenerational conflicts to a greater degree than the Italian dinner practices. The children in the U.S. families would, for instance, protest about specific food items, and the parents used food as reward to a greater extent than Italian families.

A series of studies on mealtime activities in Estonia, Finland, Italy, Sweden, and the U.S. have shown that Western middle-class families tend to set up such procedural rules for what to eat *in what order* in (e.g., "first real food, then sweets"; Aronsson & Gottzén, 2011; Brumark, 2006; Grieshaber,

1997; Ochs et al., 1996). Such rules are intimately linked to the ways in which children's consumption patterns and taste are socialized through parents' and other elders' ways of talking about food. As discussed by Ochs et al. (1996), in their analyses of mealtime conversations in two cultures, local ideas of what is tasteful or distasteful are intimately linked to language socialization patterns. Whereas both Italian and U.S. parents gently insist on children finishing their food, the Italian parents tend to foreground food as pleasure more than U.S. parents, who tend to foreground food as reward and food obligations, bargaining about dessert or no dessert (depending on the child's eating patterns) and invoking notions such as "a happy (empty) plate." Obviously, procedural rules about finishing food before sweeets in term build on children's and parents' local categorizations of food—for example, of what is "real food."

In our Swedish data, family mealtime negotiations similarly concern procedural rules (Aronsson & Gottzén, 2011), as can be seen in the following excerpt where a little boy tries to eat the dessert before he has finished the main course:

Extract 1   Negotiations between Emil (5 years) and his mother about mealtime procedural rules

1	Emil:	*(starts eating a package of nut-cream sweets)*
3	Mom:	But you have to eat your food first
4	Emil:	But there was one for me and one for you
5	Mom:	No that's not what I said
6	Emil:	But yes

In accordance with the local mealtime rules in his family, Emil is not entitled to his dessert (in this case a package of nut-cream sweets), as he has not finished the main course.. But he defiantly starts eating the sweets even though he still has not finished eating his main course (line 1). But his mother protests; he first has to eat his food ("proper " food). She tells him that he is not entitled to the sweets, presenting a social account: "you have to eat your food first." He has already tried to grab the sweets during the same meal, backing up his rule-breaking by another social account (that he was only hungry for sweets, not for food). This time, he tries to invoke an egalitarian account: there is one sweets package "for you and one for me," that is, one for his mother and another one for him. But the procedural rule of "first proper food—then sweets" overrides other rules, such as the ideology of egalitarian sharing. Like other family members, he is entitled to his share, but only at the point in time when he deserves it, that is, when he has finished his proper food.

It should be noted, though, that Emil's mother backs up her request with an account embedded within a series of other accounts and mitigations

(Aronsson & Gottzén, 2011). This young Swedish boy is not just *told* what to do, he is gently urged to comply with his parents' (and older brother's) requests to finish his food. During parts of these negotiations, his older brother (10 years of age) even positions himself as something of an adult or a co-parent, aligning himself fully with his parents in trying to make his little brother finish his food. But toward the end of the meal, the older brother positions himself as his little brother's play partner, another five-year old as it were, engaging in clownish squirting and scatological jokes, which shows that generation is at times a matter of *generational positionings* (Aronsson & Gottzén, 2011), rather than fixed age status.

HOMEWORK TIME AND PARENTS' TIME REGULATIONS

In several families, homework is regulated in terms of when it is to be done (e.g., before game play or TV time). By and large, though, homework in Sweden is not a major issue in family life, and the children themselves decide *how much time* to spend on it (Forsberg, 2007; Wingard & Forsberg, 2009). The negotiations generally concern *when* homework is to be done (e.g., before or after gaming, or before going to bed). Children display agency by *bargaining for time* (Sirota, 2006), finding various creative reasons for postponing homework until later. But parents also allow or invite their children's participation to varying degrees, depending on whether they *tell* or *ask* them what to do (Craven & Potter, 2010; Curl & Drew, 2008). For instance, a parent could either just tell a child "do your homework!" or ask him or her, "could you do your homework?"

Moreover, the U.S. parents tend to spend more time on monitoring their children's homework than the present Swedish families. In the U.S. setting, homework negotiations often start already in the car back home from school. Wingard (2006) shows how *first mentions* early in the afternoon are ways of alerting children to the homework issue. Children are told or reminded that homework has to be done, but they do not need to do it immediately, which makes the task somewhat less off-putting. Yet, even in Swedish families, homework at times involves time bargaining (Forsberg, 2007), as can be seen below.

> **Extract 2** **Participants: Niklas (13 years) and his mother.**
> **Context: Niklas is computer gaming, seated on his bed but his mother wants him to prepare for a test (see also Forsberg, 2007)**

1 Mother: Now you'll sit down with your homework
2   now!
3 Niklas: Xxx
4 Mother: And that before I'll get angry.

```
 5          (3.0)
 6  Niklas: Hm I'm just—just going to do one.
 7          (continues playing)
 8          (4.0)
 9  Mother: You have four days left to study Niklas.
10  Niklas: Yeah (.) I know, I will (continues to
11          play)
12  Mother: Yeah (.) but it doesn't seem like you
13          know that.
14          (6.0)
15  Mother: Now you are going to take those ((books))
16          with you to the kitchen table and sit
17          down there and read so that I can see you
18          (.) and you'll answer the questions(.) I
19          can't understand that you don't
20          understand that it is for your own good.
21  Niklas: (34.0)
22          (continues to play, while Mother stands
23          in the doorway waiting for him to quit)
24  Mother: Why don't you quit?
25  Niklas: But I've got to save (arranges his game)
26          (12.0)
27  Niklas: (rises from his bed, quitting his game)
```

In trying to postpone homework, Niklas bargains for time in several ways. First, he presents a mitigating account: he will just do "one" (referring to one round; line 5). Secondly, he just does not move in the requested direction (toward the kitchen) or show any other nonverbal sign of compliance. There is a striking lack of uptake to his mother's requests (lines 3, 5, 10–11, 14, and 21).

In response to her rhetorical question "Why don't you quit?", he finally provides another account, an excuse in the terminology of Scott and Lyman (1968) in that he tells her that he first has to "save," that is, save his game arrangements, before quitting (line 25).

This dispute thus revolves around homework time against gaming time. Niklas implicitly agrees that he will do his homework, "but later." His mother, in turn, seems to think that "later" will not materialize. Unless he does his homework then and there, it probably just will not happen. This dispute then involves both homework time and gaming time. As can be seen, his mother first just *tells* him what to do (line 1), and she then mitigates her demands on his time, *asking* him to do his homework in that she provides him with a couple of accounts: he only has four days left to study (line 9) and it is for his own good (line 20). Parents' regulations are, of course, partly shaped by larger societal concerns: the mother can be seen to convey a certain sense of urgency, based on what she knows about his curriculum (there are only four days left to a test at school). In terms of social time, Niklas' mother is thus in an in-between postion between the school's time demands (test soon) and her son's demands for more game play time.

GAMING TIME AND CHILDREN'S TIME BARGAINING

Contemporary debates about new technologies tend to oscillate between romantic notions on the one hand, celebrating computing as a royal road to advancement and new knowledge, and dystopic notions or moral panic, on the other, discussing new technologies in terms of over-exposure and of arrested development (Buckingham, 2001). One of the parameters in gaming is time spent in gaming. In game play contexts, time refers both to duration and to points in time (e.g., 'after homework', 'before bedtime'). In contemporary households, gaming time is often regulated by parents, and many of the present children recurrently engaged in negotiations about gaming time (Aarsand, 2007; Aarsand & Aronsson, 2009). These negotiations both concern how long children are to engage in gaming, and at what time of the day (e.g., before or after homework; before or after dinner). Several families have local rules about gaming regulating the time per day or per week that may be spent on the computer (gaming, chatting or playing around). Intergenerational conflicts are also linked to a generational divide. Both children and parents can be seen to exploit generational differences in game play competence. Parents or grand-parents may, for instance, position themselves as not in the know as a way of securing shared play time the child. The adult may (strategeically) position the child as the master or instructor, as a way of having some time together, while children may exploit generational differences in order to secure more gaming time, for instance, by bargaining for 'just one more round' when the adult partty does not realize that 'a round' may take many hours or even days (Aarsand, 2007).

Moreover, Aarsand and Aronsson (2009) have shown that traditional distinctions between public and private space often break down within family life. When game playing, children, for instance, appropriate the family's living room or other public areas of the household, dominating this area with loud game noises (car races, shooting, etc.) in such a way that other family members cannot easily use this very space for the time period concerned. This means that appropriation of space also involves an appropriation of family time, as will be seen in the next excerpt.

> Extract 3 Participants: Emil (5 years), his brother Filip (10 years), their father and Filip's friend Samuel (10 years). Context: Father would like to watch a golf program on the TV (occupied by the boys playing a computer game)

1	Father:	Hey listen (.) but Samuel you and Filip
2		couldn't you go upstairs and play a
3		little in your room Filip with your-
4		e:r- arranging some soldiers may I just
5		get to watch some golf here?
6	Emil:	NO::! *(Father looks at Emil who's shouting)*
7	Filip:	Okay then
8		(5)
9	Father:	Follow them and you'll get to play with
10		your little soldiers Emil!
11	Emil:	No
12	Filip:	Then we'll get to play
13	Father:	Yeah then you'll get to play a little

As in our prior episodes, the father does not just *tell* the children what to do (e.g., "stop playing!"). In contrast, he gently *asks* the boys if they "couldn't go upstairs and play a little..." (lines 1–5), backing up his request with an account, and more specifically with an excuse: He has to watch some golf. Moreover, his request is mitigated in several other ways as well, containing several downgradings of his request, for instance, both a modal verb ("could"), a negation, and a diminutive construction ("a little"; on downgrading directives, see Aronsson & Cekaite, 2011; Craven & Potter, 2010; Curl & Drew, 2008). But little Emil is at first completely unwilling to negotiate ("NO::!"—marking his unwillingness both by shouting and by an outdrawn articulation of his refusal; line 6). In contrast, his elder brother, Filip, agrees to go upstairs and play, letting their father use the TV (line 7). But Filip first engages in a brief negotiation with his father, checking that this is a temporary arragement, and that they will later be able to continue their computer gaming ("Then we'll get to play") and his father confirms that this is indeed the case (lines 12 and 13). This is a neat case of time bargaining, initiated by one of the children.

Such negotiations are, of course, partly shaped by local age and gender hierarchies (Ochs, 1992). Modern children may have a say in family life, but they are partly at the mercy of their parents' regulations of everyday life, which are, in turn, shaped by the child's age and by preschool and school schedules (including expectations of children's hours of sleep, preparations for school) and other societal framings of family time.

FUTURE TIME, DIRECTIVE TRAJECTORIES, AND ACTIVITY CONTRACTS

Families are organizations that involve a lot of routine work (e.g., brushing one's teeth, cleaning one's room and other cleaning activities). Parts of everyday life is organized in terms of cyclic time: getting dressed; having breakfast; leaving for school, work, and so on. Most households have rules for who is to do what and when, and parents tend to assume executive control of getting things done, that is, of monitoring children's engagement in such routine practices. Directives, like "brush your teeth" (or "could you, please, brush your teeth now") are recurrent elements of parents' surveillance of children's cleaning activities. In work on directives in family life (Aronsson & Cekaite, 2011; Cekaite; 2010; M. H. Goodwin, 2006; C. Goodwin, 2007), it has been shown that directives are often extended affairs that involve *directive trajectories* rather than isolated directives. Parents ask children to do their homework, or take a shower, or go to bed, and children procrastinate or bargain for time in varied and creative ways. Parents are at times at a loss about how to get things done. One way of securing children's compliance is to have them promise to do something in the future. Recently, it has been documented that parents initiate what has been called *activity contracts*, that is, promises about future action (Aronsson & Cekaite, 2011) as one way of securing children's compliance. Activity contracts thus involve the child's future actions, and they involve moral accountability in that the child has actually promised to do something at a future point in time, which means that she or he will be held morally accountable for failing to do so, provided that time x has come or that specific conditions are fulfilled (e.g., "after gaming," "after dinner," "after reading"). In the Swedish parent–child negotiations, such contracts were initiated a quarter of an hour before an activity, a day before, or even about a week before an activity (Aronsson & Cekaite, 2011).

Each emergent contract was tracked from its early instigation to the actual execution of a target activity, including specific moves such as drafts of contracts, ratifications, invocations, and revisions. Directive trajectories were thus analyzed in sequential detail, with a focus on participation frameworks and affective indexing of interactional contributions (on affective stances, cf. Ochs, 1996; M. H. Goodwin, 2006; C. Goodwin, 2007; Cekaite, 2010).

In order to illustrate the concept of activity contract, an atypically brief episode will be documented below:

Extract 4 **Participants: Ludvig (3 years) and Mother (M) are having breakfast.**

1	Mother:	I have to call Anna today and see if we can get an
2		appointment for your haircut ((to Ludvig))

```
3              (2)
4    Mother:  So that you'll see things (looking at Ludvig, caressing,
5              "combing" his fringe)
6              (0.3)
7    Mother:  Will that be ok?
8    Ludvig:  M:hm
9    Mother:  Mhm. (turns back to her plate)
```

In line 1, Mother can be seen to initiate an activity contract about little Ludvig getting a haircut, in that she informs him about her plan to call the hairdresser for an appointment on his behalf. Thereby, she can also be seen to initiate a contract about him getting a haircut. Initially (line 2), he does not ratify her plan; in fact, he does not respond. His mother then provides an account (cf. Goodwin, 2006; Sterponi, 2003, 2009), that is, a reason for why she is inflicting the target activity on him (so that he will be able to see things; line 4). It is in his own best interest. Otherwise, he will not be able to see. Sequentially, her offer (or announcement) has now been transformed into a mild warning (Sacks, 1995); if he does not comply, he may not be able to see. Compliance is therefore an individual choice, a personal responsibility, rather than a matter of blind obedience or subordination to someone higher in the generational hierarchy.

The pause after Mother's reason-giving, that is, her explanatory account (line 4), can be seen as a second slot for a response to her initial announcement. However, little Ludvig still does not respond, and Mother then explicitly checks if he accepts the suggested course of action ("Will that be ok?"). It is first at this point that he provides a minimal confirmation (line 6), agreeing to her terms of the contract: a haircut in the unspecified future. He has thereby promised to undergo the target activity, and what is important in the present context, is that he can later be held morally accountable to Mother (and Father or other family members) for fulfilling or not fulfilling their mutually ratified agreement. In our data, contracts recurrently emerged as such family affairs, where individual members were accountable to other members for promises initially made to but one family member. A father could later invoke a promise made to the child's mother and vice versa.

This interaction occurred at least one day prior to the moment when the target activity was going to take place. This shows that immediate compliance is not necessarily the primary goal of parental requests (and directives). Some parents may start to pursue a goal and lay the ground for mutually ratified agreements (contracts) long before the moment when the target activity is going to take place. Directive trajectories testify to the importance of intergenerational negotiations. Through activity contracts, children are not only introduced to a culture of negotiations, where they are gently monitored into compliance; they are also held accountable in the future, expanding their time horizons of moral order to that of future actions.

CONCLUDING DISCUSSION

The examples in this chapter have shown ways in which time and timing are important aspects of moral order. In some cases, parents regulate children's time by just *telling* them what to do in what order (e.g., mealtime procedures, such as first food then sweets) or in their attempts to make children comply immediately, for instance, to quite computer gaming. Similarly, children at times merely protest by refusing to undertake requested actions. But in many cases, time is a part of mutual and at times extended sequences in that children successfully negotiate about when or for how long to engage in target activities.

On the basis of the present conflicts, Table 5.1 documents a series of contrasting versions of representing time in intergenerational disputes about time. These conflicts also form something of a hierarchy:

Activity contracts
   Time bargaining
   Adults' time regulations and child's contestation
   Adults' procedural rules and child's contestation

At the bottom of this hierarchy, contested time may merely involve the child's flat refusal or protest when facing parents' procedural rules and time regulations. This means that the child's uptake may just involve non-action or unmitigated verbal protests (e.g., "No!'"). On the higher two levels, the protests also involve mutual negotiations, such as time bargaining and activity contracts. These types of disputes move beyond flat refusals or protests in that they involve negotiations. The two parties' social accounts (Buttny, 1993; Scott & Lyman, 1968) form important element of such negotiations. In various ways, both parents and children back up their positions by explaining, justifying, and excusing themselves, presenting themselves as moral persons who invoke a social and moral order.

In the present data, such time negotiations were recurrent features of adult–child interactions. However, it should be noted that time negotiations start quite early on in children's lives. The little boy in Extract 4, who is merely three years old, is already recruited as a conversational partner in the interactional accomplishment of a rudimentary activity contract, that is, a mutual regulation of when and on what conditions, a dispreferred activity (here, his upcoming haircut) will take place. In this specific case, it is the mother who does the social account work. But in the other three cases, it can be seen that the children themselves also engage in accounting for when and how they will indeed agree to engage in dispreferred activities.

This chapter extends prior work on family politics (Ochs & Taylor, 1992) and everyday accounts in family life (Sterponi, 2003, 2009) by showing ways in which family politics is often a matter of what we have here called time politics.

APPENDIX:
TRANSCRIPTION NOTATIONS

:	: prolonged syllable
[ ]	: encloses overlapping utterances
(.)	: micropause, i.e., shorter than (0.5)
(2)	: pauses in seconds
x	: inaudible word
° °	: speech in low volume (*sotto voce*)
YES	: relatively high amplitude
(( ))	: transcriber's-comments
<u>ki</u>ssa	: sounds marked by emphatic stress
heh	: laughter

NOTE

1. The Alfred P. Sloan Foundation funded the project "Everyday Lives of Working Families: Italy, Sweden, and the United States." Clotilde Pontecorvo, La Sapienza, Rome, led the Italian part of the project, and Elinor Ochs, UCLA, initiated and led the larger U.S. research. Thanks are extended to colleagues in all three sites. Last but not least, I would like to thank the participating families for opening up their homes and lives.

REFERENCES

Aarsand, P. A. (2007) Computer and video games in family life: The digital divide as a resource in intergenerational interactions. *Childhood, 14,* 235–256.

Aarsand, P., & Aronsson, K. (2009). Computer gaming and territorial negotiations in family life. *Childhood, 16*(4), 497–517.

Aronsson, K., & Cekaite, A. (2011). Activity contracts and directives in everyday family politics. *Discourse & Society, 22,* 137–154.

Aronsson, K., & Gottzén, L. (2011). Generational positions at family dinner. Food morality and social order. *Language in Society, 40,* 1–22.

Bauman, Z. (2003). *Liquid love. On the frailty of human bonds.* Cambridge, UK: Polity Press.

Beck, U. (1997). Democratization of the family. *Childhood, 4,* 151–166.

Blum-Kulka, S. (1997). *Dinner talk: Cultural patterns of sociability and socialization in family discourse.* Mahwah, NJ: Lawrence Erlbaum.

Bourdieu, P. (1991/1977). *Outline of a theory of practice.* Cambridge, UK: Cambridge University Press.

Bourdieu, P. (2003). *Distinction: A social critique of the judgment of taste.* New York, NY: Routledge. (Original published in 1979, in French)

Brumark, Å. (2006). Regulatory talk and politeness at the family dinner table. *Pragmatics, 16,* 171–212.

Buttny, R. (1993). *Social accountability.* London, UK: Sage.

Capps, L., & Ochs, E. (1995). *Constructing panic: The discourse of agoraphobia.* Cambridge, MA: Harvard University Press.

Cekaite, A. (2010). Shepherding and other embodied moves in adult-child directive sequences. *Text & Talk, 30,* 1–25.

Craven, A., & Potter, J. (2010). Directives, contingency and entitlement in action. *Discourse Studies, 12,* 1–24.

Curl, T., & Drew, P. (2008). Contingency and action: A comparison of two forms of requesting. *Research on Language and Social Interaction, 41,* 129–153.

Edwards, D. (1997). *Discourse and cognition.* London, UK: Sage.

Fasulo, A., Loyd, H., & Padiglione, V. (2007). Children's socialization into cleaning practices: A cross-cultural perspective. *Discourse & Society, 18,* 11–33.

Forsberg, L. (2007). Homework as serious family business: Power and subjectivity in negotiations about school assignments in Swedish families. *British Journal of Sociology of Education, 28,* 209–221.

Giddens, A. (1992). *The transformation of intimacy: Sexuality, love and eroticism in modern societies.* Cambridge, UK: Polity Press.

Goffman, E. (1983). The interaction order. *American Sociological Review, 48,* 1–17.

Goodwin, M.. H. (2006). Participation, affect, and trajectory in family directive/response sequences. *Text and Talk, 26,* 515–544.

Goodwin, C. (2007). Participation, stance and affect in the organization of activities. *Discourse and Society, 18*(1), 53–73.

Grieshaber, S. (1997). Mealtime rituals: Power and resistance in the construction of mealtime rules. *British Journal of Sociology, 48,* 649–666.

Heath, S. B. (1983). *Ways with words. Language, life, and work in communities and classrooms.* Cambridge, UK: Cambridge University Press.

Heritage, J. (1984). *Garfinkel and ethnomethodology.* Cambridge, UK: Polity Press.

James, A., & Prout, A. (1990). Re-presenting childhood: Time and transition. In A. James & A. Prout (Eds.), *Constructing and reconstructing childhood* (pp. 227–246). Basingstoke, UK: Falmer Press.

Luckmann, T. (1983). Remarks on personal identity: Inner, social, and historical time. In A. Söderberg Widding (Ed.), *Identity: Personal and socio-cultural* (pp. 67–91). Uppsala, Sweden: Almqvist & Wiksell International.

Ochs, E. (1992). Indexing gender. In A. Duranti & C. Goodwin (Eds.), *Rethinking context. Language as an interactive phenomenon* (pp. 335–358). Cambridge, UK: Cambridge University Press.

Ochs, E. (1993) Constructing social identity: A language socialization perspective. *Research on Language and Social Interaction, 26*(3), 287–306.

Ochs, E., Pontecorvo, C., & Fasulo, A. (1996). Socializing taste. *Ethnos, 61*, 7–46.

Ochs, E., & Schieffelin, B. (1984). Language aqcquisition and socialization. Three developmental stories and their implications. In R. A. Schweder (Ed.), *Culture theory: Essays on mind, self and emotion* (pp. 276–320). Cambridge, UK: Cambridge University Press.

Ochs, E., & Taylor, C. (1992). Family narrative as political activity. *Discourse & Society, 3,* 301–340.

Pontecorvo, C., Fasulo, A., & Sterponi, L. (2001). Mutual apprentices. The making of parenthood and childhood in family dinner conversations. *Human development, 44,* 340–361.

Potter, J. (1996). *Representing reality: Discourse, rhetoric and social construction.* London, UK: Sage.

Prout, A. (2005). *The future of childhood.* London, UK: Routledge.

Rogoff, B. (2003). *The cultural nature of human development.* Oxford, UK: Oxford University Press.

Sacks, H. (1992). *Lectures on conversation. Vol. II.* Cambridge, MA: Blackwell.

Scott, M., & Lyman, S. M. (1968). Accounts. *American Sociological Review, 33,* 46–62.

Sirota, G. K. (2006). Habits of the hearth: Children's bedtime routines as relational work. *Text & Talk, 26,* 493–514.

Sterponi, L. (2003). Account episodes in family discourse: The making of morality in everyday interaction, *Discourse Studies, 5,* 79–100.

Sterponi, L. (2009). Accountability in family discourse. Socialization into norms and standards and negotiation of responsibility in Italian dinner conversations. *Childhood 16,* 441–459.

Vygotsky, L. (1998). *The collected works of L.S. Vygotsky. Volume 5. Child Psychology.* New York, NY: Plenum Press.

Wertsch, J. V. (1998*). Mind as action.* New York, NY: Oxford University Press.

Wingard, L. (2006). Mentioning homework first in parent-child interaction. *Text & Talk, 26,* 573–598.

Wingard, L., & Forsberg, L. (2009). Parents' involvement in children's homework in American and Swedish dual-earner families. *Journal of Pragmatics, 41,* 1576–1595.

CHAPTER 6

MONEY TALKS

Children's Consumption and Becoming in the Family

Lucas Gottzén

INTRODUCTION

Every fifth year, the major Nordic-Baltic bank Swedbank publishes a report on children and pocket money. In their last report, they present findings from a survey with 3,505 pupils in Swedish elementary school (approximately 7–12 years old). About 65% of the children report that they receive pocket money on a weekly or monthly basis, while approximately 28% receive pocket money only when needed. The younger children tend to get a weekly allowance, while the older ones normally get a monthly allowance from their parents. According to Swedbank (2006), children's pocket money has increased over the years. Since 1986, when the bank conducted its first survey, the real increase has been about 30% for children under the age of nine and about 50% for the 12-year-olds. The children mainly spend their pocket money on sweets and savings. Girls save to buy trips, pets, and things for their pets, cell phones, video games, and clothes; boys save for video games, computers, cell phones, and toys.

Children, Childhood, and Everyday Life, pages 91–107
Copyright © 2012 by Information Age Publishing
All rights of reproduction in any form reserved.

In its report, Swedbank (2006) argues that it does not want to set a standard for how much pocket money children should receive. However, they argue that children should get enough allowance so that they can save some money, and, preferably, they should also receive a small amount of money for specific contributions to the household. Pocket money is seen as part of a "learning process" where children with age are given increased responsibility: "We argue that it is important that at an early age children should learn how to handle money and plan their economy" (Swedbank, 2006, p. 23; author's translation). Children should learn the value of money, what money is used for, and what their "real" expenses are. Children are allowed to make mistakes, but they should also take some responsibility for their possible mistakes. In this way, they will in time be better prepared for having their own budget when moving away from home.

A basic premise in Swedbank's argument is that children have to learn and internalize adult society's values of consumption and money. Obviously, these are not new ideas, but could be seen as folk versions of developmental and socialization theories, in particular of what has been conceptualized as consumption socialization theory (John, 1999; Moschis, 1987; Ward, 1974). In line with this, Swedbank argues that money and consumption constitute a learning process with a particular aim—that children in time (should) become responsible, adult consumers. However, childhood scholars have pointed out that such perspectives are problematical since the emphasis on what children will become in the future precludes a focus on what children are and do here and now (e.g., Prout & James, 1990). Nevertheless, developmental and socialization theories *do* have a point when arguing that childhood is a changing state, that age is crucial and that children gradually learn about consumption from the surrounding society.

In this chapter, I will discuss children's consumption and becoming, but avoiding the particular teleology of traditional developmental theories—that there is an adult final stage in children's consumption socialization. Instead, I will propose a different way of understanding children's consumption departing from the philosophy of Gilles Deleuze and Fèlix Guattari (1987/2004). This poststructuralist framework helps us to understand children (as well as adults) as incomplete and developing "becomings," where their identity, agency, and consumption are created in relation to and in dependence of other humans and non-humans (cf. Lee, 2001).

The empirical data are taken from a larger ethnographic study of family life in a midsize city in Sweden[1], where a research team has documented the lives of eight families that involve two or more children, and where at least one child is between 8 and 10 years old. In total, 25 children between 2–16 years of age participated in the study. The main method of documenting the eight families in the study was participant observation with video camera during the course of a week. Each family has been filmed up to

45 hours, covering both mornings and evenings on weekdays and weekend days. Interviews were then carried out with the eight- to ten-year-old child and both parents, covering issues such as everyday routines and leisure activities. The fieldwork was carried out between April 2003 and March 2004 (cf. Aarsand & Forsberg, 2010).

CONSUMPTION SOCIALIZATION AS THE "DOMINANT FRAMEWORK"

As with studies of childhood in general, developmental and socialization theories have for a long time been central in research on children and consumption (cf. McNeal, 2007). Consumer socialization theory and research has emerged as a major framework during the last decades (e.g., John, 1999; Moschis, 1987; Ward, 1974). Within this framework, consumer socialization is understood as the process where children "acquire skills, knowledge, and attitudes relevant to their functioning in the marketplace" (Ward, 1974, p. 380). Consumer socialization research may be divided into two strands: those researchers focusing on children's cognitive development and those focusing on the social context of children's socialization into consumers.

In an influential research review, John (1999) combines her reading of Piaget's cognitive developmental psychology with later theoretical developments, such as theories on "information process" in order to explain children's socialization into consumption. John (1999) argues that consumer socialization could be divided into three universal stages: the "perceptual stage" (3–7 years old), the "analytical stage" (7–11 years old), and the "reflective stage" (11–16 years old). With age, the child's possibility to process information and to take other's perspectives increases, competences that are argued to be crucial for how children, for instance, perceive commercials, negotiate with family members, and make decisions regarding consumption goods. John's (1999) basic argument is that consumption behavior is mainly driven by the individual child's cognitive development, and to a lesser extent by social relations. Even though calling for research focusing on the social relations of children's consumption, John argues that socio-cultural theories "are less accessible than those documenting age as a driver" (John, 1999, p. 205).

Recently, McNeal (2007) has developed a theory of consumption development that focuses on the child's early years. Even though he pays greater attention to the importance of physical development (e.g., motor skills), he pinpoints a pivotal argument within the consumption socialization paradigm:

> Consumer behavior patterns develop in stages that can be described and explained. It appears that consumer development begins at birth, or shortly

after birth—after reflexes decline—and continues in orderly stages to at least around the age of 100 months when a person is at a level of competence to be considered a bona fide consumer.... The stages are orderly, or invariant, in the sense that one must take place before the next one can. There is no skipping. (McNeal, 2007, p. xvii)

Other researchers have emphasized the social aspects of children's socialization into consumption. In a classic article, Ward (1974) argues that consumption socialization is not only an issue of children's cognitive development, but that social relations are also important. Even though he argues that the main influence on consumption socialization literature comes from psychological theories on socialization and development, he acknowledges the contribution of sociological theorists such as Talcott Parsons, who argued that children learn basic skills and understanding of consumption not only from parents, but also from peers, media, and school (Parsons, Bales, & Shils, 1953)[2]. While children learn "rational" (goal-directed) aspects of consumption from their parents and "expressive" (affective) aspects from friends and media, school teaches children the "adaptive" functions of consumption through preparing the child for taking part in consumption society. In another influential article, Moschis and Churchill (1978) combine a cognitive framework with a neo-Skinnerian social learning approach, and emphasize the importance of so-called "socialization agents." In the socialization process, these agents "transmit" norms, attitudes, and behaviors to the child. For instance, the child learns from the socialization agent through reinforcement (i.e., reward/punishment) and by imitating the adult.

While the first cognitively oriented strand of research considers biological age as the main force in children's consumer socialization, researchers within the latter, socially oriented strand argue that the surrounding society play a crucial role for how children learn to consume. However, despite these differences, both perspectives are based on traditional theories on children's socialization and development. In the early 1990s, scholars within the so-called "new" sociology of childhood (NSC) paradigm criticized these theories for constructing children as unfinished social actors without ontology and agency (James, Jencks, & Prout, 1997; Prout & James, 1990; Qvortrup, Bardy, Sgritta, & Wintersberger, 1994). The "new" childhood sociologists argued that within traditional socialization theories, children were mainly understood as "becomings" rather than as "beings" with a possibility to define their own life here and now. As a result, these theories were argued to be inadequate to explain children's everyday life and precluded researchers from taking a child's perspective and understanding children on their own terms. Prout and James (1990) argued that traditional developmental and socialization theories should be considered as a "dominant framework" not only within child studies, but also as an implied way for how parents, policymakers, professionals, and market actors understand children.

As shown, the dominant framework has been articulated in research on children's consumption, but different market actors, such as Swedbank, also express popular versions of consumption socialization. We also find the dominant framework in parents' attitudes toward their children's consumption. For instance, in a recent British study (Evans & Chandler, 2006), the parents emphasize the educational aspects of consumption goods as important criteria for what they argue is children's "good" consumption. The more "educational" consumer goods are, the greater chance the parents will buy it, or approve of their children buying it. In another study, conducted with Swedish, Norwegian and Danish families, the parents connect "good" consumption with learning, security, social belonging, and physical activities (Brusdal, 2007). In particular, the parents contrast between "educational" aspects of their children's consumption goods on the one hand, and "shallow," on the other. The parents often describe their children in innocent terms, in need of protection from what they see as the negative aspects of the market. An explicit aim for the parents is to teach their children to become critical consumers. Johansson (2005) finds similar tendencies in her study of Swedish children's relation to consumption and money. The main motive for parents to give children pocket money is that children learn about economy and consumption; giving pocket money is seen as a way of socializing children into consumer society and teaching responsibility.

BECOMING CONSUMER

As mentioned, researchers within the NSC paradigm have criticized the dominant framework for constructing children as "becomings" and have instead proposed that children should be understood as "beings." In order to take children seriously, children have to be seen as social actors here and now and not mainly for what they may end up doing in the future. The objective has been to take a child perspective in research by studying children's contribution to, for instance, consumption. Rather than having consumer culture imposed on them, it is argued that children creatively contribute to consumer culture (Cook, 2008; James, 1979; Martens, Southerton, & Scott, 2004; Pugh, 2009).

However, as Lee (1998) has shown, the notion of children as "beings" is built on an essentialist model of agency that preserves a privilege of the complete and mature over the incomplete and immature. Instead, the ontological ambiguity of childhood should be used to challenge any quest for completeness and essentialism within social research. Departing from Deleuze and Guattari (1987/2004), Lee proposes that children and adults alike should be seen as becomings, as unstable and incomplete: "Humans, regardless of age, are constitutionally unfinished. They are always indebted to someone or something else, and this indebtedness opens human life to adaptability and change.... [I]t makes little sense to talk about human beings in isolation" (Lee, 2001, p. 114).

Through emphasizing both adults and children as becomings, a Deleuze-guattarian perspective may move beyond fixed dichotomies—for instance, between one of responsible versus irresponsible actors. But rather than emphasizing maturity and the individual's agency, it understands agency as a social attribution (Lee, 2001). Deleuze and Guattari (1987/2004) argue that identity is formed in *assemblages*, in relation between humans, non-humans, and materiality. For instance, a child does not become a consumer on his or her own, nor does she or he become a consumer through merely internalizing cultural values of consumption. Rather, she or he becomes a consumer when entering in an assemblage with money, consumer goods, parents, and so on. Assemblages are not stable entities, but are open to change and may alter when coming into conflict with other assemblages, that is, other relations of humans and non-humans.

A Deleuzianguattarian perspective might not entirely alter the research focus for research of children and their consumption, but it takes it in novel directions. Instead of focusing on how children are socialized into consumption culture or at what age children are mature enough for a particular commodity (as in consumer socialization paradigm), and instead of focusing on children's competence or how they contribute to their own consumption and socialization (as in NSC paradigm), the focus is set on power relations between adults and children, in particular on what assemblages are available for adults, how they "become adult," and which are extended to different groups of children. Thus, in a Deleuzianguattarian sense, there is a difference between studying how children become consumers and how they are *becoming consumers*. While the first perspective focuses on a final stage, the latter studies how a *constant* becoming of consumption is carried out in relation to humans and non-humans.

Deleuze and Guattari highlight the power relation between individuals and society through discussing how different "strata" structure our identities and bodies into stable entities. One strata that Deleuze and Guattari mention is *subjectification*—which refers to the social necessity of being a subject and having a stable identity. As they put it, the strata's imperative to people is: "You will be a subject, nailed down as one, a subject of the enunciation recoiled into a subject of the statement—otherwise you're just a tramp" (Deleuze & Guattari, 1987/2004, p. 177). Within each stratum, the subject takes a united and hierarchally positioned identity. These identities are constructed through binary and hierarchal dichotomies, such as man/woman, White/Black, adult/child, and responsible/irresponsible. Taking dichotomous and hierarchal aspects of consumer socialization theories into account, I would argue that they could be understood as strata that aim to structure children's identities and consumption cultures into stable entities. Although the strata are powerful, people are never complete subjects to stratification. Since, according to Deleuze and Guattari, human ontology is in constant flux, it is impossible to be once and for all determined and stable. There is always a possibility of becoming-other, of creating a line of flight, and to some extent escape the strata's structuration.

WORKING FOR POCKET MONEY

In the present study, I asked the children between eight and ten years of age if they received any form of weekly or monthly allowance. Most children in the present study receive pocket money from their parents on a regular basis. Seven out of eight children report that they receive pocket money in a way or another. One child does not receive a weekly or monthly allowance, but often gets money from his grandmother. The children receive between 40 and 100SEK (approximately $5–15 US) every month. The pocket money is used for consumption, either immediately or in the near future. According to the children, the main advantage to a regular allowance is the possibility to do whatever you want with your pocket money; you could immediately spend the money or save to buy something more expensive. Some children save up for video games, others for toys. One girl said she saves up money to buy her favorite magazine each month and another girl that she normally saves up to buy clothes and shoes. Money that is not saved is normally spent on sweets and toys. For instance, Jens (9 years old) told us that he bought clothes and a new wallet with his last monthly allowance.

Children's pocket money is a social phenomenon; that is, it is a practice set in complex social relations, in particular between children and parents, who are the main distributors of pocket money. Pocket money often becomes an issue of discussions and negotiations between parents and children. How much should the child receive? What are the conditions for the allowance? Sometimes these negotiations are relatively collaborative; at other times the negotiations are characterised by conflicts (Zelizer, 2002). In the following, I will present some examples of how children in the present study negotiated with their parents about pocket money.

Let me start with Filip, who is 10 years old. He is one of the children in the study who receive most in respect to monthly allowance (200SEK, approx. $30 US). In the following episode, he is in the kitchen together with his parents and younger brother, Emil (5 years old), eating dessert after dinner. Mom raises the issue of going to a marketplace in a nearby town.

> **Mom:** Are we going to Storköping Market on Thursday?
> **Dad:** ((To Emil)) Don't you like the chocolate ice cream?
> **Emil:** No.
> **Dad:** But you like chocolate sauce?
> **Emil:** Mm.
> **Dad:** Mm.
> (3.0)
> **Filip:** Then I want my monthly allowance.
> **Mom:** Well, didn't you get it?
> **Filip:** No.
> **Dad:** But you do have!
> **Filip:** When did I get it?
> **Dad:** Well, you've got your allowance for an entire year.
> **Filip:** I have not. Uh!
> **Mom:** You'll have to cut some lawn again.
> **Filip:** I've actually helped out at home.
> **Mom:** Collect return bottles.
> **Dad:** I said that Filip could get some work to do on Thursday if he's free.
> **Filip:** No, I'm going to Storköping's market.
> (2.0)
> **Dad:** Well really?
> **Filip:** With my pocket money.

Apparently, Dad and Filip disagree whether Filip has already received his monthly allowance or not. When Filip says he wants his pocket money before going to the market, Mom curiously asks him if he has not already received it. In contrast, Dad argues that Filip has received enough money for a while, even though he is not able to answer when Filip got his allowance last time. In a later interview, when I asked him about the present discussion, he explained their arrangement:

> **Lucas:** And why didn't your parents think you should have the two hundred?
> **Filip:** Because they didn't think I needed it. But if I help out more at home I get it.
> **Lucas:** So, what was the deal then?
> **Filip:** That I need to help out uh I think it's when they say they need help then I have to help out if I can.
> **Lucas:** Mm, so you do that?
> **Filip:** Yes, mostly.
> **Lucas:** Did you think you needed those two hundred?
> **Filip:** Mm.

As a social and cultural phenomenon, money has different meanings; depending on origin and use of money, people mark money differently (Zelizer, 1994). Johansson (2005) argues that there are four different types of money in Swedish families. An example of what Johansson calls *distribution money* is the monthly allowance, which is connected to an idea that money should be evenly distributed in the family, and often also to an idea that children should do some household work as an exchange. *Gift money* is not conditioned in the same way as distribution money and is the main income for the children in Johansson's study. *Salary* is defined as money that children earn by working at home or on the job market. In contrast to salary, which is regarded as the children's private money, *collective money* is the family's common money. However, Johansson argues that this type of money is rare.

The sort of money that Filip and his parents are discussing typifies both distribution money and salaried money. The work Filip's parents suggest he should do could, on the one hand, be seen as a way for Filip to get a salary. He is encouraged to cut the lawn, help is father work on the house on Thursday, and collect return bottles (depending on size, each bottle gives 0.5–4 SEK, or 7–60¢ US). On the other hand, it seems as if the family members mainly orient toward the suggested work as a part of their arrangement regarding monthly allowance and distribution money (apart from collecting bottles). Filip wants his allowance (distribution money), which he argues is given under the condition that he "helps out" at home. But according to his father, Filip is not entitled to more allowance, although he could gain some more money by helping him with the house.

I would argue that there is one particular assemblage at work here, namely the "child-money-work" assemblage. This assemblage conditions the allowance and makes it into an educational project through which Filip has to learn the value of money in general ("you've got your allowance for an entire year") and more specifically the relationship between money and work (e.g., "You'll have to cut some lawn again"). In a study of children's work in Sweden, Samuelsson (2008) shows that despite their loose connection to the formal labor market, children report that they can get money if needed, often by doing household chores. However, much of this work is not seen as "real" since parents' payment for children's work is regarded as a part of the allowance. Similarly, Zelizer (1994) argues that allowance and pocket money position children beyond the market, while at the same time socializing them to consumer and producer values. Working and helping out at home are regarded as educational projects that are carried out under the parents' supervision (cf. Klein, Graesch, & Izquierdo, 2009). It is true that Filip positions himself as a competent consumer; he wants to go to the market with his pocket money. But even though Filip argues that he should have his entitled allowance money, he seems to agree on the basic condition—that he has to "help out" at home once in a while. Thus, in order to become what he desires, *becoming consumer*, he needs to position himself in the child-money-work assemblage, and, consequently, accept his parents' educational project that aims at teaching him the capitalist ethics of work and money (cf. Weber, 1930/2001).

BECOMING TEENAGER, BECOMING FAN

Now let us focus on some of the somewhat older children, those between 12 and 13 years of age. Within Western culture, these years are often constructed as years of transition from childhood to teenage years. In Sweden, for instance, these are the years when children end the intermediate level (*mellanstadiet*) and move to the senior level (*högstadiet*) of the compulsory school, which often also implies a physical move to another school. According to Wærdahl (2005), clothes and other consumption goods are crucial for children during these years as a way of anticipating their (future) identity as teenagers and adults. Similarly, König (2008) argues that parent–child negotiations about consumption goods do not only regard the goods in themselves, but also the child's "presentation of the juvenile self," which is done by consciously choosing specific clothes or brands and creating a unique style. The negotiations also regard the conflict between teenagers' urges for increased independence and the parents' wishes to control their consumption.

This type of conflict is illustrated in the negotiations between Lisa (12 years old) and her parents. During our week of observations she was planning to go to two concerts featuring her favorite group, the Swedish rock band Kent. The discussions started early on Saturday morning, when she was going downtown to buy a pair of Converse shoes. Lisa and her parents discussed for a long time how much money she should bring with her to town and how much she could spend at the concert in the evening on, for instance, buying a T-shirt. During this discussion she asks her father if he can take out some money from a nearby cash machine.

> **Lisa:** DADDY! (1.0) DADDY!
> **Dad:** Yes.
> **Lisa:** Could you pick up some money today? Please.
> **Dad:** Uh, I have, uh I have two, three hundred in my account otherwise I have to go to the office and transfer money.
> **Lisa:** Yeah, but can't you do that?
> **Mom:** But it's enough for a t-shirt. ((giggles))
> **Lisa:** Yes.
> **Mom:** Lisa thinks.
> **Dad:** Oh my god! But you can buy a t-shirt tomorrow.

Lisa: TOMORROW? Then they'll all be gone!
Dad: Bah.
Lisa: It's uh, yeah, dad?
Dad: Yeah. ((smiles))
Lisa: They are coveted.
Dad: Yeah, but you can buy one some other time.
Lisa: No dad, stop it! It's actually important. What if I don't get any?
Dad: Yeah, but I'll check.
Lisa: What if I get one that's too big? That's no fun, right?
Dad: But isn't it enough if you bring money tonight, right?
    Because are you coming home?
Lisa: Yeah.
Dad: Right.

This is an example of the goal that many children in the present study had: wanting to acquire money, or what Bourdieu (1986) calls *economic capital*, in order to obtain *symbolic capital* (e.g., prestige, honor, attention), for instance, through particular clothes. Here, Lisa is positioning herself in an assemblage consisting of relations between teenager, money, and symbolic consumption. Initially, she asks her father to withdraw money. When he says that she can buy a t-shirt tomorrow, she argues that they all will be gone by then. She points out the value of the t-shirts by arguing that "they are coveted," and then by saying that the whole issue about buying the t-shirt tonight is important to her since she is afraid of not getting any. It should be noted that the t-shirt is constructed as not merely a garment. It has great symbolic value to her as a fan. Apart from desiring the t-shirt, she already has pictures of Kent gathered on a table in her bedroom, creating what could be seen as a small shrine devoted to the band. Fiske (1992) argues that in contemporary Western society, fandom is an important part of young people's identity constructions through which the fan draws on the semiotic resources of different cultural commodities (e.g., band t-shirts and posters) to position themselves in relation to other fans, and in opposition to those who are not fans of the particular artist. Lisa's t-shirt and the shrine could consequently be understood as parts of her symbolic consumption, and the value of the t-shirt may not be so much related to its "practical" usefulness as in relation to other Kent fans. The t-shirt, as a non-human part of her assemblage, is positioning her as a devoted Kent fan; it is becoming a part of her subjectivity and is crucial for how she understands who/what she "is."

While the children's goal is to attain symbolic capital through buying consumer goods, the parents lead a rearing project with the aim to teach children how to manage money and become responsible consumers. In this example, Lisa's father does not orient to the t-shirt as a resource for her fan assemblage; rather, his main issue is *when* she has to have the money in order to buy the t-shirt. Her father's arguments are mainly related to temporality. He first argues that she can by a t-shirt tomorrow (she is going to the artist's concerts two days in a row), then he says she can buy the t-shirt "another time," and finally he argues that she does not need the money now since she is coming back home after her trip to town. The father's argument revolves around Lisa's need to postpone her consumption since he does not have any money to give her. Similar to the case with Filip, the father here emphasizes the value of money. But while Filip was mainly taught the relationship between work and money, Lisa is faced with the argument that money is not an endless resource, that her parents do not always have money to give her whenever she desires.

RESPONSIBLE CONSUMERISM

Above, Lisa's father argues that she has to postpone her consumption. This argument is an expression of what I would call a child/teenager-money-responsible consumption assemblage that the parents in the present study often presented. In the following, I will further discuss the issue of responsible consumerism. The next example is taken from the same morning where Lisa and her parents are discussing how much money she should bring to town. During this discussion she tells her mother that she also needs money for a new key holder (with Kent's logo).

> **Lisa:** But I have to buy a t-shirt tonight, you know. Right, mom? Please? Only one, and a key holder. Look, mine is broken, mine is broken, mom. Look, it's falling apart.
> **Mom:** No, now I think you're getting annoying.
> **Lisa:** No, but it's falling apart, I can't have it in school.
> **Mom:** But take away everything else that's on it and only have the keys
> **Lisa:** But look! Look!
> **Mom:** You'd better put in a claim for it then.
> **Lisa:** ((Rolls her eyes and sighs))

The interesting point here is that, in her argumentation, Lisa positions herself within a teenager-money-responsible consumption assemblage, an assemblage that normally the parents present. She argues that she needs a new key holder and wants to buy one tonight, one that has Kent's logo on it. However, she is mainly giving practical reasons for why she needs a new key holder: it is broken, it is falling apart so she cannot have it in school, and she even shows her mother how torn the key holder is. However, for her mother it is not enough that the key holder is broken. Maybe she thinks that Lisa does not *really* need a new key holder for practical reasons, but simply wants one featuring the band's logo. Whatever is the case, Lisa's mother draws on another aspect of the responsible consumer assemblage, that is, that you have to be careful with your belongings ("take away everything else"), and if something breaks even if you are careful, you should go back to the store and put in a claim for it ("You'd better put in a claim for it then"). Thus, through not buying into Lisa's arguments, the mother disapproves of her daughter's version of the responsible consumption assemblage. In order to become a responsible consumer, you cannot simply buy new commodities when they are broken, you have to be careful with what you buy and, if necessary, make use of your rights as a consumer.

Finally, let us now look how another child of the same age negotiates about money for consumption. It is Saturday morning, 13-year-old Niklas plans to go downtown with his friends. Before leaving, he tells his mother about his plans for the day, including joining a friend when he shops for shoes.

> **Niklas:** Uh yeah, I'll go, and he and so uh around ten and uh and then we check ((inaudible)) at noon.
> **Mom:** Mm.
> **Niklas:** And then we call Pelle or Sara, or should I take money with me so I can buy shoes as well? Cos Pelle's buying.
> **Mom:** No, no, then I'd really like to be with.
> **Niklas:** Uh well, all right.
> **Mom:** ((Nods, looks at Niklas)) Mm, I want to.
> **Niklas:** Why? ((Puts his head on her shoulder and his arm around her))
> **Mom:** ((Giggles)) Because I really want to be with.
> **Niklas:** Why? ((Comes closer, almost hugging Mom))
> **Mom:** Because I want it to be specific kind of shoes and that you don't come home with some dancing shoes or something.
> **Niklas:** ((Holding Mom's arm)) Well it doesn't matter what kinda— What? DANCING SHOES?
> **Mom:** Well but something that stands the weather.
> **Niklas:** I know what shoes I want. But! Uh! I take it as treachery ((Lets go of Mom's arm and walks away))

In this episode, the difference between Niklas' and his mother's assemblages regard the issue of competence. While Niklas positions himself in an assemblage of teenager-money-symbolic consumption, his mother positions him in an assemblage of child-money-responsible consumption. In other words, as Lisa did in the previous examples, Niklas relates to consumption as an issue of attaining symbolic capital and emphasizes his competence regarding what has symbolic value ("I know what shoes I want"). His mother, in contrast, emphasizes his incompetence, that he will not be able to buy the shoes she has in mind. In her argument, she argues that Niklas will buy "dancing shoes," which could be understood as her arguing that Niklas will only buy shoes as a way to attain symbolic capital among his peers. Instead, she wants him to buy "specific" shoes that "stand the weather." According to König (2008), in order to present a "juvenile self" you have to stop dressing like a child and consciously choose specific clothes or brands. Not being able to choose your own clothes, to let parents decide and thereby run the risk of being dressed as a child, is seen as negative among the teenagers in her study. In similar terms, Niklas is positioned in a child-money-consumption assemblage in that his mother wants to go with him to town and control what shoes he buys. While Lisa was seen as competent enough to buy her own t-shirt (even though she has to beg for money), Niklas is not given the same responsibility. Thus, while Niklas, in Deleuze and Guattari's terms, is trying to create a line of flight—to become-teenager—his mother "nails" his subject as an incompetent child in need of parental supervision.

CONCLUSION

In this chapter, I have proposed an anti-essentialist understanding of children's becoming and consumption. I have argued that both consumption socialization and the "new" sociology of childhood could be useful for studying children's consumption, but that they are inadequate in order to fully understand children's pocket money and consumption as social and cultural phenomena. While the former pays one-sided attention to what children will or should become as adults, the latter is built on an essentialist model of agency and competence, which obscures the importance of non-human actors, the developing nature of human beings, and the complexity of parent–child power relations. Instead, I argue that Deleuze and Guattari's framework is helpful to understand how children are *becoming consumers* and how their consumption is constructed in assemblages, in complex relations to parents, money, commodities, and friends, as well as discourses on childhood.

In particular, I have shown how a notion of learning and development is salient in much previous research on children's consumption, in market actors' arguments, as well as in mundane parent–child negotiations on pocket money. In all these areas, I discern a stratifying structure where children with age are argued to develop "proper" consumer competence. In my ethnographic data, parents create assemblages wherein children's need for learning the value of money and consumption goods is central. The first assemblage, which I have called children-money-work, emphasizes the value of money through connecting money and work together. In order to gain money, whether as a part of the allowance or as a salary, children have to deserve it. Obviously, this is a capitalist ethic that permeates most of Western adult society, but within the allowance system, young people's household work is disguised as learning and, consequently, their work is not seen as "real" work (Samuelsson, 2008; Zelizer, 1994).

The second assemblage that the parents propose is what I call child-money-responsible consumer, which emphasizes the necessity for children to become critical and responsible consumers. This may include the purchasing of consumer goods that are "practical," care for consumer goods, or that withholding one's desires and postponing their consumption. This assemblage can be contrasted to the assemblage to which the 12- to 13-year-olds in the study orient, namely teenager-money-symbolic consumption. Within this assemblage, young people's identities are constructed in relation to consumer goods with symbolic value, such as particular brands or band t-shirts. Symbolic consumption could be seen as a way for children *becoming teenagers*, to create new identities as they create lines of flight away from the stratifying dominant framework. In becoming teenagers, children's consumption is given a different meaning than as future responsible consumers. They may not be responsible or competent in adult terms, but from their own perspective, symbolic consumption is desirable and a way for them to construct themselves as something else than as a child or an adult responsible consumer in being.

NOTES

1. The Swedish study is part of an interdisciplinary ethnographic project documenting the everyday lives of middle-class families in Italy, Sweden, and the U.S. (cf. Ochs, Graesch, Mittman, Bradbury, & Repetti, 2006). The project has been generously financed by the Alfred P. Sloan Foundation and in Sweden been led by professor Karin Aronsson, Stockholm University. A scholarship from the Swedish Research Council for Working Life and Social Research for a 12-month postdoctoral Fellowship at University of California, Los Angeles has made the finalizing of this chapter possible. I am thankful to Angela Orlando, Linda Schultz, the members of the The Nordic Network for Researching Children's Everyday Lives, and my colleagues at the Department of Child and Youth Studies, Stockholm University, for their invaluable comments on earlier drafts of this chapter.
2. It should be noted that psychoanalytic theorists, in particular Sigmund Freud, heavily influenced Parsons.

REFERENCES

Aarsand, P., & Forsberg, L. (2010). Producing children's corporeal privacy: Ethnographic video recoding as material-discursive practice. *Qualitative Research, 10*(2), 249–268.

Bourdieu, P. (1986). Forms of capital. In J. G. Richardson (Ed.), *Handbook for theory and research for the sociology of education* (pp. 241–258). New York, NY: Greenwood Press.

Brusdal, R. (2007). If it is good for the child's development then I say yes almost every time: How parents relate to their children's consumption. *International Journal of Consumer Studies, 31*, 391–396.

Cook, D. (2008). The missing child in consumption theory. *Journal of Consumer Culture, 8*(2), 219–243.

Deleuze, G., & Guattari, F. (1987/2004). *A thousand plateaus: Capitalism and schizophrenia.* London, UK: Continuum.

Evans, J., & Chandler, J. (2006). To buy or not to buy: Family dynamics and children's consumption. *Sociological Research Online, 11*(2). Retrieved June 29, 2009 from: http://www.socresonline.org.uk/11/2/evans.html

Fiske, J. (1992). The cultural economy of fandom. In A. L. Lewis (Ed.), *The adoring audiences: Fan culture and popular media* (pp. 30–49). London, UK: Routledge.

James, A. (1979). Confections, concoctions and conceptions. *Journal of the Anthropological Society of Oxford, 10*(2), 83–95.

James, A., Jencks, C., & Prout, A. (1997) *Theorising childhood.* Cambridge, UK: Polity Press.

Johansson, B. (2005) *Barn i konsumtionssamhället.* Stockholm, Sweden: Nordstedts Akademiska förlag.

John, P. R. (1999). Consumer socialization of children: A retrospective look at twenty-five years of research. *Journal of Consumer Research, 26*(3), 183–213.

Klein, W., Graesch, A. P., & Izquierdo, C. (2009). Children and chores: A mixed methods study of children's household work in Los Angeles families. *Anthropology of Work Review, 31*(1), 98–109.

König, A. (2008). Which clothes suit me?: The presentation of the juvenile self. *Childhood, 15*(2), 225–237.

Lee, N. (1998). Towards an immature sociology. *The Sociological Review 46*(3), 458–482.

Lee, N. (2001). *Childhood and society: Growing up in an age of uncertainty.* Maidenhead, UK: Open University Press.

Martens, L., Southerton, D., & Scott, S. (2004). Bringing children (and parents) into the sociology of consumption. *Journal of Consumer Culture, 4*(2), 155–182.

McNeal, J. U. (2007). *On becoming a consumer: The development of consumer behavior patterns in childhood.* Oxford: Butterworth-Heinemann.

Moschis, G. P. (1987). *Consumer socialization: A life-cycle perspective.* Lexington, MA: Lexington Books.

Moschis, G. P., & Churchill, G. A. (1978). Consumer socialization: A theoretical and empirical analysis. *Journal of Marketing Research, 15*(4), 599–609.

Ochs, E., Graesch, A., Mittman, A., Bradbury, T., & Repetti, R. (2006) Video ethnography and ethnoarcheological tracking. In M. Pitt-Catsouphes, E. Ernst,

& S. Sweet (Eds.), *Work and family handbook: Multi-disciplinary perspectives and approaches* (pp. 387–409). Mahwah, NJ: Lawrence Erlbaum.

Parsons, T., Bales, R. F., & Shils, E. A. (1953). *Working papers in the theory of action.* Glencoe, IL: The Free Press.

Prout, A., & James, A. (1990). A new paradigm for the sociology of childhood? Provenance, promise and problems. In A. James & A. Prout (Eds.), *Constructing and reconstructing childhood: Contemporary issues in the sociological study of childhood* (pp. 7–34). London, UK: The Falmer Press.

Pugh, A. (2009). *Longing and belonging: Parents, children, and consumer culture.* Berkeley, CA: University of California Press.

Qvortrup, J., Bardy, M., Sgritta, G., & Wintersberger, H. (Eds.). (1994). *Childhood matters: Social theory, practice and politics.* Aldershot, UK: Avebury.

Samuelsson, T. (2008). *Children's work in Sweden: A part of childhood, a path to adulthood.* Umpublished doctoral dissertation, Department of Child Studies, Linköping University.

Swedbank (2006). *Veckopengen V.* Stockholm, Sweden: Institutet för privatekonomi, Swedbank.

Ward, S. (1974). Consumer socialization. *Journal of Consumer Research, 1*(2), 1–14.

Wærdahl, R. (2005). "Maybe I'll need a pair of Levi's before junior high?" Child and youth trajectories and anticipatory socialization. *Childhood, 12*(2), 201–219.

Weber, M. (1930/2001). *The protestant ethic and the spirit of capitalism.* London, UK: Routledge.

Zelizer, V. (1994). *The social meaning of money: Pin money, paychecks, poor relief and other currencies.* New York, NY: Basic Books.

Zelizer, V. (2002). Kids and commerce. *Childhood, 9*(4), 375–396.

CHAPTER 7

FOSTER PARENTING AS CULTURAL PRACTICES

Foster Parents' Developmental Goals and Strategies for Their Foster Children

Oddbjørg Skjær Ulvik

INTRODUCTION

"We just want her to become an ordinary child." This was a common expression in an interview study with Norwegian foster parents. The subject of this chapter is foster parents' developmental goals and strategies for their foster children, as they are expressed in narratives of their everyday practices. In Norway, fostering is a care arrangement organized by the child protection services and it is modeled on the biological nuclear family.

A universal task of parenting is to support children's acquisition of the skills necessary to function adaptively in their local community (Tamis-LeMonda, Way, Hughes, Youhikawa, Kalman & Niwa, 2007). The goal for parental care practices in all cultural contexts is that children should develop to be "unremarkable" in their own society. This is how it was formulated by Jean Briggs, who studied Inuit children in Newfoundland (Briggs, 1998). It

Children, Childhood, and Everyday Life, pages 109–124
Copyright © 2012 by Information Age Publishing
All rights of reproduction in any form reserved.

is the same goal that is expressed by foster parents in the quote above: "an ordinary child."

A theoretical premise in this chapter is that foster parenting, as well as parenting, should be analyzed as a cultural practice. That means that the agents involved appropriate and use available cultural tools in their meaning making (Bruner, 1990; Wertsch, 1998). Contemporary discourses of children and childhood constitute cultural tools for parents, as well as for foster parents, and of course also for the children. The cultural context in which the analyzed care practices take place is a developed country in the Western world, where ideologies of individualization are predominant (Beck & Beck-Gernsheim, 2002; Giddens, 1991; Gullestad, 1997) where the norm of autonomy (Rose, 1999) is part of folk psychology (Bruner, 1990). The analytical interest is how care practices are *accounted for* by the foster parents. Thus, analyzing foster parents' narratives of their everyday practices provides an opportunity to understand constructions of a "normal," "unremarkable," or *a culturally adequate child* (Ulvik, 2007).

Within socio-cultural developmental psychology, it is the children's involvement in everyday life practices and their various interactions with adults and children that make up their developmental conditions (Hedegaard, 2002; Hedegaard & Fleer, 2009; Rogoff, 2003; Valsiner, 2007; Vygotsky, 1998). Within this tradition, children not seen as objects of the adults' developmental efforts, but as social participants who continually take part in the practices of everyday life, and thus negotiate the care practices they are involved in (see the introduction to this book). Accordingly, it is relevant to explore how the caregivers understand the children they care for, as well as the caregivers' ideas, ideals, goals, and strategies for a particular child's development. Caregivers' developmental goals and strategies are widely ignored in traditional developmental psychology (Bruner, 1990; Burman, 2008; Haavind, 1987; Keller, Demuth, & Yovsi, 2008). From a socio-cultural position, caregivers' intentional practices make up a relevant area of research (Haavind, 1987; Weisner, 2009). The socio-cultural concept *developmental support* refers to the adults' practices oriented towards the child, practices that are directed towards developmental movements and that have progressive goals. The concept of developmental support does not have a predetermined content: The content and the direction of the developmental support provided in a given cultural context have to be analyzed.

Through history and across cultures, fostering arrangements have had various functions and significances. An example is kinship fostering in East Africa. The practice that children frequently reside within a household other than that of their biological parents is a widespread care arrangement, thoroughly studied by anthropologists (Goody, 1982; Notermans, 2008). In Norway, as in most countries with organized child protection services, foster care is a widely used arrangement when the care a child is offered is considered to violate certain cultural standards (Colton & Williams, 1997; Schwartz, 2005). Goody (1982) refers to this practice as crisis fostering. The mission implicitly given to foster parents in such an arrangement is to normalize the child's developmental conditions and to compensate for the inadequate developmental support to which a child has been exposed before the placement. In other words, foster parents' task is to contribute to the development of a culturally adequate child.

As a care arrangement, the foster family differs from its model, "the family," in several ways. The relationship between the child and the adults may be temporary, and fostering is a paid activity and a public mission. These differences, however, make foster parents a suitable group for studying normativity. Foster children already have developmental stories for which the foster parents are not responsible and of which they are only partially aware. The children's care stories are widely seen as culturally inadequate. The fact that foster parents are not responsible for the child's problems offers them a special frame of interpretation for a foster child's ways of being. Foster parents may display a child's problems more freely than parents who might risk being blamed for having provided inadequate care. For the same reason, foster parents might also provide more explicit narratives of their developmental strategies for the child. Their status as selected and competent caregivers gives them elevated positions to speak from. Studies from what is an exceptional care arrangement could thus also contribute to an understanding of developmental goals and strategies in general within a given cultural context.

Aspects of care practices that distinguish foster care from other more general parental care practices are highlighted in the analyses. The questions addressed in this chapter are: What characterizes developmental support for children in an extraordinary care arrangement, a foster family? What are the developmental goals and strategies that the adult caregivers have for their foster children? And how do the care practices reflect societal conceptions of what is a "normal" and "unremarkable" or culturally adequate child in this specific socio-cultural context?

METHODOLOGY

This chapter is based on an interview study with 18 Norwegian foster families. The foster parents belong to the working and lower-middle classes, and vary in age from late twenties to late fifties. Children and adults were interviewed repeatedly over a two-year period, the children were interviewed separately while the foster parents were interviewed together (Ulvik, 2007). Only the interviews with the foster parents have been selected as the empirical material for this chapter. The narrators in the examples in this chapter are predominantly foster mothers, which reflects foster parenting as a gendered activity. Developmental goals and strategies (which are analytical concepts used by the researcher and not by the informants) could not be studied fruitfully in isolation, but have to be deduced from analyses of narratives of everyday life in these families. The children in their turn respond to their caregivers' developmental goals and strategies through their everyday practices. Accordingly, narratives of these practices are the basis for exploring developmental goals and strategies, and thereby constructions of a culturally adequate child. Life mode interviews were used for this purpose. Through a detailed examination of the events and practices of the preceding day, the informants' understanding of and reflections on the practices in which they were involved were explored jointly by the researcher and the informant. Thereby the informants' subjective meaning making is explored. Hanne Haavind (1987) developed this methodological approach in her study of mothers of small children, and it has since been developed and applied in a broad range of studies.

The analytic framework developed in this study of foster parents' developmental goals and strategies is introduced by a short narrative from one foster mother:

> Eleven-year-old Tom's foster mother describes yesterday's family breakfast. She says that she generally prepares Tom's lunch box, explaining that she deliberately decided to do this for him, even though he could manage it himself, because she wanted to show him that adults should be responsible. Tom has a history of neglect, having had to manage things on his own and to take care of his younger siblings. His foster mother wants to show him that things have changed. She says that adults differ from children and Tom should be relieved of an excessive burden of responsibility. The child welfare worker told Tom's foster mother to support the boy's autonomy and self-management. But the foster mother says she prioritizes teaching him the meaning of being a child in a family.

In this short narrative of an everyday life situation, the foster mother implicitly expresses her concept of development, her developmental goals for this particular child, and her strategies for achieving these goals. The making of the lunch box is given a special significance. The significance attributed to this practice may be seen as a strategy for achieving a more abstract goal. Simultaneously, aspects of the construction of a culturally adequate child could be derived from this narrative.

Preparing lunch for a child is a common care practice in a Norwegian context. But the foster mother's account shows how this care practice in this case is directed towards a foster child. Providing satisfactory nutrition is not given as the main reason for this care practice, which the foster mother uses to assist in achieving an overarching developmental goal. Her perception of what is preferred and normal is for children to be relatively free from responsibility, with adults being responsible for them. As part of the foster mother's corrective program, Tom has to learn how to be cared for by adults. Preparing his lunch box can thus be analyzed as a strategy for *cultural correction*: a strategy to achieve more abstract developmental goals by correcting the child's culturally incorrect perception of the meaning of being a child in a Western society in late modernity. Implicitly, "child" and "adult" are constructed as dichotomous categories of significance. While the foster mother is aware of and supports the developmental goals of autonomy and self-management as part of the cultural agenda, for this particular child with his particular care history, she makes other priorities. The construction of a child as having limited responsibility is culturally specific. In some parts of the world, children younger than Tom care for themselves and even have responsibility for younger siblings (Ochs & Izquierdo, 2009; Rogoff, 2003; Tamis-Le-Monda et al., 2007; Weisner & Gallimore, 1977). While children's care practices for other children are valued in some cultural contexts, the issue is one of concern in Western countries and is described using terms such as "parentified child" (Jurkovic, 1997).

In this chapter, developmental goals are analyzed on two levels, as shown in the example above. The strategies directed toward the overarching developmental goals, which implies constructions of a culturally adequate child, are conceptualized as cultural correction. The concept will be further explained.

THE CONCEPTUAL DISTINCTION BETWEEN "DEVELOPMENTAL SUPPORT" AND "CULTURAL CORRECTION"

Comparison on a descriptive level of care practices in foster families and other families is of limited interest. In both arrangements, children learn to brush their teeth and have their lunches prepared. The same types of practices could, however, be attributed to various types of underlying reasoning. The analytical focus is thus on the accounts of the care practices. As we can see in the example above, foster parents have complex and culturally embedded developmental goals for their foster children and employ complex strategies to achieve them. The empirical material in this study made evident the need for conceptual specification: the aspect of developmental support which has as its purpose to normalize, adjust and return or introduce the child to an adequate developmental trajectory is in this study conceptualized as cultural correction. The foster parents' developmental goals comprise the children's ways of being, self-presentation, understanding of self, emotional wellbeing, relationships and intentions. Cultural correction is an analytical concept. It is not synonymous with behavioral correction, which it may comprise, but is not limited to. Some ways of behaving, like stealing and lying, are obvious targets for efforts to instill change, while some skills and competences may be lacking and have to be taught—for instance, attending to personal hygiene. Behavioral change is not a primary goal for the foster parents in this study. Cultural correction represents developmental goals at a second, more abstract, level.

As already mentioned, socio-cultural theory presupposes that developmental support is embedded in a cultural system of norms and significance. That means that all kinds of developmental support include the correction and adjustment of the child's ways of being. The cultural direction of the developmental support is implicit in the socio-cultural development concept. The concept cultural correction may thus appear superfluous. However, in order to highlight the caregivers' intentionality as cultural agents, a distinction between the two concepts was required in these analyses of foster parents' practices. Developmental support is a more comprehensive concept than cultural correction, but cultural correction is one aspect of it. The distinction will be further clarified through empirical examples.

FOSTER PARENTS' DEVELOPMENTAL SUPPORT FOR THEIR FOSTER CHILDREN

The foster parents in this study report a broad range of developmental strategies, of which a large proportion is of a corrective, adjusting nature. In order to bring the child into an acceptable developmental pathway, they make detailed and repeated observations of a broad spectrum of the child's ways of being. They call upon different kinds of expertise and professional assistance and they build up and organize advanced care systems around the child. Foster children have experienced developmental conditions that violate established standards in the relevant cultural context. In some ways, they often do not appear "unremarkable" (Briggs, 1998). Many foster parents in this study report about their foster children's subtle code violations, of which they have gradually become aware. This may involve a lack of basic knowledge, such as a 13-year-old not knowing the seasons of the year. Or the child may behave in ways which are not regarded as age- or gender-adequate, or may lack skills and competencies. A precondition for carrying out this process of observation and interpretation is living everyday life continuously with the child. Code violations and gaps in general knowledge are first discovered, and then interpreted. The next challenge is to elaborate strategies for change. The foster parents present various explanations for the children's conspicuous ways of being. The foster parents may be preoccupied with the consequences of a particular way of being, for instance with the child's opportunities for social participation with peers. Or foster parents focus their attention on the origins of the way of being. Their interpretations account for their corrective strategies and developmental support.

Clean Children versus Self-Initiated Showering: Developmental Goals at Two Levels

Personal hygiene was an important area of concern, and the foster parents provided several narratives on this topic. Foster parents had several analyses and strategies to accomplish their goal, the first level of which is *clean children*, with the second level being *self-initiated showering*. As the foster mother of 13-year-old Fred explained:

> When he comes out of the shower, he is still dirty. He just lets the water run over him and looks even worse afterwards. Soap is dangerous. We started to put him back in the shower. If he still smells, then he has another turn in the shower. If he goes back in for a second time, I go in with him. That is a setback for him. But we have to do it. . . . It is not only showering, it is tooth-brushing and everything. I do not understand what it is. I think it is worse for him to take a shower than for someone else to run a marathon. He does not need to be clean. He thinks of it as something he does for me: He takes a shower out of duty. I do not want to have to pay him pocket money for taking a shower. That is what I want to change. So we have thought a lot about what to do about cleanliness, how to handle it. We have tried the good way and we have tried the bad way.

As this narrative shows, that the boy simply takes a shower is not sufficient for his foster mother. "Showering out of duty" is too low an aspiration. The foster mother has critical reflections about her own strategies. Her second-level goal is that the boy should see the need for a shower and even want one. On the first level, the goal is to shower properly and by forcing the child to do so this goal can be attained. But this strategy is seen as illegitimate and possibly even harmful to the attainment of goals at the second level; which could be conceptualized as an issue for cultural correction. Similar situations are reported by other foster parents. A foster mother of two boys, aged 9 and 11, have these reflections:

> That is something all foster parents are focused on, I think, cleanliness. Many try to enforce it at regular hours. At that day, at that time, you have to take a shower. I think that is not right, it is a military approach. I think showering is something we should have a feeling for: Now we are sweating, now we have taken exercise, now a shower will do us good. I did remind them every time: Isn't it good to have a shower? . . . Sometimes I almost have to threaten them. I thought we had fixed it: One of them came home and said, "Now I've been skiing, a shower will be good." But it did not last. Now I have to nag again.

The developmental goals in these examples are not limited to hygiene: It is not sufficient that the child gets *clean*. The goal is that the child should have a *feeling for it,* which is part of a larger program of cultural correction. The showering should be self-initiated: The abstract developmental goal is self-governed children, and that is what constitutes the cultural correction. Developmental goals at that level are more complex to accomplish, and require more advanced strategies from the caregiver.

Being Aware of One's Needs

Being aware of one's needs is a related developmental goal on the foster parents' agenda. A foster mother of an 11 year old boy explains:

> I tell him to go out and feel the temperature. "What should you wear?" He often asks about that. "Stand in the doorway and feel what it is like," I say. And then I let him put on whatever he wants. If he is too cold or too warm, he can just come back and change. It works much better now.

This foster mother's strategy is complex. The boy asks for direct advice, but the foster mother does not respond to his request. Instead, in a quite directive way, she stages a situation that provides the boy with an experience that enhances bodily awareness, and simultaneously gives the boy the experience of being the one to make a decision. "Feel what it is like" also sends a message to the child that his own perceptions are valid. This training is done within a framework where the foster mother controls the consequences of the boy's choices. She evaluates the results of the strategy positively, and attributes them to her own efforts. Proper dressing is a goal at the first level, but it is not the main issue. The foster mother's main developmental goal for the child, her goal at the second level for which cultural correction is needed, is for him to become a self-governed individual aware of his own needs. Awareness of one's own needs is a competence that does not come from "within," but is social in its nature. It has to be developed through certain kinds of social participation, as we can see from this narrative of the interaction between the adult and the child.

Learning to Make Choices

Here a foster mother of a nine-year-old boy tells about various and individually adapted activities the child participates in, which were chosen on the basis of the child showing any interest for a topic:

We try not to push him in any one way. We may actually try to lead him a little in a certain direction, but I think he should learn to choose. If he makes the wrong choices, then okay, we will tell him. If he starts on an activity, he is not allowed just to drop out; he has to carry on with it for a while.

Learning to make choices on your own is the developmental goal in this narrative. It is a goal at the second level. While "pushing someone" is not a worthy parental practice, in this foster mother's words it is legitimate to "lead a little," if necessary. She is talking about making responsible choices. "Making your own choices" carries an implicit obligation on the child—an obligation that is defined by the adults. The foster mother is not only correcting the child if he makes a wrong choice, but more importantly she is highlighting the importance of the child learning to choose, which includes being responsible. We should be aware of the subtle—and culturally important—distinction in this narrative between "pushing" and "leading a little," which represents the limits of the caregiver's agency.

Speaking Up for Oneself

Speaking up for oneself is a competence that is highly valued by the foster parents in this study, with many expressing the view "it is better for the child to speak up too much than too little." Expressions of feelings like anger, protest, and discontent are tolerated and even encouraged, being regarded as progress. Expressing one's needs, and asking for what one wants, are related competences. Thirteen-year-old Lilly is regularly trained in the competences of speaking up and asking for what she wants:

The foster parents want her to learn how to ask for money. They encourage her: "Ask for money, and you will get it." They think this is a lacking competence due to her care history. If she asks for a cartoon magazine in the shop, they say, "No, but ask for money, and you can buy one." They want her to say: "That is something I want." But she never does. When her friends get new clothes, she never asks for some for herself. She appreciates being in shops, but otherwise she never expresses preferences. Her foster mother doubts that she has any preferences. When Lilly is asked, "Isn't this pullover nice?" She always agrees. But she would agree about another one too. The foster mother asks her: "Do you prefer the red one or the yellow one? Say what you really think, not what you think I'd like to hear." And now they can see some results of this strategy. Now Lilly can say that she decides herself. And in a conversation, she can say: "Now I am talking." The foster parents regard this as progress. The only desire she has expressed is for a dog. And the foster parents tell her that a precondition is for her to take more responsibility. She has to carry out several tasks on her own initiative, without encouragement. The foster parents think her desire for a dog may act as a motivation for her.

This girl is failing to present herself as an autonomous individual. The foster parents are aware of the cultural obligation of "being oneself," the obligation for individuals to continually create and display a self (Giddens, 1991; Gullestad, 1997; Rose, 1999). They use several everyday life situations to train her to acquire the lacking competences this implies: to be self-representing, to express preferences that underline her individuality, to be self-assertive and self-governed. By expressing a personal wish, Lilly shows her foster parents that she is developing in the preferred direction. When her wish for a dog is not instantly met, it is used as a strategy to enhance the preferred development of more self-construction (Giddens, 1991). These efforts are part of a comprehensive program of cultural correction in this foster family.

The Children as Partners in Their Own Developmental Projects

During the study, it became clear that an expectation exists among foster parents that the children should be partners in their own developmental project. They are supposed to support the foster parents' developmental goals for them. If a child declines the invitation to participate in the joint project, the foster parents/foster child relationship might be threatened. Here the foster mother of 13-year-old Annie explains her frustration:

> I was fed up and wanted to give up. She gave nothing in return, she lied and tried to cheat me. We had an episode in the bathroom. I had to monitor her, to check that she washed her hair. We did actually threaten her, saying that she had to leave. If you are not interested in helping yourself, why should we care? She does not do it for our sake. We were hard on her, and it is debatable if that is the right thing to do to a child. But we had to say it. We would feel more like parents if she gave something in return.

Annie does not share the foster mother's developmental goals for her. She is not self-governed in the sense that she feels a need to wash her hair on her own initiative. The sentence "she does not do it for our sake" expresses the child and the foster parents as individualized parties with different interests. The trivial negotiation on personal hygiene is simultaneously a negotiation of the whole relationship. This narrative, like the other narratives in this study, expresses an expectation of a reciprocal relationship between the child and the adults. "Helping oneself" is the articulated goal here, and the expectation is that the goal should be shared. The foster mother's frustration is due to the child's lack of engagement. In this narrative, engagement and shared goals are preconditions for the relationship. The girl's way of expressing her attitude to hygiene is not interpreted as autonomy, and is not supported. When the adults threaten her with ending the relationship, they approach her as the autonomous individual they want her to become. The foster mother's self-reflective comment, "it is debatable if that is the right thing to do to a child," shows the illegitimacy of abandoning a child, which she is aware of.

Gender- and Age-adequate Participation

The concept of the culturally adequate child is not free of gender- and age-related considerations. In the caregivers' developmental goals, the gender- and age-adequacy of the girl or boy is implicit. Gender and age are basic social categories that give direction to people's own ways of presenting themselves, and to other people's interpretations of them. In a late modern society, gendered practices are not complementary. Men and women, girls and boys do not have normatively separate repertoires of behavior. The significance of gender is constantly negotiated in specific cultural contexts (Lareau, 2003; Thorne, 1993).

Age and gender have implications for caregivers' developmental support. In families in general this may be implicit in the organization of everyday life, and direct corrections are rarely necessary. Many of the foster children in this study are regarded by their foster parents as less gender- and age-adequate than their peers and as persons who are at high risk of code violation. Foster parents seem to be competent to assess this risk. Gender-adequacy is not, however, expressed as an explicit goal by the foster parents. That might be due to an illegitimacy of expressing such goals. Six-year-old Sara's foster mother tells about the girl's development after spending a year in the foster family's care, and the strategies the foster parents have used to support this development:

> She was tough, dressed in silk shorts and boxing gloves, preoccupied with fighting and war toys. You do not buy swords for such children, you try to soften them a little. Her mother had reinforced her boy-like manners. We gradually removed the war games. We asked her, "Do you see any of your girl-friends playing with these?" Girls do not have to play with dolls, but there was nothing feminine about her. In the toy store, she went straight to the boys' department. She does the same in clothes shops. I say, "Here is the girls' department." She can climb trees and wear appropriate clothes for that, but for her first day at school, I thought it was important for her to wear a dress. We did not care about it, but she would have been conspicuous if she had been the only one in trousers. Now Sara has such a nice smile, she has grown to be a very soft and nice girl. She even lets her hair grow long.

Play related to war toys is in this narrative interpreted as gendered behavior, and the communication with the child also follows the gendered line: "Do you see any of your girlfriends playing with these?" An alternative interpretation of the aggressive and defensive play could be related to the child's care story and her possible need for protection, which is not brought into consideration here. Gender-adequate self-presentation is not presented as a separate goal. The social consequences of being inadequate are presented as the reasons for the efforts. Strategies are continually evaluated. Other children are used as models. The foster mother presents herself as tolerating gender unconventional behavior, and she points to the reactions of other people, who are supposed to be more gender conventional. The care practices in this narrative could be characterized as conventional, or the foster mother could be characterized as culturally sensitive. When she points to her own tolerant attitude contrasted to the expected conventional attitudes of others, this could be interpreted as an expression of the cultural mission implicit in foster parenting.

Foster Parents' Ambitious Developmental Goals

There is a widespread expectation among the foster parents in this study that the children will be conspicuous when they arrive at their home as their foster children. Some foster parents were surprised to see that the children "did not look like foster children at all." Few expect the child to be "unremarkable" at the beginning of their relationship, but it is a widely shared expectation that they will come to be so as a result of the foster parents' efforts. This implies that the impact of their own efforts is positively assessed. Foster parents negotiate implicitly both with the child and the child protection workers as to what should be developmental goals for the child. Some of the foster parents have more comprehensive developmental goals for the children than the children themselves, and are also more ambitious than the child protection workers who assigned them the task.

The foster parents of 13-year-old Tina reflect:

> We have to realize that she will never be like other kids. We still hope that she will be, but sometimes we doubt it. She doesn't worry about the future, she will get money somehow. That is a frightening attitude, and we have told her that this is no way to think. When it comes to the child welfare services, we are making the mistake that we want to succeed. We get clear messages that the day she moves out, she will be a social client. So why should we bother? They tell us that we are competent, but that we will never succeed, and it is not our fault. But I would regard it a real setback. We want her to have a job and to manage on her own as an adult.

For these foster parents, their developmental goal for her of "managing on her own" is essential for constituting the meaningfulness of their efforts. The cultural correction carried out by foster parents and the developmental support they give their foster children are not explicitly described in the task handed to them. Foster parents' developmental goals should not, however, be regarded solely as their individual initiatives and personal preferences. "Managing on one's own" represents a widely shared norm within modern Western culture (cf. Giddens, 1991). The developmental support they offer and their ambitious developmental goals have to be understood in the light of worthy parental practices in their cultural context.

CONSTRUCTIONS OF A CULTURALLY ADEQUATE CHILD

The above narratives show a variety of developmental goals that foster parents have for their foster children, and which in this analysis are characterized as part of a program for cultural correction. In this study, the empirical content that ultimately could represent a construction of a culturally adequate child is as follows:

- knowing what it means to be a child in a family
- having limited responsibility for oneself and siblings
- being self-governed and showing initiative
- being aware of one's needs
- asking for what one wants
- speaking up for oneself
- making (responsible) choices
- being a partner in one's own developmental project
- behaving gender- and age-adequately
- managing on one's own in adult life

To sum up, the discourse of the individualized child, or more specifically, *the self-constructing child* (Giddens, 1991) represents an implicit developmental goal towards which the foster parents employ the various developmental strategies we have seen in the preceding examples.

CONCLUDING REMARKS

The discourse of the self-constructing child is not synonymous with a self-centered, non-social child, and it is not opposed to a socially relating child. On the contrary, children's self-construction, their ability to display individuality, is seen by the foster parents as a precondition for solid relationships with caregivers as well as with peers (Ulvik, 2007). The dichotomous divide of "individualism" and "collectivism" as conceptual categories with the associated developmental goals "autonomy" versus "relatedness," is challenged by several scholars (Kagitcibasi, 1996; Tamis-Le-Monda et al., 2007). Instead, both theoretically and empirically, it is suggested that there is a variation within individuals and cultures, and both developmental goals of relatedness and autonomy are valued (Tamis-Le-Monda et al., 2007). Likewise, the developmental goals which are analyzed in this chapter, and the implicit construction of a culturally adequate child in the foster parents' narratives, transcend the mentioned dichotomy. The tension is not along the axis "autonomy" and "relatedness." A contrast to the discourse of the self-constructing child may rather be the discourse of the externally governed, shaped child, which in this study seems to be regarded as highly illegitimate. This further entails that parental practices could be discredited if the children appear as dependent, shaped, and governed persons, who do not speak up and articulate their own wishes. The examples in this chapter could be seen as paradoxical in that the developmental goal of being self-constructing and self-governed is achieved by encompassing strategies of shaping and governing. This could be seen as an example of a paradox in the general cultural developmental agenda in a late modern society: We govern and shape actively to contribute to the development of the self-governed, self-representing, and choice-competent individuals of tomorrow.

Developmental support that is clearly intended to result in self-constructing children could be interpreted as embodying a subtle mode of discipline, as part of a larger movement from external control to internal and self-control in care practices in late modernity. As discussed by Foucault (1999), modern self technologies do not merely involve the behaviors of the parties concerned, but their ways of thinking and feeling. We have in this chapter seen examples of how the foster children are invited by their foster parents into the kind of social interaction that enhances self-construction. The "self-constructing child" is not a "natural" phenomenon, but developed through social interactions of certain kinds. In other words, the self-constructing child develops by social participation.

The discourse of the self-constructing child serves as a cultural tool (Wertsch, 1998) for the foster parents' care practices, which they master and widely appropriate. Some of the narratives presented in this chapter may arouse moral indignation directed towards the foster parents. I suggest that we rather locate the contradictions and the tensions in how they talk about their practices to the cultural context of which they are part. The foster parents could be interpreted as being culturally sensitive caregivers who are aware of the competences that are demanded in a late modern society (Beck & Beck-Gernsheim, 2002; Giddens, 1991; Gullestad, 1997). Although focusing their attention towards the individual child, the foster parents could be seen as participants in a collective endeavor in which they constantly negotiate the meaning of childcare and of conceptions of a culturally adequate child.

REFERENCES

Beck, U., & Beck-Gernsheim, E. (2002). *Individualization: Institutionalized individualism and its social and political consequences.* Thousand Oaks, CA: Sage.

Briggs, J. (1998). *Inuit morality play. The emotional education of a three-year-old.* New Haven, CT: Yale University Press.

Bruner, J. (1990). *Acts of meaning.* Cambridge, MA: Harvard University Press.

Burman, E. (2008). *Deconstructing developmental psychology.* London, UK: Routledge.

Colton, M., & Williams, J. (1997). *The world of foster care.* Hants, UK: Arena.

Foucault, M. (1999). Technologies of the self. In L.H.Martin, H. Gutman, & P.H. Hutton (Eds.), *Technologies of the self* (pp. 16–49). London, UK: Tavistock.

Giddens, A. (1991). *Modernity and self –identity: Self and the society in the late modern age.* Cambridge, UK: Polity Press.

Goody, E. (1982). *Parenthood and social reproduction: Fostering and occupational roles in West Africa.* Cambridge, UK: Cambridge University Press.

Gullestad, M. (1997). From "Being of use" to" finding oneself": Dilemmas of value transmission between generations in Norway. In M. Gullestad & M. Segalen (Eds.), *Family and kinship in Europe.* (pp. 202–219). London, UK: Pinter.

Haavind, H. (1987). *Liten og stor. Mødres omsorg og barns utviklingsmuligheter.* [Small and big. Mothers' care and children's developmental possibilities].Oslo, Norway: Universitetsforlaget.

Hedegaard, M. (2002). *Learning and child development.* Aarhus, Denmark: Aarhus University Press.

Hedegaard, M., & Fleer, M. (2009). *Studying children. A cultural-historical approach.* London: Open University Press.

Jurkovic, G. J. (1997). *Lost childhoods: The plight of the parentified child.* London, UK: Routledge.

Kagitcibasi, C. (1996). *Family and human development across cultures: A view from the other side.* Mahwah, NJ: Erlbaum.

Keller, H., Demuth, C., & Yovsi, R. D. (2008). The multi-voicedness of independence and interdependence: The case of the Cameroonian Nso. *Culture & Psychology, 14,* 115–144.

Lareau, A. (2003). *Unequal childhoods: Class, race, and family life.* Berkeley, CA: University of California Press.

Notermans, C. (2008). The emotional world of kinship: Children's experiences of fosterage in East Cameroon. *Childhood, 15,* 355–377.

Ochs, E., & Izquierdo, C. (2009). Responsibility in childhood: Three developmental trajectories. *ETHOS, 37,* 391–413.

Rogoff, B. (2003). *The cultural nature of human development.* New York, NY: Oxford University Press.

Rose, N. (1999). *Powers of freedom: Reframing political thought.* Cambridge, UK: Cambridge University Press.

Schwartz, T. T. (2005). *Parenting for the state: An ethnographic analysis of non-profit foster care.* New York, NY: Routledge.

Tamis-LeMonda, C. S., Way, N., Hughes, D., Yoshikawa, H., Kalman, R. K., & Niwa, E. Y. (2008). Parents' goals for children: The dynamic coexistence of individualism and collectivism in cultures and individuals. *Social Development, 17,* 183–209.

Thorne, B. (1993). *Gender play: Girls and boys in schools.* Buckingham, UK: Open University Press.

Ulvik, O. S. (2007). Seinmoderne fosterfamilier. En kulturpsykologisk studie av barn og voksnes fortellinger. [Foster families in late modernity: A cultural psychological study of children and adults' narratives]. Oslo, Norway: Unipub.

Valsiner, J. (2007). *Culture in minds and societies. Foundations of cultural psychology.* London, UK: Sage.

Vygotsky, L. S. (1998). *The collected works of L. S. Vygotsky.* Volume 5. Child Psychology. New York, NY: Plenum Press.

Weisner, T. S. (2009). Culture, development, and diversity: Expectable pluralism, conflict, and similarity. *ETHOS, 37,* 181–196.

Weisner, T. S., & Gallimore, R. (1977). My brother's keeper: Child and sibling caretaking. *Current Anthropology, 18,* 169–190.

Wertsch, J. (1998). *Mind as action.* New York, NY: Oxford University Press.

CHAPTER 8

FAMILY PROBLEMS

Exploring Dilemmas and Complexities of Organizing Everyday Family Life

Dorte Kousholt

INTRODUCTION

This chapter discusses professional support to families who are defined as having 'special problems' by drawing on knowledge of *general dilemmas* in children's and parents' everyday lives in Danish society. This demands conceptualizations of family life that take into account the complexities and challenges of arranging a family life. Moreover, it entails an understanding of parents' and children's problems as connected to problematic life conditions. Children's and parents' problems are seen as linked to dilemmas and conflicts in relation to arranging an everyday life that is shared as well as separate. The point here is to turn our attention to how children's lives in other contexts with other children and adults shape the interplay between parents and children in the family context. This focus makes it possible to link parental care to the everyday life of the child across different contexts.

Expanding our understanding of parenting requires theoretical concepts that situate family practices in societal structures (Dreier, 2008). Concepts

Children, Childhood, and Everyday Life, pages 125–139
Copyright © 2012 by Information Age Publishing
125

about family life form understandings of family problems and, in turn, how to support families with problems. Thus, situating the interplay between parents and children in everyday life contexts challenges the treatment of "isolated family relations" as the pivotal focus in professional support to families. The possible consequences of the theoretical approach, developed in this chapter, are discussed in relation to developing professional interventions directed at children and families in troublesome life conditions.

I argue that a focus on *family conduct of life* can contribute to working with the conflicts and problems parents and children face in their everyday life. This goes together with transgressing dichotomies between "normal" and "abnormal" problems—and separating the abnormal form the normal in concepts as well as in professional practice (treatment of special problems often takes place in special institutions separated from parents' and children's common life).

The chapter draws on a qualitative study of the everyday lives of children and parents in a Family Development Center[1], a residential institution for families in Denmark. The study investigated children's and parents' perspectives on their life and difficulties and the cooperation between the families and the professionals. The analysis centres on the conflictual processes of organising family life (Kousholt, 2011a).

THE EVERYDAY LIFE OF CHILDREN ACROSS SOCIAL CONTEXTS

The sociological and anthropological childhood research tradition (e.g., James, Jenks, & Prout, 1998) has contributed with research into the social life of children in diverse everyday contexts such as schools and neighborhoods (e.g., Mayall, 1994; Rasmussen & Smidt, 2002; Thorne 1993) and has introduced significant methods for engaging children in research (e.g., Christensen & James, 2000). In recent years scholars within this tradition have explored children's perspectives on various topics in relation to home and family life (e.g., care, upbringing, food practices) (Alanen & Mayall, 2001; Brannen, Heptinstall, & Bhopal, 2000; Brannen & O'Brien, 1996; Jensen & McKee, 2003). Such research provides insights into childhood as part of societal structure and children's agency.

Furthermore, recent contextual developmental psychology in Nordic countries has contributed to our understanding of children as *participants in sociocultural practices* and highlighted *children's perspectives* as central to the study of children's lives (e.g., Andenæs, 1997; Haavind, 2005; see also Højholt, this volume). Children's perspectives signify an analytical approach that informs my research interest and design. It has to do with focusing on children's positions and their participation in social practices—investigating what children do, and how they understand the different life contexts in which they participate with other children and adults. This entails looking at how the contexts that children live in are structured and at adults as conditions for children's lives.

Children's everyday life in Denmark takes place in several contexts—for example, the home, the day care institution, the school. That means that children's developmental possibilities are formed across different contexts (Fleer & Hedegaard, 2010; Højholt, 2008). As Singer (1993) points out, the care of children in today's Western world is divided between parents and professionals and must be understood as *shared care*. In each context, children face difficulties and social conflicts that are often related to (problematic) connections between these contexts. Whereas adults in day care institutions or schools act within delineated areas of the child's development (e.g., the teacher is responsible for ensuring that the child learns the curriculum), parents are responsible for the "entirety" and for the *connections* between the child's life contexts. Parental care thus involves considering and acting in relation to the coherence of the child's life. To do so parents must cooperate with different professionals in, for example, day care or school. The cooperation with different professionals in turn influences the parents' possibilities for supporting their child—as illustrated by the examples later in the chapter.

Family life is formed in interplay *with other contexts* in the child's life. Focusing on this interplay yields important insights into *conditions* for family life. Investigating family life as part of children's everyday life across different contexts broadens the perspectives on family life. This approach builds on the feminist critique of family research that focuses on the family as a unit whose "content within" is studied as disconnected from societal structures (e.g., Leira, 1993). It points to the need to broaden our perspective in research on families by investigating the family as both forming and being formed by societal structures.

THE FAMILY THEORIZED AS SOCIAL PRACTICE

In line with cultural-historical research traditions (e.g., Chaiklin, Hedegaard, & Jensen, 1999; Holland & Lave, 2001), my aim is to investigate the dialectic relations between the individual and the social. Humans relate productively to their conditions of life in collaboration with each other (Axel, 2002; Stetsenko, 2008). I draw on social praxis theory (Lave, 2008) integrated with conceptualizations of human beings as *participants* in social practice (Dreier, 1997, 2008; Højholt, 1999, 2008). The concept of participation points out that human beings are always *taking part* in some societal arrangement in *collaboration* with other people. Social practices are historically formed as part of more encompassing structures. This implies investigating the family as a part of *structures of social practice* and through the ways in which it is a part of children's and adults' everyday life. Family life is not an isolated practice—it is connected to and separated from other practices in specific ways that influence how family members can move between and combine practices in their life. People's lives and commitments are always distributed between several contexts. Therefore, we must turn our attention to *possibilities of participation across contexts*. By investigating the everyday life of children *across different life contexts* we focus on how the meaning of what goes on in the family is created in interplay with other places and relations in the life of the child. Thus, family life is investigated in relation to the everyday lives of children.

The family is theorized as connected to other practices through the concept of *family conduct of life* (Dreier, 2008). The concept of conduct of life opens up possibilities for dealing with people's everyday struggles to make their life work across these various contexts (Holzkamp, 2011). The conduct of life serves as a concept for analyzing mediating levels between sociostructural characteristics and subjective meanings and action possibilities. My interest has been in expanding our understanding of the social and collective processes involved in what can be called the shared or coordinated conduct of everyday life (Højholt & Kousholt, 2009).

FRAMING THE STUDY

In order to develop the analytical points, I draw on practice research with a Family Development Center, a residential institution for families in a suburb of Copenhagen (Kousholt, 2011a; Højholt & Kousholt, 2011). The study explored everyday life in the institution and at the same time analyzed the professional intervention from the *perspectives* of parents and children and *related* to the children's lives in other contexts (e.g., day care institutions or schools). I followed the lives of the families who lived at the Family Development Center over a year and a half. I spent time with the families in the afternoon and evening where children and parents were together. Furthermore, I did interviews with parents and children and arranged meetings with the professionals, where we could reflect upon and discuss preliminary analyses. In that way, the aim of the study was to expand our knowledge of how families make meaning and use of professional interventions.

Professional interventions are always *a part of* people's lives. A lot of other things are going on in children's and parents' lives at the same time that influence how and in what way children and parents can connect the professional intervention to what they experience as problems and difficulties in their lives. Focusing on children's lives across different contexts turns our attention to children's difficulties in connection with the possibilities of participation across contexts. Furthermore, it brings to the fore the fact that parenting involves caring for the compound life of children.

Families are placed at the Family Development Center because of concerns from the social services about whether the parents are able to provide the necessary care for their child. In addition, there is often an explicit concern on the part of professionals (e.g., teachers) in contact with the child(ren) in a day care institution or school. Families stay in the Family Development Center from three months to one year. During this time the children attend their regular day care institution or school. The professionals employ videotaped observations of everyday activities, conversations, and multiple family activities to support the families in working towards establishing and achieving different goals for the development of the family. The Family Development Center participated in the research project as a means of transcending individualized paradigms of treatment. They aim at developing cooperation with the families in ways that support parents and children in dealing with the difficulties they face in their lives.

In the study, I employed ethnographically inspired methods to follow the children across their different life contexts (Huniche & Jefferson, 2009). I spent time with the children in the family institution, the day care institution or the school, and the after-school center. These periods of participatory observations provided insight into challenges and conflicts in the everyday life of the families that I further explored through interviews with children, parents, and relevant professionals. In that way the study produced knowledge about the lives of the children in different settings, from different perspectives, and over time. This enables a multifaceted understanding of complex and changing problems and life situations.

I developed the participatory method and analytical approach in an earlier research project about the everyday life of middle-class families in a small town in Denmark (Kousholt, 2008, 2011b). This study provided insight into how the families make everyday life work and brought my attention to *conflictual processes of organizing family life,* and the *connections* between family life and the life children have in other contexts (such as day care institutions and schools) together with other children and adults. In the present study I wanted to further develop this knowledge by shifting my focus to families who were defined as having problems and in need of professional support. In that way, I developed my analytical approach by going across the dichotomy between the "normal/ordinary" and the "abnormal/special" in relation to family life and family problems (see also Andenæs, in press). Among other things, I did this by using knowledge of problems and dilemmas in "ordinary" family life to challenge understandings of families with "special needs."

TREATING "RELATIONS WITHIN THE FAMILY"

The study this article draws on involved "reflection meetings" with the family work professionals. During such meetings, professionals and researchers discussed the fact that parental support of the everyday life of the child across different contexts tends to fall outside of the realm of the professional focus. This is not uncommon. Previous research has also shown how professional practices tend to treat the family as an isolated and private enterprise (Dreier, 2008). This entails a risk of narrowing problems connected to difficult life conditions into relational difficulties. This "psychologizing" of social problems is connected to the development of psychological theory and practices for treating individual problems (Danziger, 1990). Jones (1999) describes how during the early nineteenth century, researchers and clinicians reframed their descriptions of "problem mothers" in terms of the emotional dynamics of parent–child relationships. This went hand in hand with the emergence of a psychoanalytic framework that increasingly replaced more class-based interpretations of misbehavior—for example, poverty as an explanation for a parent's role in "delinquency causation" (Jones, 1999).

This means that problems tend to be located *within* the individual family members. Consequently, the professional interventions concentrate on the emotional and relational aspect of the family's problems. Examinations of the parents' "relational competences" often take place in *isolated* situations that are rather *disconnected* from the concrete life conditions.

I will illustrate some aspects of this problem using an example from the everyday life of one of the families. The family consists of the mother, Claire; a 4 ½-year-old girl, Sara; and her little brother John, who is one year old. Claire has other children who do not live with her at the moment. She has troublesome relations with the children's fathers, and when she is referred to the Family Development Center she has no place to live. Her daughter Sara is considered to be "a little behind in her development"; however, she is functioning fairly well in her day care institution.

The professionals are concerned because they think that the contact between Claire and Sara is predominantly "negative"; they point out to me that Claire often rejects Sara, and that they have many conflicts. Claire tells me that she has difficulties in dealing with Sara; she feels that "something is wrong" with her. She experiences Sara as very restless and unfocused. Sara has now started to go to the family's own room to watch TV when she comes home from the day care institution. Claire, who is concerned that Sara is not able to concentrate and play by herself, sees that as a positive development—that she is now able to sit down for a while and concentrate. Claire connects the changes in Sara's behavior to a more peaceful time at the Family Development Center. They used to stay in a house with another family; now they have a house for themselves. The professionals, however, are very concerned that Sara has withdrawn from her mother and has "given up on the contact." They talk about when "to draw the line" and react on their concern for the girl's development.[2]

The example illustrates that both the mother and the professional identify problems *within* the family. However, they perceive them very differently. The mother points to positive changes in the family's life conditions and she connects these changes to opportunities for her and Sara in relation to how they can make their everyday life work. The professionals interpret the changes as a weakening of the relation between mother and child. During this period in the family's life, the professionals become more concerned and preoccupied with how to assess and control the development of the family.

The point here is not to assess which interpretation of the situation is correct, but to show that the professional explanations direct our attention to the mother–child relation. As pointed out by Burman (1994) and Seymour (2004), for example, the mother–child relationship has been foregrounded as *the* most important relation in the child's life that overshadows any other relationships. Ochs and Shieffelin (1994) show that in middle-class Western society, dyadic interactions between caregiver and infant are regarded as pivotal for the process of socialization. This can furthermore be seen as related to theories of dyadic attachment as the primary basis for the development of children (as put forward by, e.g., Bowlby and Ainsworth). I stress this to underline that it would be a reduction to point to lack of competence among the professionals working in this field. The example illustrates that, despite the professionals' ambition of understanding the families' difficulties connected to their life conditions, the intervention appears to concern the emotional interplay and a rather *isolated* relation between mother and child. The more practical aspects of organizing a family life, which can support the everyday life of the child, fall out of focus.

The opportunities to develop the interaction between mother and daughter are inextricably entangled in the everyday practices of the family. Like other parents, Claire must continuously arrange a daily life with children who demand different and often conflicting things from her. She must prioritize her own resources and involve other parties when she needs help with the children. The organizing of a family practice is connected to her other priorities and to the distribution of her limited resources and time. This is not to say that Claire and Sara have no problems. The point is that any kind of problem must be understood in relation to personal possibilities of participating in conflictual social practices

In a later interview, when the family had moved to their own apartment, Claire explained that to her, the biggest relief and support in her everyday life was her new boyfriend, who helped her prepare the meals and feed

John so that she could spend more time with Sara. In that way, she indirectly expressed her need for *practical help* and support from another adult. This exemplifies that Claire's and Sara's problems must be understood in connection with *the conditions* for the conduct of everyday life for the family.

The interviews I conducted with the parents showed that when professionals focus interventions on "repairing" or "building up" relational competences, this generates a strong sense of insecurity among the parents. It seems to foster "performative compliance"—that is, doing things for the sake of the professionals to get good evaluations. When the professionals' increasing concern leads to a narrowing of focus to the mother–child dyad, it foregrounds dilemmas between support and control. When families enter family treatment, many types of difficulties have a tendency to become "problems-within-the-family": within an individual person or within an isolated relation between parent and child. Paradoxically, it seems that the *more worried* the professionals are about the well-being of the children, the more likely it is that the problematic life conditions of the family will fall out of the professional focus. This can be seen as related to the way parenting is often understood as an "ability" (as "inner psychic processes" developed, and harmed, in the mother's own childhood) that you either possess or do not possess. When the professional get very concerned for the child's welfare, the pressure on their professional judgement increases—and that seems to intensify the divide between "normal/ordinary" and "abnormal/ special" and to problems being individualized. It seems that the professional worry draws focus away from conflictual everyday practices and inwards to problems-within-family-relations. In that light, conflicts between parents and professionals can appear as "lack of progress" and opposition or resistance from the parents. In such cases, the professionals talk about feeling powerless and frustrated in relation to supporting the parents.

PARENTING AS SUPPORT TO THE EVERYDAY LIFE OF CHILDREN ACROSS DIFFERENT CONTEXTS

Turning to another family, I will show how the mapping of the everyday life of the child across different contexts may offer important information about the difficulties of the family. It provides knowledge about the child's perspective living in the Family Development Center. The example also turns attention to opportunities for working professionally with the aspects of parenting that are connected to supporting the everyday life of the child.

Mona is the mother of Peter (7 years old) and Maria (4 years old). The example focuses on Peter's difficulties connected to his life among his peers in school and what this means for his mother and the everyday life of the family. After a very problematic divorce, Mona has moved to another part of the country. Mona describes herself as "stressed out"; she does not sleep at night, she cries a lot, and she is very anxious about how to manage her children. Mona is very concerned about her son Peter, who has uncontrollable fits of anger. He often wets himself, and sometimes vomits. Mona cannot find a place to live, and after some months of staying with relatives the family, she has moved to the Family Development Center. Peter has been hospitalized because of his physical symptoms, and the overall conclusion is that his problems are "psychological" and related to a "low self-esteem."

> Mona tells me that Peter is often very sad in the morning and sometimes pretends to be sick (he recovers very quickly when he is allowed to stay home from school). Mona connects this to conflicts among some of the boys in his class. Mona tries to establish a good dialogue with the school about Peter's difficulties in relation to the other boys. However, she does not feel that it is going very well. She is very frustrated about her cooperation with the school, and she sometimes feels like giving up.

Mona experiences Peter's problems as anger and physical symptoms that become practical difficulties in their everyday life. Her conflicts with Peter in the mornings as well as her worries and frustration are connected to Peter's life in school, his conflicts with the other boys, and her feelings of "not getting through" in the dialogues with Peter's teacher.

> Peter tells me that he is friends with all his classmates except for three boys who tease and hit him. At school, Peter organizes soccer games with the other boys. Peter invests most of his energy in the breaks. The children's activities in the breaks involve many physical conflicts, accusations, interruptions, and new starts. Peter also tells me that he is unhappy because he cannot have friends home to play in the Family Development Center—because "there are other families living there and it will disturb them."

When Peter is not allowed to invite friends home, it limits his possibilities to build friendships and relations in school. One could say that it limits his attempts to link the two contexts. This does not mean that the solution to Peter's problem is letting him invite friends over; however, it points to the everyday practical aspect of living at the Family Development Center and what that might mean to Peter. For Peter, "self-esteem" is very much linked to his interplay with the other boys in school and how to connect his interest with activities together with the other children.

Peter is concerned with what games he likes and his relations to the other boys in the class. Peter's engagements and conflicts in school point to other ways of understanding what constitutes difficulties for him. Peter's possibilities for dealing with what he experiences as problems are connected to his daily life across contexts and his possibilities for connecting experiences, engagements, and making friends.

> A professional who works with Peter at the after-school center tells me that there have been some conflicts between the boys in the class; they have had difficulties getting play activities going without anyone being excluded. They have, as professionals, paid attention to it and tried to help out. She describes Peter as a somewhat fragile boy—he gets very upset when the other boys do not want to play with him. However, "he is always part of some activities with other children and we do not see much of him," she says.
>
> Peter's teacher tells me she works very hard on the well-being of the children in her class and the relations between them through different "social games." However, she also states that when it comes to what goes on during the breaks she is "in the dark"; she does not know what goes on. She points to that Peter has some problems sitting still and paying attention—like some of the other boys.

The teacher and after-school center professionals work in their own ways with the conflicts among the boys. However, they are also—as the teacher says—"in the dark" in relation to many aspects of the boys' interplay. Mona and the professionals who know Peter see him differently. His difficulties look different in different contexts; they are described and understood differently and connected to different aspects of his life. The descriptions can be seen as connected to the different tasks the adults have in relation to Peter. Peter's difficulties are complex and interwoven with what goes on at school and between the boys. The different adults' diverging perspectives are a part of his life condition and developmental possibilities. This *multiplicity* of different perspectives and contradictions between different perspectives are matters that the mother in some way must *relate* to and deal with when she tries to *explore* what is at stake for her boy: why he sometimes is so angry and sad and how she can understand his physical symptoms.

Mona tells me that the professionals at the Family Development Center help her in the cooperation with the school. Mona often worries and is very insecure about what to do. The professionals discuss with her how she can involve the teacher and they support her in organizing dialogues with the school. They accompany her to meetings at the school and they try to help her investigate what goes on in Peter's life among his friends and how to react. For instance, she talks to them about when Peter is feeling sick and sad in the morning—should she force him go to school?

It is interesting to note that the *meaning* of Peter's problems changes in relation to how the problems can be handled in other places. For example, when the professional in the after-school center helps Peter with clean underwear—without making a fuss about it—so that Peter can continue playing with the other boys, the physical problem becomes less salient for him as well as his mother. This points to the possibility of thinking of intervention as a form of support that is linked to the practical implication of children's and parents' difficulties in their everyday life contexts.

Mona must evaluate differences and contradictions in the information she receives from the professionals and try to integrate these bits and pieces into a compound picture of what goes on in her son's life. How Mona can understand and relate to Peter is influenced by her relation to the professionals at the school. Her difficulties cannot be understood in isolation from Peter's life at school. The way in which she can provide relevant support to Peter is connected to her insight into how Peter experiences difficulties in his life. Furthermore, Mona's possibilities to develop relevant support for Peter are influenced by her cooperation with professionals in Peter's life. Getting support as a family increases the number of professionals that parents must relate to and cooperate with in order to take care of their children. In that way, professional support can be "just one more professional" to relate to. However, as the examples illustrate, those professionals also support parents in relating to and making meaning of multiple perspectives conflicting demands.

FAMILY CONDUCT OF LIFE

The examples illustrate that family conduct of life must be arranged in relation to dilemmas and social conflicts in other contexts than the home. Family members conduct their lives in *relation* to a multitude of demands from various places. The focus on family conduct of life turns our attention to the work of arranging a complex practice where different lives, interests and perspectives must be integrated and coordinated to *make family life work*. Developing everyday practices in my life is not only my individual project. Everyday practices must be created and negotiated and may involve struggling with other people with whom one's conduct of life must be co-ordinated. Such continuous processes involve the constant handling and overcoming of conflicts and dilemmas. Solutions are often temporary and bring new conflicts and dilemmas (Kousholt, 2011b). Thus, conducting life as a parent is connected to exploring ways of arranging life in relation to conflicts and dilemmas, as well as in relation to possibilities for dealing with practical issues in everyday life.

Children's and parents' different perspectives are anchored in different locations and positions in the family and connected to different lives and possibilities in other places. Significant parts of family life are arranged in relation to the everyday lives of the children in other places. The relation between parents and professionals influences parents' possibilities for supporting the development of their child in fundamental ways. Problems in the family are often connected to *conflicts between different contexts* (and between adults) in which the children take part. The examples have drawn attention to the way in which parents must organize the life of the family in relation to a multitude of demands from various other contexts—such as a day care institution or a school.

CONCLUSION

My ambition in this chapter has been to direct our focus away from treating isolated and de-contextualized parent–child relations and towards discovering how to work with the conflictual processes of organizing family life. I have suggested that working with the concept of "family conduct of life" opens opportunities for understanding family life and family problems in ways that go beyond dichotomizing between "ordinary" and "special." This implies turning our focus in the direction of contradictions in life, social conflicts, and general dilemmas in the common life that humans live together.

The interaction between Mona and Peter and how Mona perceives Peter's developmental possibilities and her own choices as a parent are affected by the family's relation to the school. The problems the family experiences are connected to conflicts at school and how Peter can create links between the two contexts. This does not mean minimizing our view on the influence of families (as Harris, 1995, seems to suggest). My point is that the family's influence must be comprehended in connection to what goes on in other contexts. The family's situation is interwoven with conflicts and dilemmas in the everyday life of the parents and children.

I suggest that the examples show the importance of working with difficulties in children's and parents' lives in a way that is meaningfully connected to their everyday practices. This does not mean that professionals should refrain from working with relational conflicts within the family. The point is to go beyond individualized treatment of personalities and to work with the possibilities of participation in daily life in different places (Højholt & Kousholt, 2009). It means that the professional must—in cooperation with the families—explore the dilemmas and complexities of organizing a family life and support the continuous work of the families who are struggling with their daily life. The examples have illustrated that professional worry can direct the intervention to a rather *isolated* relation between mother and child or individualized understandings. I wish point to open *exploration* of conflict and dilemmas in the conflictual practices that the families take part in. To do so, the professionals need to explore the perspectives of parents and children, their experiences and reasons for acting in concrete situations, and *as part of an everyday life* across different contexts. I have pointed to the fact that the opportunities to develop the interaction between parents and children are entangled in the everyday practices of the family. This point has consequence for the way family problems are understood—and for how we arrange support to families.

Professional support to families could support children's interaction with peers and the parents' possibilities of getting involved in their children's lives. This change of the professional focus means turning professional attention toward *other places and relations,* and to the cooperation between parents and professionals and between different groups of professionals.

The professionals in the Family Development Center talk about getting on "shaky ground" and at the same time getting "more work and strengthen focus." New perspectives on family life—and on family problems—change the professionals' view on their professional task; it changes what constitutes support to families in difficulties. There is a need for research into how professional intervention becomes part of people's everyday struggles with dealing with conflicts and problems in their life across different contexts.

NOTES

1. With this terminology the Head of the Family Development Center wants to signal a change in the professional focus: from "treatment" to "collaborating with the families"—as part of an aim to transgress individualized ways of understanding children's and parents' problems.
2. The examples in this chapter are condensations of interview transcripts and observations notes.

REFERENCES

Andenæs, A. (1997). Theories of development from the perspective of the children, their parents and the scientists. *Researching Early Childhood. 3,* 51–73.
Andenæs, A. (in press). From "placement" to "a child on the move": Methodological strategies to give children a more central position in Child Welfare service. *Qualitative Social Work*
Alanen, L., & Mayall, B. (Eds). (2001). *Conceptualizing child-adult relations.* London, UK: Routledge Falmer.
Axel, E. (2002). *Regulation as productive tool use: Participatory observation in the control room of a district heating system.* Roskilde, Denmark: Roskilde University Press.
Brannen, J., Heptinstall, E., & Bhopal, K. (2000). *Connecting children: Care and family life in later childhood.* London, UK: Routledge Falmer.
Brannen, J., & O'Brien, M. (Eds.). (1996). *Children in families: Research and policy.* London, UK: Falmer Press.
Burman, E. (1994). *Deconstructing developmental psychology.* London, UK: Routledge.
Chaiklin, S., Hedegaard, M., & Jensen, U. J. (1999). *Activity theory and social practice: Cultural-historical approaches. .* Aarhus, Denmark: Aarhus University Press.

Christensen, P., & James, A. (Eds.). (2000). *Research with children: Perspectives and practices*. London, UK: Falmer Press.

Danziger, K. (1990). *Constructing the subject*. New York, NY: Cambridge University Press.

Dreier, O. (1997). *Subjectivity and social practice*. Center for Health, Humanity and Culture. Aarhus, Denmark: Aarhus University Press.

Dreier, O. (2008). *Psychotherapy in everyday life*. New York, NY: Cambridge University Press.

Fleer, M., & Hedegaard, M. (2010). Children's development as participation in everyday practices across different institutions. *Mind, Culture and Activity 17*(2), 149–168.

Haavind, H. (2005). Towards a multifaceted understanding of children as social participants. *Childhood, 12*, 139–152

Harris, J. R. (1995): Where is the child's environment? A group socialization theory of development. *Psychological Review, 102*, 458–489.

Holland, D., & Lave, J. (Eds.). (2001). *History in person: Enduring struggles, contentious practice, intimate identities*. Oxford, UK: SAR Press. James Currey.

Huniche, L., & Jefferson, A. (2009). (Re)searching for persons in practice: Field-based methods for critical psychological practice research. *Qualitative Research in Psychology, 6*(1), 12–27.

Højholt, C. (1999). Child development in trajectories of social practice. In W. Maiers, B. Bayer, & B. D. Esgalhado (Eds.), *Challenges to theoretical psychology* (pp. 278–285).

Højholt, C. (2008). Development through participation in social communities. *Journal of Australian Research in Early Childhood Education, 15*(1), 1–13.

Højholt, C., & Kousholt, D. (2009, May). *Researching conduct of life across children's life contexts*. Paper presented at ISTP Conference, Nanjing, China.

Højholt, C. & Kousholt, D. (2011). Forskningssamarbejde og gensidige læreprocesser. [Research Cooperation and Mutual Learning Processes]. In C. Højholt (Ed.), *Børn i vanskeligheder. Samarbejde på tværs*. [Children in Difficulties. Cooperation across contexts] Copenhagen, Denmark: Dansk Psykologisk Forlag

James, A., Jenks, C., & Prout, A. (1998). *Theorizing childhood*. Cambridge, UK: Polity Press.

Jensen, A. & McKee, L. (2003). *Children and the changing family: Between transformation and negotiation*. London, UK: Routledge Falmer.

Jones, K. W. (1999). *Taming the troublesome child: American families, child guidance and the limits of psychiatric authority*. Cambridge, MA: Harvard University Press.

Kousholt, D. (2008). The everyday life of children across early childhood institution and the family. *Journal of Australian Research in Early Childhood Education 15*(1), 13–25.

Kousholt, D. (2011a). Muligheder i familiearbejde set fra børns og forældres hverdagsliv.[Possibilities in Family Work seen from the perspectives of Children and Parents]. In C. Højholt (Ed.), *Børn i vanskeligheder. Samarbejde på tværs*. [Children in Difficulties. Cooperation across contexts] København: Dansk Psykologisk forlag

Kousholt, D (2011b). Researching Family through the Everyday Lives of Children across Home and Day Care in Denmark. *Ethos,*

Lave, J. (2008). Situated learning and changing practice. In A. Amin & J. Roberts (Eds.), *Community, economic creativity, and organization* (pp. 283–296). Oxford, UK: Oxford University Press.

Leira, A. (Ed). (1993) *Family sociology—Developing the field. Conference proceedings.* Oslo, Norway: Institute for Social Research.

Mayall, B. (Ed.). (1994). *Children's childhoods: Observed and experienced.* London, UK: Falmer.

Ochs, E., & Izquierdo, C. (2009). Responsibility in childhood: Three developmental trajectories. *Ethos 37*(4), 391–413.

Rasmussen, K., & Smidt, S. (2002). Children in the neighborhood—The neighborhood in the children. In M. O'Brien & P. Christensen (Eds.), *Children in the city: Home, neighborhood, and community* (pp. 82–100). Abingdon, UK: Falmer.

Seymour, S. (2004). Multiple caretaking of infants and young children: An area in critical need of a feminist psychological anthropology. *Ethos 32*(4), 538–556.

Singer, E. (1993). Shared care for children. *Theory & Psychology 3*(4), 429–449.

Stetsenko, A. (2008). From relational ontology to transformative activist stance on development and learning: Expanding Vygotsky's (CHAT) project. *Cultural Studies of Science Education, 3,* 471–491.

Thorne, B. (1993). *Gender play: Girls and boys in school.* Buckingham, UK: Open University Press.

SECTION III

SCHOOLS AS SOCIAL ARENAS

CHAPTER 9

A PARADOX OF INCLUSION

Administrative Procedures and Children's Perspectives on Difficulties in School

Maja Røn Larsen

INTRODUCTION

In Denmark, as in many other countries, inclusion has been a central issue in the political and theoretical rhetoric of school development. In the wake of the Salamanca statement (UNESCO, 1994), it has been emphasized that all children have the right to participate in the regular school system, no matter what difficulties they might be in[1].

However, different research approaches continuously question the apparent contradiction between the ambitions of inclusion on the one hand and the tendency of exclusion to different special education institutions on the other (e.g., Allodi & Fischbein, 2000; Hjörne, 2004). In Denmark there has been an increasing focus on "inclusive school for all." Simultaneously, however, the Danish school system is steadily excluding an increasing number of children, streaming them out of their ordinary classes in state schools into different kinds of special education (UVM, 2003). In the period between 1997 and 2007, the number of pupils in state school (age 6–16)

Children, Childhood, and Everyday Life, pages 143–160
Copyright © 2012 by Information Age Publishing
All rights of reproduction in any form reserved.

143

increased by 18.3 %. In the same period, the number of pupils in extensive special education increased by 48% (Andersen & Pedersen, 2008). The institutional logic of this somewhat paradoxical development of the school system seems to be that, in order to include children in school, they have to be excluded, helped, and then re-included (e.g., Hjörne, 2004; Mehan, 1993). This discloses an underlying point, that when a child is assumed to have "special needs," the focus seems to change so that the *special needs*, as something to be compensated for, become foregrounded and the *child as a person* living among others becomes backgrounded. In this way the child as a subject with personal perspectives and commitments becomes invisible—and the "special needs" become the decontextualized and desubjectified objects of special education.

The chapter addresses some of the dilemmas of how professionals understand and work with the inclusion of children that for academic or behavioural reasons are placed in the borderline territory between "normal" and "deviant" education—those children defined as having "special needs." The dilemmas in the work of inclusion will be explored by relating an analysis of *children's social perspectives* on difficulties in school with an analysis of *the institutional arrangement*, in which the conceptualization of children's special needs is used and developed in relation to specific conditions for social practice. The category of "special needs" is in this way analyzed in relation to *the social practices in which it works*—as developed and maintained by a number of different participants with common as well as different and sometimes even contradictory interests at stake.

The following section will unfold my theoretical and methodological approach to children's perspectives, on the one hand, and institutional procedures on the other. Subsequently, this is followed by analysis and discussions of the relations between special class practices, working explicitly with the ambitions of inclusion, and the administrative practices of referral. In conclusion, the different lines of analysis and results are summed up.

THEORETICAL AND METHODOLOGICAL APPROACH

This chapter is based on a research project, positioned within a tradition of critical psychology, originating from Klaus Holzkamp (e.g., 1995, in press) and in the Danish context developed primarily by Ole Dreier (e.g., 2008a, 2008b). The tradition has its roots in critical, historical activity theory (CHAT) (Nissen, 2009) and advocates a critical and decentered approach to phenomena in human life. Basically, in relation to this specific chapter, it means that to understand what is going on in one social practice, for instance the special education classroom, we sometimes have to look elsewhere, into other social practices involved in the institutional arrangement of helping children in difficulties in school. This is relevant for the analysis of the children's as well as the professional's perspectives. In relation to children's perspectives; in order to understand their actions in one context, we will have to follow their trajectories of participation into other contexts.

In the same way, when we explore professional dilemmas in the work of inclusion in the practice of special education, it becomes relevant to analyze the social practice of defining difficulties and processing *case files* in relation to specific institutional conditions.

My specific analytical focus concerns the relation between children's perspectives on difficulties *in their life* in a special education class and the administrative practice and procedures of "children with special needs" that posit them primarily as *cases* or *case files*. In this analysis the concept "institutional arrangement" is used to grasp structural conditions not as abstract determinants of subjective agency, but as conditions produced and reproduced in a conflictual process of cooperation between subjects acting with different interests developed in their trajectories, in and across different life contexts (Dreier 2008a, 2008b).

THE EMPIRICAL STUDY

In the Danish school system, education within state schools (municipal primary and lower secondary schools) and special education are organized, managed, and financed separately within two different pillars of administration. This organization is anchored in the Danish welfare tradition, where the individuals' rights to support are administered on an individual level in order to secure the priority of those in greatest need of support. In practice this means that if a child runs into severe difficulties in school, he or she can be referred and transferred individually between the separate systems through a referral process. In this process, "special needs" are defined as "maladjustments" or "dysfunctions" for the individual child. This separation of "normal" children on the one hand and "special/deviant" children on the other is reproduced throughout all institutional arrangements as well as in research traditions—for example, the separation between pedagogy and special pedagogy.

In order to analyze the dilemmas of professionals involved in working with children assumed to have special needs, the research project was designed as an ethnographic field study across the different institutional arrangements of social practice featured in the care of children with difficulties in relation to school. During a year and a half, I conducted participatory observation among children and professionals in a special education class. In the same period, I observed administrative meetings of referral to special education. In addition, I conducted interviews with teachers, parents, social workers (pedagogues), psychologists, and administrators.

TOWARD A SITUATED STUDY OF CHILDREN'S PERSPECTIVES

In the sociocultural tradition, children's development has been conceptualized as situated in concrete historical and cultural contexts (e.g., Burman, 1994; Hedegaard, 2002; Højholt, 2008; Rogoff, 2003; Woodhead, 1997). These perspectives have been part of a broad theoretical critique of the so-called traditional developmental psychology's universalistic concepts. Several researchers have criticized the historical use of individualizing psychological or medical categories of deviance and disabilities within the special educational practice. "Since the beginning of the twentieth century, psychological theory—along with the medical model of individual pathology— has formed a cornerstone of special education practice" (Sigmon, 1990, p. xi). The tendency to decontextualize and individualize children's difficulties in their school lives has been criticized from several theoretical perspectives (e.g., Danziger, 1997; McDermott, 1993; McDermott & Varenne, 1998; Mehan, 1984, 1993).

A main theme in the different approaches is the critique of the way individualizing understandings of development, learning, and difficulties retracts the focus from the historical, institutional, organizational, or cultural contexts (e.g., McDermott & Varenne, 1998; Skrtic, 1991, 1995). Within the different approaches to "difficulties in school," the institutional and societal context in which the difficulties appear is emphasized. As Mehan, Hertweck, and Meihls (1986) put it, "If children are handicapped only in school, then it is possible to say, that the school itself creates or generates the handicap" (p. 161). Mehan and his colleagues' central point is that the institutional practices of school, referral, and special education sometimes seem to contribute to the difficulties they are intending to overcome.

In continuation of the critique of individualizing concepts of disabilities and attempts to contextualize the difficulties in institutional organisational and cultural contexts, there has been a growing interest in developing knowledge from children's perspectives on difficulties in school (Morin, 2008; Morris, 1997). The following analysis is an attempt to elaborate on children's difficulties through the perspectives of the children themselves. This attempt is inspired by Holzkamp's claim that all psychological knowledge must be developed from the standpoint of the subject (e.g., Holzkamp, in press). By this I do not mean that we, in some kind of existentialist way, "enter" into children's minds and observe the world through their eyes, but that children's perspectives are *analytic,* indicating that the research process takes the point of view *of* the child as a subject participating in social communities among other subjects instead of focusing *on* the child as an object (Hedegaard, 2002; Højholt, 2008; Kousholt, 2008; Rogoff, 2003).

In my observations, I have attended to the direction of children's focus and actions—what is their purpose and trajectory and what are they part of? These observations turn the analytic focus to the situations in which the children participate: The observations and analysis of phenomena situates them in social contexts. *Participation* becomes a key concept, since it gives us the possibility to understand that what are seen as problematic actions are often meaningful in relation to the social communities the children are part of (e.g., Hedegaard, 2002; Højholt, 2008; Rogoff, 2003, 2008). Children orient themselves in relation to each other doing whatever they do as an integral part of the production of their shared life conditions (Holzkamp, 1995). Sometimes children's participation conflicts with what we as adults or professionals would characterize as "the right way to participate," and as a consequence the actions is considered as "symptoms" of the children's inner disabilities and described as indicative of some kind of lack of ability to participate. However, analyzing children's actions as participation related to the conditions of a specific practice or community, from their position in contexts among other children, they rather seem to be exercising legitimate ways of participating. By attending to participation as a key concept, what can be seen as children's individual disabilities instead appear as linked to the conditions for participating in communities with others (Lave & Wenger, 1991; Rogoff, 2008; Røn Larsen, 2004; Stanek, 2008). When observing children described as having concentration difficulties in the classroom, they do not simply lack the ability to focus. Instead they seem to be focusing elsewhere—on the other children in the classroom, watching what they are doing and trying to relate to this. In this way their focus on the school exercises seems missing but can actually be seen as a consequence of the conflicting purpose of orientating among peers. This draws attention to children as subjects with their own purposes following their particular agendas in their participation in communities among peers, and, as a consequence, they may appear as disturbances to the agenda of the social practice of doing schoolwork in class.

However, as will be argued on the basis of observations in a special class, children as participating subjects are often overlooked by professionals working with children defined as having "special needs." This phenomenon of "desubjectifying" children in difficulties will be analyzed in relation to the specific institutional arrangements of the professionals—specifically the processes of referral.

THE PARADOX OF INCLUSION/EXCLUSION

In her dissertation, "Excluding for Inclusion," Eva Hjörne (2004) explores and criticizes the institutional processes of excluding a child by defining its individual difficulties as a premise for working with inclusion. In continuation, she points out how the exclusion and categorization of children in difficulties as individually dysfunctional restricts the possibilities of inclusion of the child both by shaping the child's identity in a certain way and by the individualizing pedagogical strategies they are exposed to. In my empirical material a teacher from a special class reflects dilemmas related to this in the following way:

> If we wish to include children with difficulties in their "normal" state school classes, we need access to understand how the problems occurred in the first place. Who is part of it and so on? A lot of these children have a history of being bullied by others. And sometimes this has led to violence from these children towards other children, but the others are not innocent.

Even though the teacher is pointing to the need for more situated perspectives on the social contexts of difficulties, my observations from a family class[2] illustrate how the intention of a situated perspective on children's difficulties seems to be difficult to fulfill in practice. The following observation shows a conflict between Arthur and Ali:

> Arthur is sitting by the window opposite of his mother. He is surrounded by screens that can be raised or lowered in order to protect him from disturbances from the other children.
>
> Another boy, Ali, is tumbling around on the floor with a large plastic ball that the children are sometimes seated on, in order to calm them down. Ali is singing loud, and pushes the ball into Arthur, who shouts at him, "Go away, you shitty little brat." Arthur's mom steps in between the boys, who are trying to hit and kick each other, and one of the teachers says "Ali, you shouldn't tease Arthur like that." Arthur pulls his screens up. Ali crawls around on the floor, shouting; "Arthuuur, I'm touching your things now"— and reaches out to grab Arthur's schoolbag. Arthur shouts and attacks Ali, who is sneering at him. Arthur's mother catches Arthur and says to the teachers: "This is too much, he can't take it." Arthur is seated behind the screens—guarded and protected by his mother. He is still shouting abuses at Ali. The two teachers hold on to the still shouting and singing Ali, pulling him back to his table. They are talking to each other: "I have tried to put him on the ball3, but it doesn't seem to be working for him." One teacher addresses Ali in a loud tone of voice: "You can't play with this ball, Ali. You can sit on it and that will calm you down." The two teachers are trying to seat Ali on the ball, but his body is like spaghetti. He is still shouting and laughing at Arthur. Arthur jumps up and runs out the classroom door; on the way, he pushes Ali's table.

The professionals describe Arthur as a fragile child reacting aggressively to disturbances and having a lot of "impulsive outbreaks." As a consequence, the professionals put a lot of energy into protecting and guarding Arthur from the other children. This is why the screens have been constructed to be raised if he, his mother, or the teachers think he is being disturbed. However, analyzing this through the perspective of the child as a participant it could be argued that the professional understanding of Arthur and his difficulties reflect a decontextualized and individualizing perspective, isolated from the concrete situation. In relation to this, the screens become a symbol of the decontextualization within the social practice of special education.

At an interdisciplinary meeting about two months later, when Arthur has been medicated with Ritalin, he is described as having fewer impulsive outbreaks but with a rising tendency to be depressed as a side effect of the medication. Again, the understanding of him draws on a desubjectifying comprehension that leaves little room for exploring the conditions in relation to which his reactions make sense. Both his impulsive outbreaks and his depression are related to chemical reactions within the brain, and disconnected from the situation in which they occur.

The other boy Ali is described as a child who "disturbs." Here the ability to disturb is desituated and seen as a (dis)ability of this specific child. Ali is considered "a typical ADHD," as one of the professionals says. The physiotherapeutic artefact accentuates the decontextualization, as it is described as helpful for ADHD children—and therefore is used to "calm him down." The point is that nobody in the situation focuses on the *social conditions* for the boys' participation when it comes to understanding their difficulties.

CHILDREN'S PERSPECTIVES: ARTHUR AND ALI

Because the observations stretch over the complete school day, it has been possible to analyze the boys' actions as part of their trajectories of participation. Observations from earlier periods that day show Arthur asking a third boy (Hassan) to come and visit him at home some day. The encounter between the boys is interrupted by one of the professionals, who wants Hassan to do something else in relation to an exercise of schoolwork. In the situation it seems that Arthur thinks he is being rejected, and he leaves the situation looking down into the floor. Later on Hassan and Ali are playing together under a blanket. Arthur is watching them from a distance with an angry look on his face.

This might very well be a prelude for the scene we saw in the previous example. It could look as though Arthur's and Ali's outbursts are closely connected with the social life of the children. By observing the children over time, it becomes clear how they engage extensively in negotiating and fighting over their relations with each other but with very limited possibilities for participation. This calls our attention to the life conditions and possibilities of participation of the boys in the special education class. By the referral to special education, they are placed in a situation where they are separated from their previous classmates and put together with just a few other children, often of different ages. In this way the children's outbursts and difficulties are contextualized by a situation with restricted possibilities for participating in the children's communities. A mother of another 9-year-old boy explains in an interview her son's frustrations in relation to his peers, quoting him as screaming: "I don't know where I belong—here or there. I don't even know if my friends [from state school] know me anymore."

In the classroom, children's difficulties tend to be individualized and related to their innate, individual defaults or "special needs" by the understandings of the professionals. In contrast, observations of the classroom situations from an analytic children's perspective show how children's difficulties are situated in social contexts and connected to possibilities of participation with other children. The social perspective seems absent in the professional practice, even though the social context of difficulties in school are acknowledged by the professionals as crucial to the work of inclusion, as we saw it in the previous quote from a teacher in a special class. In the following section, I will search for the conditions for this apparent paradox by analyzing the institutional arrangement within which the tasks of professional work with children in difficulties are formulated.

ADMINISTRATIVE PRACTICE AND PROFESSIONALS' CATEGORIZATIONS

A number of researchers, often inspired by a poststructuralist approach, have explored the connections between dominant psychological categories and concepts and specific historical contexts (e.g., Danziger, 1997; Mehan, 1993; Rose 1998; Woodhead, 1997). As an extension of these lines of investigation, but posed within a slightly different theoretical framework, the contribution of the present analysis is to contextualize the professionals' understanding of and work with children in difficulties. It is a general analytical standpoint in my analysis that perspectives (i.e., the professionals' perspectives on children as having individual "special needs") are related to specific positions in social practices (Dreier, 2008b). Parallel with analyzing the children's perspectives in relation to the context in which they participate, professionals' perspectives are similarly considered in relation to the contexts in which they are positioned.

Inspired by poststructuralist analyses of categorization processes, both researchers and politicians have suggested that the main problem concerns the categories of the difficulties themselves. As an alternative, my analysis focuses on the social practices where categories work and where they are being both reproduced and changed by different participants.

The construction of children's difficulties as their "special needs" is in the present analysis explored as a social practice with specific institutional conditions. Professionals' available categories and concepts for understanding children's difficulties are comprehended as something developed and negotiated among different participants acting with common, as well as different interests and purposes, being positioned in concrete institutional conditions and arrangements (Dreier 2008a, 2008b; Højholt, 2006). In order to understand why individualizing understandings seems to be so powerful, we must analyze the very institutional arrangement in which they work. The important issue here is to analyze the dilemmas and problems in professional work in relation to concrete practice instead of questioning the individual professional.

Juxtaposing the described critical psychological perspectives with a more sociologically inspired perspective on bureaucratic organization facilitates an analysis of the relations between *conditions* for the professionals' work and *challenges* of working with children's difficulties.

In this respect, my research project has a cross-contextual focus on the interdependence of different social practices involved in the institutional arrangement around "children with special needs."

The relevance of this, in continuation of the above, is that professionals' understandings of children's difficulties and concrete institutional practices are closely linked to the professional conditions and action possibilities in relation to the children's developmental possibilities.

REFERRAL AS A STEP-BY-STEP PROCESSING OF "SPECIAL NEEDS"

The research process across different social practices involved in the institutional arrangement of supporting children with difficulties makes it possible to study the apparent discrepancy between professional intentions and practices in relation to inclusion as related to the institutional conditions of the special class practice. In this way, it becomes possible to analyze the institutional arrangements and logic in which an individualizing understanding of children's difficulties becomes dominant. I have therefore followed the procedure of defining the child's special needs "backwards" through the institutional arrangement of defining and working with difficulties. Following this track took me into the administrative and interdisciplinary practice of referral between the state school class and the special class, where the task of supporting the child is defined and the placement in a special school is decided. By observing the referral processes it was possible to see how the specific social practice of defining professionals' tasks in relation to children's "special needs" leads to certain understandings of their difficulties.

The Referral Practice

The process of referral begins when children are referred to special education by the heads of the state schools. The referral committee defines the task of helping the child and matches it with a relevant and available special institution. The basis of decisions is the case file that contains descriptions of the child, assessments, and psychological test results delivered by a range of involved professionals. The referral meeting is organized and divided into three stages with different, changing participants. In the first stage, the different professionals involved in the different life contexts (typically, head of state school, teacher, social worker from after-school child care institution, family counselor, psychologist) of the child present their perspectives on the child's "special needs" to both the headmasters of the relevant municipal special education institutions and three administrative leaders of different departments of childcare.

In the second stage, the different professionals who know the child leave and the heads of the special education institutions propose or deny their institutions as options for the specific child—"bid in" as they call it. Then they leave the room. In the final, third stage, just four participants are present: The three different administrators of municipal childcare and a psychologist. They make the final decision about where to place the child. The process of handling one case through all three rounds takes about 20 minutes.

A central question to understanding the gap between an individualizing and a contextualizing perspective on children's difficulties is then: What kind of information is considered important at the referral meetings in the process of defining children's difficulties and the special support needed? Observations of the referral process show an overrepresentation of information about the single child isolated from context and situation. The following observation is selected from the referral of Arthur, as he is being relocated from the family class to another special education institution. Normally the state school is the "delivering institution," but in this specific example it is the family class:

Round 1:
   Head of Family Class: He has been a very expensive boy for the system—he requires one teacher by himself at all times.

Teacher of Family Class: Since we suggested his case for referral, Arthur started a Ritalin treatment. That has clearly calmed him down. The number of impulsive outbreaks has declined and his concentration is better.

　　The parents want us to emphasize that the medication is helping him, so that he won't be sent out to a bad place. Arthur displays a strong spillover effect of the behavior of the group he's in.

　　There was a meeting two weeks ago at the children's psychiatric department, and they are planning to check him for an autistic superstructure, when the ADHD is toned down.

Head of Pedagogical Psychological Counselling (PPC): (Looks around) Anything else you need to know? (Nobody responds)

Round 2

Head of Social Administration: He could be a boy for Little House. [An institution specialized in Autism]

Head of Little House: I think, we can have him, but let's wait for the diagnosis.

Head of Kids Field (Another special education institution): We have a boy just like him in Kids Field already. But this boy is taking up a lot of resources as it is, and it's important for the staff to get a success with this boy [who is already there] before we bring in a new one.

Round 3

Head of PPC: He needs to be replaced immediately; he is taking up too many resources on several budgets.

Head of School Administration: Let's place him in Little House, then.

When comparing the kind of knowledge presented and the specific aims of the three rounds, it is worth noticing that situated knowledge form the child's life plays a still smaller part in the negotiations during the rounds. Instead, another type of knowledge becomes dominant, such as standardized categories of cultural or family background or presumptions of a diagnosis—typically different labels from the autism spectrum or variations of ADHD. The observation illustrates a very consistent characteristic for the practice of referral, namely the lack of knowledge of the situations in which difficulties occur. The only comment on Arthur's involvement in children's communities seems to be the mentioned concern of him "displaying a strong spillover effect of the behavior of the group he's in." In this way the child's community is described but with an absence of his subjectivity—the contextualization is reduced to Arthur simply mirroring the social context where he is located. The contextualizing, situated knowledge of the child's difficulties, the knowledge important to understand Arthur as a participant is absent. This aspect seems underlined by the organizational characteristic that professionals and parents with concrete, situated knowledge of children's lives do not have access to participate in the process of deciding of what is best for the child. A central question is then: How is this reasoned as a meaningful process? Attempts to answer this question through an exploration of the structural arrangements as antagonistic conditions for the different participants will be the continuing theme of the following sections.

The Replacement Agenda

Another interesting feature in the second round, where the different special education institutions "bid in" on the children, is that it appears as a kind of jigsaw, where the exercise is to make the children and institutions fit each other. In this way, the categories for understanding children's difficulties seem influenced by the availability of institutions. A piece of conversation between two heads of administration in relation to Arthur's case illustrates this:

> "He needs to be replaced immediately; he's taking up too many resources on several budgets."

> "Let's place him in Little House, then."

During the process of referral, more wide explorations of different perspectives is turned into a question of making the children match the available institutions. In order to make the children fit the institutions; the administration needs unambiguous knowledge on which to base its decisions. Here the administrative needs seem to overrule the exploration of the children's life situations. In relation to this, it is important to remember how the legislation pertaining to special education is formulated as an individual right or privilege of the child. The premise of the referral process is individual descriptions of difficulties. The external help to problems in a classroom requires one single carrier of the difficulty. The "special need" has to belong to somebody.

The combination of an analytical approach focusing on the children's perspectives on the one hand and to the bureaucratic procedures of a certain institutional arrangement on the other makes it possible to see how equally grounded yet conflicting logics are at stake at the same time. The bureaucratic procedures of the specific institutional arrangement seems to depend on a logic about releasing resources and relocating the individual and therefore it presupposes descriptions of the single child's "special needs," and in this way the systematic lack of attention to any knowledge of the social context makes sense. At the same time we see a contrasting logic pointing at the need for detailed knowledge about and access to work with the social context of the difficulties in relation to working with inclusion (as the special class teacher pointed out earlier), and this logic seems to widen the possibilities of understanding and working with the social aspects of difficulties.

From the professionals' perspective, this contradiction is a dilemma when it comes to supporting children in difficulties. The professionals need resources to work with the difficulties, but at the same time they are reluctant to open "a case"—often with considerations related to the consequences for the child. The case becomes the path to resources and a way of handling the responsibility of the practice, where the child is in difficulties. A social worker described it like this: "In order gain help—we have to describe a monster."

In this way it can be argued that the descriptions of children's difficulties are defined in relation to the institutional arrangement in which they need to operate. The distribution of special aid depends on individual children's social security numbers and the help available is primarily support to individual children's individual learning and behavioral problems. The decontextualized understandings of children's difficulties make sense within institutionalized dynamics of gaining support. These translations of children's lives into individualized cases makes the children "replaceable" within the bureaucratic rationality dominant within the system.

In this way, the administrative need for specified categories on which to base decisions can be said to have deep implications for the work with children in difficulties. During the referral the difficulty becomes decontextualized, and will then "belong" to the single child. Therefore the obvious task for the special class teachers becomes related to this (decontextualized) child's "special needs"—thereby, any options of working in the regular class (where the difficulty once occurred), the classroom that the child is now excluded from, become restricted.

The Diagnostic Agenda and Test Psychology— Professionalism at Stake

In the process where "special needs" is meant to describe natural facts of the child's difficulties, the psychologist is given a central role (Woodhead, 1997). Throughout the processes of referral there are numerous references to psychological tests and possible ways of understanding children's difficulties through knowledge of specific IQ and skills in the sphere of learning, thinking, and remembering. The test results are often followed up by assertions of which diagnosis would best describe the child's difficulty, not only by the psychologist but from any of the professionals. In this way tests and diagnoses seem particularly important in defining children's difficulties as their "special needs." In continuation of the discussion of the logic of the social practice of referral, it seems reasonable to link the power of the psychological tests and the diagnostic language to the administrative need for unambiguous individualizing descriptions of "special needs."

An observation from a referral meeting shows a teacher describing a 7th-grade boy having conflicts with the teachers, and skipping of school. The teacher describes the boy as "on level academically." He relates the boy's difficulties to his family's problems after having been moved out of their flat into an area with a high rate of crime. The teacher is concerned that the boy "must be on his toes" to participate among the boys in the local community—and describes the boy's process of becoming "street-wise" as a part of the problem. After the teacher's presentation, the psychologist concludes on the basis of a test that the boy has attention deficits and insufficient intelligence. The teacher seems offended and challenges the psychologist:

> "I don't think that this is the whole story about him. Particularly I don't understand what you are saying about his intelligence."

> The psychologist replies: "But that's because he has a good short-term memory. That tends to cheat you into believing that he has a normal intelligence—because he follows up on what you've just said."

In the following rounds of visitation, nobody mentions the descriptions of the boy's life situation. The teacher's attempt to widen the perspective seems to be rejected by the dominance of test-psychology's decontextualizing understanding. Later on the head of the school administration comments that this particular teacher is too engaged in the boy—he is being unprofessional. The comprehension of professionalism as connected to neutrality is underlined by the structure of the referral process. The final decision makers—those who are supposed to make the best decisions for the child—are always the leading psychologist and three heads of administration. In this way, the persons who are by definition furthest removed from the daily life of the child are given the power of definition over the difficulties of the child. Moreover the decontextualization of the child seems to be an immanent characteristic of the referral process, connected to the described notions of professionalism.

The mutual supportive relation between expertise about individualized needs and the rationality of administration reproduces conditions for decontextualizing children's difficulties. The administrative procedures are structured in ways that require standardized categories that are possible to administer and base decisions on. Test-psychology as a specific form of professional expertise produces such knowledge and is therefore valued above contextualized, situated descriptions of children's difficulties.

CONCLUDING DISCUSSION

The apparent paradox of inclusion could have been analyzed from multiple angles. For example, it could have been relevant to make a much deeper analysis of the practices that the children are excluded from—the state school. However, this analysis has primarily intended to shed some light on conditions under which certain understandings of children and their difficulties are privileged in relation to others within a certain institutional arrangement. The importance of this analysis is primarily connected to the way organization and categorization seems to be crucial to the scope of possible actions within in the professional practices of working with children's difficulties.

By analyzing the institutional arrangements of securing children's rights to special education, it has been pointed out how a range of different participants with both common and contradictory interests and conditions are involved in supporting children in difficulties. This implies that there are other interests than those of the child involved in the production of the institutional arrangement, meant to secure the children's needs. For example it seems to be an arena of different professionals struggling for acknowledgement. The institutional arrangements frame these struggles according to an agenda that values individualized, decontextualized descriptions of children's difficulties higher than contextualized ones.

In this way, the conditions of understanding "children's difficulties within a context" as an inseparable unit, are restricted. The possibility of approaching children in difficulties as persons with their own perspectives—as participating subjects, living lives across different life contexts and together with others—seems limited, even though this understanding seems central for success in the professional work of actually including children with difficulties.

To sum up, the initial problem of this article, the paradox of inclusion, is unfolded—namely that we seem to have structured the institutional arrangements for inclusion of children described as having "special needs" in a way that presupposes an individualized/decontextualized understanding that leads to exclusion because these kinds of descriptions give us privileged information on which to base decisions. Within the specific institutional arrangements, individualized perspectives are equated with "professional expertise," which at the same time devalues a social contextual perspective as "unprofessional." The administrative need for system efficiency and the dominance of expertise as professionalism seems to form a powerful self-referring relation that frames the reproduction and maintenance of the specific institutional arrangements. But one severe consequence of the described processes is that possibilities of actually working with including children in regular classrooms by analysing their own perspectives on their everyday lives are restricted.

The described differences between the perspectives on difficulties in children's lives become relevant since the different perspectives point to dramatically different strategies of pedagogical work in relation to inclusion. When taking the "individualistic point of view," children's difficulties are something to be compensated for in order for the child to develop and learn in a proper way. But taking the perspective of children's difficulties as something developing in practice with a number of other participants involved means that strategies of inclusion must focus not only on the single child as object for change, but also on the community or group in which the child is participating.

NOTES

1. In this chapter I will be using the phrase "being *in* difficulties" rather than "*having* difficulties" since a specific point of the chapter is concerned with understanding difficulties as part of a social context. Therefore, difficulties do not "belong" to a single individual, as something he or she "has."

2. The family class is one of the special classes that have opened their classrooms for my observations. It is a special education institution, where the child's parents attend together with the child three days a week, inspired by the Marlborough Model (Asen, Dawson & McHugh, 2001). The ambition of the family class is inclusion of the child in the regular school system. A further discussion of the family class will exceed the frames of this chapter. In this chapter, the family class will merely represent an institution working outside the state school explicitly with helping children to solve their difficulties and over time re-include them in the state school. (For further discussion of the family class see, e.g., Knudsen, 2009.)

3. She refers to a large ball, a physiotherapeutic artefact designed to strengthen children's motor coordination and ease their behavioral challenges; the ball should be helpful for restless children to sit on during class.

REFERENCES

Allodi, M.W., & Fischbein, S. (2000). Boundaries in school: Educational settings for pupils perceived as different. *European Journal of Special Needs Education 15*(1), 69–78.

Andersen, J., & Pedersen, A.H. (2008, January 14). *Folkeskolens vidtgående specialundervisning—Skoleårene 1996/97–2006/07* [Extensive Special Education in the

State Schools—School years 1996/97–2006/07] The website of the Danish Ministry of Education. Retrieved from http://www.uvm.dk/~/media/Files/Stat/Folkeskolen/PDF07/071231_vidtgaaende_2006.ashx

Asen, E., Dawson, N., & McHugh, B. (2001). *Multiple family therapy: The Marlborough model and its wider applications.* London, UK: Karnac.

Burman, E. (1994). *Deconstructing developmental psychology.* New York, NY: Routledge.

Danziger, K. (1997). *Naming the mind: How psychology found its language.* London, UK: Sage.

Dreier, O. (2008a). *Psychotherapy in everyday life.* Cambridge, UK: Cambridge University Press.

Dreier, O. (2008b). Learning in Structures of Social Practice. In K. Nielsen et al. (Eds.), *A qualitative stance: Essays in honor of Steinar Kvale* (pp. 85–96). Århus, Denmark: Aarhus University Press.

Hedegaard, M. (2002). *Learning and child development.* Århus, Denmark: Aarhus University Press.

Hjörne, E. (2004). *Excluding for inclusion? Negotiating school careers and identities in pupil welfare settings in the Swedish school.* Göteborg, Sweden: Acta Universitatis Gothoburgensis.

Holzkamp, K. (1995). Alltägliche Lebensfürung als subjektwissenschaftliches Grundkonzept. *Das argument, 212,* 817–846.

Holzkamp, K. (in press). Psychology: Social self-understanding on the reasons for action in everyday conduct of life. In U. Osterkamp & E. Schraube, (Eds.), *Turning psychology upside down. Writings of Klaus Holzkamp.* Basingstoke, UK: Palgrave Macmillan.

Højholt, C. (2006). Knowledge and professionalism: From the perspectives of children? *Journal of Critical Psychology, 19,* 81–160.

Højholt, C. (2008). Participation in communities: Living and learning across different contexts. *Australian Research in Early Childhood Education* 15(1), 1–2

Knudsen, H. (2009). The betwixt and between family class. *Nordisk Pedagogik, 29*(1), 149–160

Kousholt, D. (2008). The everyday of children across early childhood institutions and family. *Journal of Australian Research in Early Childhood Education. 15*(1), 13–26.

Lave, J., & Wenger, E. (1991). *Situated learning: Legitimate peripheral participation.* Cambridge: Cambridge University Press.

McDermott, R. P. (1993). The acquisition of a child by a learning disability. In S. Chaiklin & J. Lave (Eds.), *Understanding practice: Perspectives on activity and context* (pp. 269–243). New York, NY: Cambridge University Press.

McDermott, R. & Varenne, H., (1998). *Successful failure: The school America builds.* Oxford, UK: Westview Press

Mehan, H. (1984). Institutional decision-making. In J. Rogoff & J. Lave (Eds.), *Everyday cognition* (pp. 41–66). Cambridge, MA: Harvard University Press.

Mehan, H., (1993). Beneath the skin and between the ears: A case study in the politics of representation. In S. Chaiklin & J. Lave (Eds.), *Understanding practice: Perspectives on activity and context* (pp. 241–269). New York, NY: Cambridge University Press.

Mehan, H., Hertweck, A., & Miehls. J. L. (1986). *Handicapping the handicapped: Decision making in student careers.* Stanford, CA: Stanford University Press.

Morin, A. (2008). Learning together: A child perspective on educational arrangements of special education. *Journal of Australian Research in Early Childhood Education, 15*(1), 27–38.

Morris, J. (1997). Gone missing? Disabled children living away from their families. *Disability & Society, 12*(2), 241–258.

Nissen, M. (2009). Objectification and prototype. *Qualitative Research in Psychology, 6,* 67–87

Rogoff, B. (2003). *The cultural nature of human development.* Oxford, UK: Oxford University Press.

Rogoff, B. (2008). Observing sociocultural activity on three planes: Participatory appropriation, guided participation, and apprenticeship. In K. Hall, P. Murphy, & J. Soler (Eds.), *Pedagogy and practice: Culture and identities* (pp. 58–74). London, UK: SAGE.

Rose, N. (1998). *Inventing our selves.* Cambridge, UK: Cambridge University Press.

Røn Larsen, M. (2004). Børnefællesskaber i den pædagogiske praksis [Children's communities in the pedagogical practice]. *VERA, 29,* 68–79.

Sigmon, S. B. (1990). *Critical voices on special education: Problems and progress concerning the mildly handicapped.* Albany, NY: State University of New York Press.

Skrtic, T.M. (1991). *Behind special education: A critical analysis of professional culture and school organization.* Denver, CO: Love Publishing Company.

Skrtic, T.M. (Ed.). (1995). *Disability and democracy: Reconstructing (special) education for postmodernity.* New York, NY: Teachers College Press.

Stanek, A. H. (2008, September). *Understanding children's communities of practice: A possible path of integration.* Paper presented at the International Society for Cultural and Activity Research (2). San Diego, CA.

UNESCO. (1994). *The Salamanca statement and framework for action on special needs education.* UNESCO website. Retrieved from http://www.unesco.org/education/pdf/SALAMA_E.PDF

UVM. (2003). *Udviklingen i specialundervisningen* [The Development of Special Education]. The website of the Danish Ministry of Education. Retrieved from http://pub.uvm.dk/2003/specialundervisning/html3/Chapter4.htm

Woodhead, M. (1997). Psychology and the cultural construction of children´s needs. In A. James, & A. Prout (Eds.), *Constructing and reconstructing childhood: Contemporary issues in the sociological study of childhood* (pp. 63–84). London, UK: Falmer Press.

CHAPTER 10

USING THE CHILD PERSPECTIVE TO SUPPORT CHILDREN WITH SEVERE IMPAIRMENTS IN BECOMING ACTIVE SUBJECTS

Louise Bøttcher

While children's learning in general is understood as arising from their motivated, subjective activity, the learning of children with neurodevelopmental disorders is often understood from a decontextualized and individualized perspective. From that perspective, different functional impairments are understood as learning impediments caused by brain lesions, while the situational, emotional, and personal aspects of children's learning remain neglected both in theoretical concepts and in the professionals' understanding of the child. The aim of this chapter is to explore the possibilities for including the perspective of subjective activity in our theoretical and practical understanding of children with severe neurodevelopmental disorders. Being disabled does not hinder the child from liking some types of activities more than others, seeking to have fun, enjoying

Children, Childhood, and Everyday Life, pages 161–177
Copyright © 2012 by Information Age Publishing
All rights of reproduction in any form reserved.

a good laugh. However, children with severe neurodevelopmental disorders are dependent on help from others to move, eat, play, and learn. At the same time, they often face severe communicational impairments and severe impediments in learning to communicate due to their motor and cognitive impairments, as illustrated in the following case of Daniel, a pupil observed at a special school for children with pervasive motor and learning impairments.

DANIEL AND HIS ROLLTALK I

Daniel, a seven-year-old boy, is observed in his school during a lesson. Daniel attends the unit for the youngest children along with five other children, two teachers, two pedagogues, one physiotherapist, one occupational therapist, and two pedagogical helpers. He and another boy are placed opposite the teacher in their standing frames (a device that holds the child fixed in a standing position). Each child has his Rolltalk (a small computer with a touch screen) placed in front of him on the table of the standing frame. First, Daniel has to play "news from home" by finding and pressing the buttons on the screen. He does this heavily supported by the teacher and smiles as he listens to what his mother has recorded. Next, Daniel pays attention and smiles as they listen to the home news of the other boy. After this, the teacher records "news from school" on the machines of both children. "Do you want the Christmas song?" the teacher asks both boys. Daniel communicates a clear "no" via facial expressions, but the teacher ignores this and records the song on his Rolltalk anyway. He communicates his dissatisfaction with grumbling sounds, but the teacher ignores this too. She later explains to me that Daniel is always saying no to everything, no matter what.

The Rolltalk is given to the children to enable them to express their emotions and wishes with greater autonomy. However, as also illustrated in the example, teaching the children to use the Rolltalk sometimes ends up with a decontextualized focus on the individual shortcomings of the child. The main point to be argued is that the development of communicative abilities hinges on social conditions and learning practices that treat these very disabled children as acting subjects in their own learning and development. The affordance concept, as developed by Costall (1995) and Bang (2009), will be used as an interpretational concept that allows the researcher to approach the perspective of the child. This means that the child perspective is approached through analytical concepts and linked to a wider understanding of development as arising from the dialectic relation between the child and his activity in different social practices (Hedegaard & Fleer, 2008).

THE THEORETICAL CHALLENGE: UNDERSTANDING THE COGNITIVE ABILITIES AND IMPAIRMENTS OF CHILDREN WITH SEVERE NEURODEVELOPMENTAL DISORDERS

Psychological research in children with severe neurodevelopmental disorders is mainly oriented towards research questions with functional approaches to cognition and how it is influenced by tissue damage. The aim of the functional approach is to describe the child's cognition as a general pattern of strengths and weaknesses and point out cognitive impairments that obstruct learning (Anderson, Northam, Hendy, & Wrennall, 2001; Rourke, Fisk, & Strang, 1986). The functional approach is useful in that it offers a nuanced conceptual framework for understanding cognition and the relation between brain areas and brain processes and cognition. Situational aspects of the assessment procedure are acknowledged but are mainly included as extrinsic to the cognitive functioning, for example as task characteristics that may impede the learning of the child due to cognitive impairments such as in attention (Baron, 2004). The case in this chapter involves a boy with severe cerebral palsy (CP). CP is caused by a pre- or perinatal brain lesion and causes impairments in motor function and control of posture, often accompanied by other impairments in, for example, perceptual or cognitive functioning (Bax, Goldstein, Rosenbaum, Leviton, & Paneth, 2005). The cognitive abilities and impairments of children with severe CP are considered extremely difficult to describe because of the simultaneous presence of motor, attentional, and communicational impairments that may cause variations in the measurements (Sabbadini, Bonnanni, Carlesimo, & Caltagirone, 2001). However, this methodological problem points to a more basic theoretical challenge to the functional approach. The reduction of cognition to one stable description is exactly what invalidates the description. Impairments in attention or verbal comprehension do not confound the evaluation of the cognitive abilities of these children; they are part of their cognition. The challenge is to approach and capture the fluctuations in cognitive abilities and understand the way cognitive abilities and situational aspects are interwoven.

Before addressing this challenge, it might be relevant to explicate why it is important. Consider a child with severe CP. The child is unable to move around on her own and only partially controls her own bodily posture. Fine motor functions mainly consist of an ability to grasp and release objects. The oral function is severely impaired and verbal expressions are restricted to unarticulated sounds. On top of these neuromotor impairments, the child has pervasive learning difficulties. Such a constellation of impairments in cases of children with severe CP makes learning difficult, because their opportunities for compensation are limited. Compensation for communicative impairments through augmentative or alternative means is impeded by impairments in fine motor function. Use of mental strategies is impeded by executive impairments. These multiple challenges stress the importance of using every opportunity to learn, because even though the movability of the impairments in children with severe CP might be smaller than that of children with mild or moderate CP, even minor gains in the ability to communicate may create a significant improvement in their quality of life (Shelly et al., 2008).

THE SITUATED COGNITION APPROACH

The perspective of situated cognition aims to understand how situational factors are intrinsic parts of the cognitive functioning of the child (Salomon, 1993). The situated cognition approach opens up for an understanding of cognition and cognitive development as activities by acting subjects related to the particular practices that constitute the social situation of the child's development (Hedegaard, 2008; Vygotsky, 1998). Consideration of cognition in practice involves linkages of cultural-historical practices and the specific activities on one hand and the cognitive, perceptual, communicative, and motive-driven activity of the child on the other. The idea of the situated cognition approach is to analyze how cognition emerges and develops as a distributed system of people, activities, and mediating artefacts (Cole & Engeström, 1993). Taking the approach by Salomon (1993), cognitive development is understood as a spiral-like movement between the individual cognitive competencies of the child and situations of distributed cognition. We are led to focus not only on how the child functions cognitively and emotionally in different contexts and activities, but on how particular activities afford and develop different types of cognitive activities by providing different opportunities. The activities the child is engaged in are part of particular practices, placed in different social institutions such as schools, special schools, or after school centers (Hedegaard, 2008). The specific practice, such as the special school, is guided by traditions and values connected to the education of children with disabilities, and these traditions and values are expressed in the different specific activities. The organization of particular practices supports the development of different cognitions and different skills, sometimes at the expense of others. The development of the child emerges from the activity of the child within this social setting as a whole. Inspired by the distributed cognition perspective (Salomon, 1993), I suggest that cognition should be understood and studied in activities in settings that afford distributed cognition in particular ways.

COGNITION AND AFFORDANCES

The affordance concept also points to an individual perspective on how the child in a situated practice perceives and participates in that very practice. The affordance concept was first coined by J. J. Gibson (Bang, 2009). One of his main aims was to capture bottom-up processes in perception: how the meaning of objects is directly perceivable from their physical forms in relation to the perceptual-motor functions of the individual animal or human being. The affordance meaning of an object is a relational property that exists neither in the individual perceiver nor in the environment, but arises from the relation between them. Any given environmental feature has multiple affordances. According to Gibson, it is the psychological states of individuals that make them perceive particular affordances and not others. Later writers have elaborated on Gibson's concept in order to stress how the affordances of objects involve much more than mere physical properties. As an elaboration, the affordance concept is used to denote reified cultural and historical processes, values, and intentions that have shaped the different objects and provided them with meanings for actions (Costall, 1995). Our common cultural-historical background often makes us perceive objects very similarly. In addition, affordances are the functionally significant properties in relation to particular individuals and their personal history and intentionality within environments with cultural-historical properties. Different individuals may perceive the same artefacts and practices differently because of their different personal histories and different goals. Stressing functional properties more than pure form foregrounds the intentionality of the perceiving subject (Bang, 2009). The affordance concept facilitates studies of the relation between the environment that includes both the historical and societal nature of artefacts and practices and the individual's intentions and perception of possibilities for actions. The aim of including the concept in the analyses is to capture resonances between the child and its environment, and how they affect the activities of the child.

Artefacts present in the school constitute environmental properties which may help initiate activities through exploration and appropriation. By definition, having a physical impairment impedes or at least changes one's ability to explore the environment. A child with severe CP might perceive the activity affordances of a playground or a toy very differently from a non-disabled child. Where a playground with swings might afford taking a swing for most children, the same playground might only afford looking at the movement of the swings for a child with severe motor impairments. Likewise with learning disabilities, by definition they impede or change the appropriation of cultural tools such as language, letters and numbers (Cole & Engeström, 1993). A child with visual-perceptual difficulties might perceive letters and words very differently from a same-aged peer who is already able to read. The affordance concept can be used to analyse and explore how having particular motor and learning impairments might affect the way artefacts and activities are apprehended *by particular persons* within specific practices.

DEVELOPMENT OF COMMUNICATION IN CASES OF SEVERE NEURODEVELOPMENTAL IMPAIRMENT

The development of communicative abilities has been chosen as an example of the dialectic between the development of individual cognition and activities that support and develop the child's individual cognitions through social interactions. In addition, the affordance concept can be used to describe how different communication aids resonate with particular children and feed into the activities the child participates in along with other children and adults. To begin with, a socially based theory of the development of communication will be outlined briefly. Next, the communicational development of children with severe CP will be characterized.

The Social Interactional Theory of Language Development

The social interactional paradigm of language development has been developed from cognitive and functional linguistics by Tomasello (1992) and Trevarthen (2001). It is in opposition to the paradigm of formal linguistics (e.g., Chomsky, 1980; Pinker, 1994), which explains language development as the unfolding of inborn language modules. In contrast, the social interactional understanding of communicative development rests on dialectic processes between the individual development and social activities. From this approach, the development of language and communication is situated and has to be studied in the reciprocal relations between the child and the activities where communication takes place. Individual communication development is based in neural networks unique to humans, but it is the social processes the infant participates in that foster the utilization of neural potential. Communication development is not located in the child or the environment, but always both in the child and the environment as well as in their mutual relations. The gradual acquisition of verbal language transforms this relation and greatly expands the ability of the child to express emotions, intentions and experiences. Communicative skills and language acquisition also mark a great step into the cultural practices around the child and the cultural mediation of cognitive functions and actions (Cole & Engeström, 1993).

During development, the precursors for proper communication skills are seen in early protoconversations and early intersubjectivity between the infant and his primary caregivers: rhythmic patterns of movement and vocalizations in time with the vocalizations, touches, and expressions of the adult (Trevarthen, 2001). Later during infancy, mutually shared attention and non-verbal communication about emotions, objects and intentions typically develop. The infant has an early competence for engaging in communicative interaction, but depends on his caregiver to initiate and regulate the dyadic interactions. Gradually the infant begins to initiate communication and gain experience in showing intentions through nonverbal communication with his caregiver: reaching ("I want that object"); "You want that rattle?"; and finally this will have an impact on their mutual activity: "Here is the rattle." Later in the language-learning process, the child begins to acquire and use simple words through imitative modeling (Tomasello, 1992): Children participate in culturally specific activities structured by adults, and their shared attentional focus within these activities allows the child to guess the meanings of words used by the adults and imitate that use in a way that goes beyond pure mimicry. The concept of imitative modelling covers the fact that the child must learn both the sound of the word and the appropriate use of it.

A second important social process in language and communication development is communicative feedback (Tomasello, 1992). Communicative feedback occurs during communicative interaction, when the child tries out her communicative means learned through imitation with various interlocutors and receives feedback from the other persons about the efficiency of her communicative efforts. Through communicative feedback, the challenge posed upon the child is to modify and elaborate communicative expressions if she wants to get her message through and maintain the interaction.

Communicative Development in Children with Severe Cerebral Palsy

Children with severe CP are often impeded in their development of language and communication (Pennington, 2008). Their impairment is double; first of all, the acquisition of language relies on basic processes of perception, attention, categorization, learning, memory, and other general cognitive processes that are often impaired. Secondly, the language learning difficulties due to perceptive and cognitive impairments are amplified because these children often lack active participation in communicative interactions that afford language learning. Typical communicative interactions might not afford active participation of these children, because they are not able to seek out interlocutors on their own or initiate conversations verbally. The process of communicative feedback is slowed down because these children's more limited communicative resources make it more difficult for them to adjust their communicative expressions. Instead, they are dependent on the activity of others to initiate or aid communication and other's knowledge about the child and the subject of conversation to be able to interpret ambiguous or idiosyncratic sounds or signs.

This double challenge calls for an augmentation of language development that focuses on both the cognitive abilities of the particular child and on cognitive and communicational affordances in the child's different practices. During typical language development, communicative affordances for language development are words and sentences used by adults within specific activities. For children with severe CP, verbal language has to be supplemented with other communicational means: signs (with hands and body), symbols on cards, concretes, Rolltalk machines. However, affordances are *perceived* possibilities for activity in relation to objects within a practice. As such, affordances are subjective; different people perceive different affordances in the same practice depending on their perceptual, cognitive, emotional, and motive gearing.

EMPIRICAL STUDY

The theoretical considerations will now be illustrated with a study at a special school for children with pervasive motor and learning impairments, mostly due to severe CP, although the school also includes children with other severe disabilities.

The study focuses on the development of communicative abilities among the children in the school through organization of the learning activities and by the inclusion of the children's perspectives in the organization of the learning activities. The study is a case study combining different qualitative methods. Observations of the focus children (N=2) during learning and after-school activities were chosen as the main basis for gathering information about activities in the practice and how children and adults (staff) participated with each other in the different activities. This was supplemented with observations at staff meetings, where the focus was on how the staff described and discussed the purposes of different activities. In addition, interviews were conducted with staff and parents of focus children in order to gather more information about the history of the child, how the child functions at different times of the day and in practices other than the school. In this chapter, the focus will be on data from observations of one of these two children and staff discussions about this child and the learning activities he participated in. This particular case was chosen because his communicational ability was the weaker of the two.

Daniel is a seven-year-old boy with severe CP. He is not able to stand, sit, or walk without support and he has a stomach pump for eating. In addition to his substantive motor impairments, he has learning impairments, poor vision due to cerebrally caused visual perceptual impairments, and communicative impairments. He mainly communicates with sounds and facial expressions; for example, he often says "yes" by smiling.

Daniel has a *Rolltalk communicator*. Most children at the school work with screen pictures with six to nine buttons that afford the possibility of following different conceptual layers of expression with a logical design: places (e.g., home, school), people (e.g., teacher, physiotherapist, mother), "I would like to do" (e.g., walk alone, play, listen to music), and many others. Both layout and content are customized to the child in accordance with his or her motor abilities and interests, and to the activities where the Rolltalk is used. By pressing the button on the screen, the child activates a voice saying a word or a sentence, musical sounds, recorded messages, or short video sequences. If the child learns to use the Rolltalk, it can enable the child to communicate about a wider range of subjects and with interlocutors without the extensive contextual knowledge that is required to understand the often idiosyncratic signs and sounds used by the child.

During a period of ten months, 30 observations of Daniel during activities in school were conducted: 20 with video, 10 written observations. In the same period, 26 staff meetings were observed. The data were interpreted in a stepwise procedure. The first step was the identification of associations between the activity of Daniel and the context: here, particular adults and activities. Secondly, recurring patterns of activities were found and interpreted in relation to the described theoretical framework.

Methodological Reflections about the Inclusion of the Child's Perspective

Given that Daniel has pervasive communication problems, this could present a serious methodological difficulty in gaining insight into his perspective. However, the inclusion of the child perspective in theoretically based analyses is necessarily an interpretive process (Hedegaard, 2008). The affordance concept is proposed as a concept that can be used to interpret empirical material in terms of both the functionality and intentionality of recorded artefacts and practices (Bang, 2009). As stated earlier, the understanding of cognition as activity in practice is closely related to the affordance concept, because individual cognition is shaped by the affordance of different objects and cultural tools. It is true for all children, but exceedingly salient in children with severe neurodevelopmental disorders, because they are so dependent on specialized artefacts to function. Artefacts present in the school constitute environmental properties, which may help to initiate activities through exploration and appropriation.

Through observations of Daniel's activities in concrete learning practices and with different artefacts, it becomes possible to trace and interpret the affordances, understood as his individual intentions and perception of possibilities for activity in relation to the artefacts.

Daniel and His Rolltalk II

Background: Since the beginning of this school year, the teachers have begun to include activities with the Rolltalk machines as part of their lessons. Regarding Daniel, the team has stated as an explicit goal that he should start to use his Rolltalk in basic communication, for example to answer "yes" or "no" to a question. The activities in the observation below follow a structure familiar to the children:

> Daniel and two other boys are sitting in chairs with their Rolltalk machines on the tables in front of them and each with an adult next to him. The teacher asks the children to find the day of the week on the Rolltalk. Daniel finds and presses the button on the touchable screen heavily supported by his helper. They do the same with the month. The teacher asks the children to look out of the window at the weather and find and press the button that describes the weather of the day. Daniel does so heavily supported by his helper. Outside it is foggy, but this option does not figure on the screen, so cloudy is chosen instead.
>
> Next, each child is telling "news from home" with his or her Rolltalk. One boy has music recorded on his machine; he plays it, the others listen, and the teacher then removes his machine from the table. Next, a second boy presses "today it is Monday" [he does this every day], then his machine is taken away. Finally, Daniel is supposed to play news from home, but he refuses and communicates with his body and with sounds that he wants to move on to the next activity of the lesson: the reading of a story about a naughty Christmas elf who teases a family. The teacher accepts this and removes his machine.
>
> During a staff meeting two months later, the learning practice described above was discussed. The agenda of the meeting involved an evaluation of Daniel's development in different areas and the formulation of new goals for the next half-year period. There was general agreement that he had not made the expected progress on his Rolltalk. The teacher stated that it was necessary to remove the Rolltalk from him during lessons, because otherwise he obstructed the learning activities for the group as a whole by pressing buttons and making irrelevant noise. One member of the team raised the concern that they in general tend to remove the Rolltalk machines too fast, leaving

Daniel and the other children with very little time to practice using it, which could be the reason for Daniel's missing progress. The staff members discussed how the team could support Daniel so that he could keep his Rolltalk on the table.

The different observations (learning activity, staff meeting) illustrate how different people in the same learning practice act very differently vis-à-vis the Rolltalk machine. The object, the Rolltalk, affords very different meanings and different ways of acting. The teacher views the Rolltalk as part of the activity of learning concepts about the world. The concepts used in the learning activity are added to the choice on the Rolltalk's different conceptual layers, and the idea is that the children get acquainted with the concepts through the learning activity. However, during lessons, Daniel and some of the other children do not use their Rolltalk to answer the teacher's questions, but find and press other buttons, for example those that make musical sounds (drums, piano, etc.). The Rolltalk thereby began to afford interruption to the teachers, and in return the teachers have begun to remove the Rolltalk machines after the short initial activity.

For Daniel, his Rolltalk affords something completely different. Despite the stated goal that Daniel should begin to use his Rolltalk for basic communication, Daniel's communicative statements, as illustrated in the observation excerpt, are by sounds, body signs, or facial expressions and not with his Rolltalk. The Rolltalk does not seem to afford communication to Daniel. What does it afford, then? A recurring theme in the observations of Daniel is "making fun by being naughty." Above, the theme is seen in Daniel's attraction to the story about the naughty Christmas elf. Also it is seen in many observations (not included in the chapter) where he refuses to follow the instructions by the therapist with a broad grin on his face, and discussed by the staff at the meeting as a recurring episode they can understand, but still see as problematic because his physical training and learning in general is based on his cooperation. Without Daniel's cooperation, there can be no motor training, no learning, and no development. This last problem with the necessity of cooperation is a general problem vis-à-vis several of the children at the school.

Returning to what the Rolltalk affords to Daniel, he is able to perceive it as "a box I can touch to make sounds/words" and possibly "a box I can touch to make different words and sounds." The stated aim is to get to the point where the affordance of the Rolltalk from Daniel's point of view is "a device I can use in my communication with other people to express how I feel, what I would like to do, what I did yesterday, and so on." This process in itself is similar to typical language learning. The difference is that the cognitive and communicative impairments of Daniel might call for more explicit teaching of categorizations and communicational rules, such as turn-taking and referencing, because his passive role in communication this far, quite typical for children with severe CP (Pennington, 2008), has deprived him of the practice children without disabilities get during their everyday activities. In addition, while verbal language is inevitably used in most activities the child participates in from birth, the use of signs or Rolltalk machines has to be introduced explicitly to practices and activities and become part of the communication taking place, before they can become part of the social processes of language acquisition. The adults need to consider and support the affordance of the communicational aid from the perspective of the child—for example, Daniel—in order to be able to treat him as an acting subject who makes contributions to a collaborative practice. Daniel making noise with his Rolltalk, Daniel being naughty by the support of his Rolltalk, has to be seen and treated as a communicating subject before he can start to use the Rolltalk as a box that produces words for communication. It could be by utilizing Daniel's motive for being naughty, for example by giving him opportunities to be naughty with the help of the Rolltalk instead of taking it away from him. As it is now, Daniel's opportunities to be and to be seen as an acting subject and not just an object for the adult's interventions are mostly by refusing cooperation. Fortunately, exceptions do exist, as will be shown in the observation excerpt in the following paragraph.

Development as a Dynamic Circle that Includes Intention, Communication, and Acting

Daniel's participation in activities that allow him to follow his emerging motives furthers his ability to become aware of and communicate motives and enhances his learning in general because of the positive emotions associated with motives. The observation excerpt below is chosen in order to show a situation, where Daniel's exploration of his intentions in an activity contributes to his development and to the shared activity:

Daniel in an after school activity at the gym hall: Two pedagogues and four boys, one of them Daniel, are in the gym hall. The pedagogue, Carl, has organized an activity, rolling a ball back and forth in a designated area of the floor marked by orange plastic cones. Carl rolls the ball to one boy, who sits on the floor. Daniel is moving independently around in his walker. He approaches Carl and makes contact by placing himself close to Carl. Carl squats next to Daniel and tries to involve him in the ball rolling activity: He takes Daniel's hand and tries to help him hit the ball, but the ball just falls to the floor without getting anywhere. Daniel withdraws his hand. Carl gets up and leaves the game in order to help another child. As soon as he has turned his back to Daniel, Daniel moves forward and manages to turn over two of the nearest cones. Carl returns, takes a step forward with his arm extended as if to stop Daniel, changes his mind, and observes Daniel instead. After Daniel has managed to turn the first two cones over, he pauses for a while with a look of great amusement on his face. Carl moves over to the other boy, squats next to him, and they both watch Daniel. Daniel moves his legs up and down, moves forward and turn over a third cone, smiles a big smile. Carl smiles too. Daniel looks attentively at the cones, moves forward, and during the next nine minutes he manages to turn over most of the remaining cones, by moving forward and around in bigger and smaller circles. The other boy follows him with his gaze and points out cones still standing by pointing to them. Carls observes and makes comments to Daniel about his progress vis-à-vis his self-appointed goal.

At first, Daniel makes contact with an adult in the manner typical for him, by moving over next to the adult. Carl, the pedagogue, responds by including Daniel in the activity. However, the ball and the rolling activity do not afford the kind of independent activity Daniel seeks, because he can neither hold nor throw the ball. Instead, Daniel acts from the motive of being naughty by disrupting the game. When Carl chooses to accept Daniel's act as a contribution to the shared activity, Daniel responds by developing and exploring a new affordance of the orange cone: their "turn-over-ness," and a new intention: *his* ability to turn over all of the orange cones. The new activity is challenging for Daniel, physically *and* cognitively: He gets to practice visuomotor coordination, sustained attention, and executive persistence, to mention some necessary cognitive processes. The observation is an example of a situation where Daniel is able to turn his motives (make contact and tease Carl, turn over cones) into active participation in the social practice by bodily communicative acts that are recognized by the pedagogue Carl. By being able to act on his motives and perceived affordances, Daniel (and Carl) create a positive developmental cycle, where Daniel evidently enjoys his ability to actively shape the activity he is part of, in a developmentally stimulating way.

As mentioned, Daniel's communication in the observation is through bodily acts only. Without communicational aids, his communication is limited to acts or gestures that restrict communication to content already in the shared focused attention—mainly the ongoing activity and persons and objects present, or passive communication in which an adult asks him questions to which he can answer yes or no. Although Daniel's bodily communication functions well in the observation excerpt, his development of further communicative skills is central in many transitions of his motives and perceived affordances to activity and participation because of his major motor impairments. Where most children become able to follow motives and act on the affordances of artefacts around them by reaching and crawling from early on, at age seven Daniel still depends heavily on others to help him do what he would like to do in most situations.

The enhancement of his development of communicational skills and his ability to use an artefact such as the Rolltalk machine could expand his ability

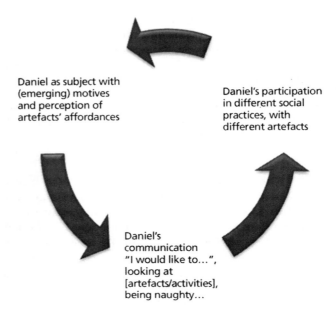

Daniel as subject with
(emerging) motives
and perception of
artefacts' affordances

Daniel's participation
in different social
practices, with
different artefacts

Daniel's
communication
"I would like to...",
looking at
[artefacts/activities],
being naughty...

Figure 10.1 The dynamic of Daniel's cognitive, communicational, and social development.

to participate actively. Learning to communicate, expressing motives, and acting in shared practices and contributing to them are not separate, but related in one circular developmental dynamic (see Figure 10.1). Therefore, the acquisition of communication skills is crucial for Daniel's ability to contribute to collaborative practices to a greater degree than is the case at present. Daniel's learning of communicational skills could be accomplished through his explorations of his intentionality in different activities in school, during after-school activities, and during activities outside of school. His participation and his experiences with different artefacts and experiences of doing things with artefacts widen the relation between Daniel and that artefact and develop the affordance of these artefacts as perceived by Daniel. Focusing on affordances as the intentionally significant properties of the environment, the child's perspective becomes central in understanding the learning and development of Daniel and other children with severe neurodevelopmental disorders.

ANALYZING THE PERSPECTIVE OF THE CHILD AS PART OF UNDERSTANDING THE DEVELOPMENT OF CHILDREN WITH SEVERE CP

This chapter began by analyzing the inadequacy of the functional approach to understand the cognition and developmental conditions of children with severe neurodevelopmental disorders. One main problem was that the functional approach separates the cognitive abilities of the child from the situated activity she is part of. This is particularly problematic in regard to understanding the learning and cognitive development of children with severe neurodevelopmental disorders, because they are very dependent on special artefacts and activities to function and develop. Another related problem is that the separation of the child from the activity leads to a view of the child as an object, making the way for practices at odds with how to get the children to participate in the organized learning activities.

The analysis of the practice at the special school revealed how theories about children with typical developmental trajectories can be useful in analyzing the developmental conditions of children with severe neurodevelopmental impairments. The inclusion of concepts such as situated cognition, affordances, and motives in the analyses of the development of children with severe CP highlighted how children with severe neurodevelopmental disorders have different conditions for developing as acting subjects, not only biologically, but socially as well. This might provide this group of children with social constraints in their development of communicative abilities in addition to their impaired biological conditions. Similar to children without disabilities, children with severe neurodevelopmental disorders need to be granted positions as acting subjects to develop their communicational skills. The ability to express oneself, non-verbally or verbally, is central to the child's ability to engage in activities the child has a positive feeling about. Through experiences of motivated activity, the child develops a motive hierarchy and an identity as a person that likes certain activities and people and dislikes or is indifferent to others (Hedegaard, 2002).

Considering cognition in practice provides a theoretical foundation for the inclusion and utilization of situational and intentional factors to enhance learning and development. Individual cognitive development is accomplished only through the individual's activity within practices that afford specific cognitive activities through particular artefacts and social activities. Furthermore, the affordance concept highlighted how different participants within the same practice might perceive the same artefacts and activities differently. I have argued that it is necessary to supplement a practice perspective with the perspective of the child, because the child perspective is indispensable for understanding and supporting a particular child's motives for developing communicative skills and for organizing activities that afford that child's development of communication and other areas of development. The intentionality of the child becomes central in understanding how his cognitive and communicational abilities are related to his social conditions. The access to the child perspective is suggested through a theoretical approach and analytical concepts aimed at including the child perspective within a wider understanding of development as arising from the dialectic relation between the child and her activity in different social practices. Analyzing children with severe neurodevelopmental disorders as acting subjects is a prerequisite for doing research that includes and works with the active transformation of the existing environment through subjects' collaborative activities: teachers, therapists, *and children*. The inclusion of the child's perspective enables analyses of how children with severe neurodevelopmental disorders contribute to the collaborative processes within learning practices. These analyses are part of a wider project of giving a group of very disabled children better conditions for contributing to the collaborative processes within their everyday practices and to enhance their learning of ways to communicate, which again improves their ability to contribute to the collaborative processes. It has been argued elsewhere (Bang, 2009) that the study of the reciprocity of the child and the environment in the constitution of an activity setting enables the study of potentials for development. Such analyses might provide a foundation for the exploration of new developmental possibilities within the environment and provide new opportunities for children to make contributions in a learning practice in which the professional adults often play the organizational master role.

REFERENCES

Anderson, V., Northam, E., Hendy, J., & Wrennall, J. (2001). *Developmental neuropsychology: A clinical approach.* Hove, UK: Psychology Press.

Bang, J. (2009). An environmental affordance perspective on the study of development: Artefacts, social others, and self. In M. Fleer, M. Hedegaard, & J. Tudge (Eds.), *Childhood studies and the impact of globalisation: Policies and practices at global and local levels* (pp. 161–181). New York, NY: Routledge.

Baron, I. S. (2004). *Neuropsychological evaluation of the child.* New York, NY: Oxford University Press.

Bax, M., Goldstein, M., Rosenbaum, P., Leviton, A., & Paneth, N. (2005). Proposed definition and classification of cerebral palsy. *Developmental Medicine and Child Neurology, 47,* 571–576. doi: 10.1017/S001216220500112X

Chomsky, N. (1980). *Rules and representations.* New York, NY: Columbia University Press.

Cole, M. & Engeström, Y. (1993). A cultural-historical approach to distributed cognition. In G. Salomon (Ed.), *Distributed cognitions: Psychological and educational considerations* (pp. 1–46). New York, NY: Cambridge University Press.

Costall, A. (1995). Social affordances. *Theory & Psychology, 5,* 467–481.

Hedegaard, M. (2002). *Learning and child development.* Aarhus, Denmark: Aarhus University Press.

Hedegaard, M. (2008). A cultural-historical theory of children's development. In M. Hedegaard & M. Fleer (Eds.), *Studying children: A cultural-historical approach.* London, UK: Open University Press.

Pennington, L. (2008). Cerebral palsy and communication. *Pediatrics and Child Health, 18,* 405–409. doi: 10.1016/j.paed.2008.05.013

Pinker, S. (1994). *The language instinct.* New York, NY: William Morrow.

Rourke, B. P., Fisk, J. L., & Strang, J. D. (1986). *Neuropsychological assessment of children: A treatment oriented approach.* New York, NY: Guilford Press.

Sabbadini, M., Bonnanni, R., Carlesimo, G. A. & Caltagirone, C. (2001). Neuropsychological assessment of patients with severe neuromotor and verbal disabilities. *Journal of Intellectual Disability Research, 45,* 169–179.

Salomon, G. (1993). No distribution without individuals' cognition: A dynamic interactional view. In G. Salomon (Ed.), *Distributed cognitions: Psychological and educational considerations* (pp. 111–138). New York, NY: Cambridge University Press.

Shelly, A., Davis, E., Waters, E., Mackinnon, A., Reddihough, D., Boyd, R. et al. (2008). The relationship between quality of life and functioning for children with cerebral palsy. *Developmental Medicine and Child Neurology, 50,* 199–203. doi: 10.1111/j.1469-8749.2008.02031.x

Tomasello, M. (1992). The social bases of language acquisition. *Social Development, 1,* 67–87.

Trevarthen, C. (2001). Intrinsic motives for companionship in understanding: Their origin, development, and significance for infant mental health. *Infant Mental Health Journal, 22,* 95–131.

Vygotsky, L. (1998). *The collected works, Vol. 5; Child Psychology.* New York, NY: Plenum Press.

CHAPTER 11

SOCIAL IDENTITIES IN TRANSITION

Contrasting Strategies of Two Boys When Changing School

Ditte Winther-Lindqvist

INTRODUCTION

The study of this chapter is inspired by cultural-historical activity theory and social representations theory, as it seeks to understand how social identities are developed in the transition between primary and lower secondary school on the verge of youth life. How do changes in the social and institutional environment affect children's development of social identities during the transition into a new school? Around which activities and values is the social order in the classroom centered? These questions are posed from a theoretical position regarding social identities as a co-constructional dialogical process, which means that identities are communicated in immediate situated action, but relying on cultural-historical constraints—in this case, the different institutional goals and demands from the schools and the different social representations of youth and youth life in the community. Development is regarded as the result of a dialectic interplay between the person

Children, Childhood, and Everyday Life, pages 179–197
Copyright © 2012 by Information Age Publishing
179

and the environment, in which the person's motives and resources are developed in dialogue with the ever (slowly or rapidly) changing affordances, demands, and possibilities for participation (Bang, 2009; Hedegaard, 2009; Valsiner, 1997). Regarding social identities as dialogically constituted, identities are always identities-in-interaction, which is a way of underscoring the local and negotiated nature of identities (Aronsson, 1998). Identifications are expressed and circulated in the group, as part of everyday life activities among peers and teachers, and they evoke emotional responses like embracement, denial, and resistance because identifications always involve normative judgment: "When we identify a person, we are obviously not simply stating a fact but assessing and labelling him" (Moscovici, 2000, p. 43). Social representations shape the outlines of possible legitimate as well as illegitimate identities on a collective level, and how people acquire them and identify with them in social practice Gerard Duveen summarizes as the developmental process of *social identities* (2002). The concept of identification, as it is used here, denotes a communicative process in which a person self-presents and is identified by others, and the identified person self-identifies with that identification and reacts upon it in various ways. A person's social identities involve both categorical and individual identification in E. Goffman's terms (1982). The categorical identification (someone's gender, age, ethnicity, etc.) melts in with more person-specific differentiating devices like that person's particular ways of participating (as someone shy, outspoken, dominant, funny, generous, mean, etc.). Identities are negotiated and solidified in practice, and they are created in patterns of interactional repetition. Those repetitions and routines always also represent potentials for changes in the course of interaction, and they are thus to be regarded as permeable and open social structures. These patterns of change and stability in social identity construction are illustrated with case material presenting two boys with marginal social identities in two 6th class classrooms. These particular boys are chosen as exemplary cases for two reasons: Their stories nicely illustrate how belonging to the classroom as someone legitimate relies on the ability to make self-presentations as a young person, recognized as such by peers, friends, and teachers, and also their stories illustrate how the school transition creates new possibilities for legitimization and marginalization because the meaning of "how to be a young person" changes.

METHODOLOGY: RESEARCHING SOCIAL IDENTITIES DURING TRANSITIONS

Social identities in a classroom environment resemble contracts between people, and sometimes they take on an almost binding character, describing and prescribing how people are expected to act towards particular others in relation to activities (Hundeide, 2004). There is thus a tendency towards solidification of social identities in everyday life despite their open character, but in times of transit changes are more likely, as the new place is anticipated and prepared for and finally actualized. In transitional periods we are "betwixt and between" as the daily routines and our usual social roles and positions are shaken and a new time starts: one of becoming (Kofoed, 2008; Turner, 1964/1979; Zittoun, 2008). When starting someplace new, like in a new school among new classmates, one is recognized anew. Transitions between institutions thus imply a demand for a change in social identity, because the person is identified and recognized differently after a transition into a new group position.

With the aim to get closer to the child's perspective, ethnographic approaches to studying children try to capture the meaning children themselves make of their activities and relationships in everyday life (Christensen & James, 2003; Greene & Hogan, 2005; Hedegaard, 2009; Hedegard, Fleer, Bang, & Hviid, 2008; James & Prout, 1997). When children are interacting with peers and friends, they "tell each other" and "are being told" who they are by making and receiving invitations, greetings, criticism, praise, recognition, exclusion, and rejections, and these identifications are aligned with and express underlying frames or rules of a local social order (Goodwin, 2004; Hughes, 1991, 1995; Winther-Linqvist, 2009). Each here-and-now situation consists of and provides potentialities for development, as every encounter and experience with oneself and others may change our ways of understanding ourselves, others, and aspects of the world (Bang, 2009). In line with these ideas, I did a motivated ethnographic study, which is a method suggested by Gerard Duveen and Barbara Lloyd (1993) and exemplified in their study of social identities of gender in a reception class environment in the UK. The method implies that it is particular aspects of the culture in question that the researcher investigates—the empirical research is thus motivated towards specific research questions, rather than aimed at understanding the wholeness qualities of a cultural system, which is the case in classical anthropological ethnography (Hammersley & Atkinson, 2007).

In the present case, the motivated ethnography aims at understanding the practice and process of children's social identity formation as it takes place within the everyday life of the classroom. Following children in their school lives, I observed the children's ways of participating in activities, their relationships, friendships and playgroups, conflicts, and status hierarchy, in order to come to understand how the questions *who am I?* and *who are you?* are posed and answered, and how these questions relate to the child's motives and rules of the social order. Recognizing that the same person inhabits several social identities in various contexts and relationships, this study focuses only on how social identities are negotiated, changed, and reified in different school contexts.

DESIGN

The majority of Danish children receive schooling in the municipal primary and lower secondary schools,[1] which in urban areas are located within the same building and with one administration. The classroom consists of 20–28 pupils who stay together all the way from reception class to 9th class. Every class has a class teacher, but teacher teams typically specialize in teaching pupils in either introduction (reception class, 1st, 2nd, and 3rd class), primary (4th–6th class) and lower secondary (7th–10th class). The empirical investigation took place in a small village in the countryside, I call it "Heatherfield," and because of its small size, this village school only offers teaching until 6th class, after which all pupils are transferred to the bigger school of 900 pupils in the neighboring village of "Greengrove." This way of organizing state schooling in the rural areas of Denmark has increased in recent years, and thus the principle of one school class is not necessarily the actual practice any longer. Children in the area around Heatherfield are typically from ethnic Danish families of lower-middle to middle-class income, many working in the capital city a half-hour drive away. I followed the children in their last four months of 6th class in Heatherfield, into their first three months of lower secondary school in Greengrove for a total of 40 school days (240 hours). I was able to follow six out of nineteen pupils between the two schools. Supplementary to observations and tape-recordings, I interviewed all children in 6th class (some in groups, some individually, and some both), and the chosen focus children I interviewed also after the transit. As part of the interviewing I asked them to do drawings of their peers in the classroom, with the only rule that they themselves should be portrayed in the picture. These drawings structured the conversations about their classroom experience among their peers. During observations and as focus points in interviews, I noticed the ways children present and recognize themselves and others through utterances like accusations, direct encouragements, or derogatory or praising comments on looks and behaviors, body-language signs, and other forms of interpellation that serve as identifiers of particular persons, perceived by other persons.

FINDINGS

Norms of the Social Order: What It Takes to Become Someone Legitimate in 6th Class

The ongoing task of finding one's place or achieve a sense of belonging in a classroom rests on the ability to perform well in scholastic activities as well as being held in high regard by peers and teachers (Abreu & Cline,

2008; Adler & Adler, 2003; Osterman, 2000; Wortham, 2006). Generally popularity involves factors like socioeconomic background, physical attractiveness, coolness, scholastic performance, and social sensitivity (Adler & Adler, 2003; Eder, 1985). As suggested in the literature, popularity shows, among other things, in *visibility* and *precocity*. What brings popularity is to practice precocity in a visible way, and thus establish whatever is considered to be ahead of social time. Social time denotes what is considered age-appropriate behaviors, attitudes, activities, and values among peers in a group like that of a school class (Hviid, 2008).

In the 6th class at Heatherfield school, social life is hierarchically organized, and the popular children are the most active and influential in making identifications of themselves and others. A few persons in the peer group personify virtues of legitimacy as those belonging, while others do not in different ways. Since the pupils are 12–13 years and on the verge of puberty, "ahead of time" means practicing youth. The children are sensitive towards whether they are identified as ahead of social time, in social time, or lagging behind social time, which in this classroom is voiced as mature or childish positions. In an interview with four girls called the "horse-girls," they for instance drew all the pupils in bubbles among their best friends. They placed themselves in a bubble in the lower corner and drew themselves as crawling babies, and playing horseback-riding eating candy, whereas the popular girls were depicted in the upper side at the center of the page in youth-marked clothing and postures. Those marginalized girls thus showed an ironic distance towards how they were identified by the popular girls, but nonetheless their social identities were defined in opposition to those popular youth-marked girls. Social representations of what is considered age-appropriate circulate in the community and feed more local interpretations of "how to behave as a young person." This social representation functions as a collectively constituted orientation point with which to evaluate one's own and others' developmental timing and social identity. Those actively defining what is age-appropriate are mainly a group of three to five girls, and their standards are consequential not only for how they are perceived but also to how everyone else is perceived in the classroom.

Friendships as Enlargements of Self in the Classroom

Friendships and friendship groups play a crucial role in relation to social identification in the 6th class classroom, both internally (in relation to who I consider myself to be) and externally (how others perceive me). This is shown among other things in the children's drawings, where friends are depicted together and also placed hierarchically on the paper. The term *friend* in Danish and among the children covers everything from a mate (someone you just like from the classroom) to a friend (someone you like and trust and sometimes see after school) or a best friend, someone you confide in, can count on when in trouble, and see frequently after school. All six boys name each other as friends in the meaning of mate or buddy, whereas the girls are more exclusive, naming only peers as friends if there is trusting of secrets involved in their relationships. Following Winterhoff's (1997) recommendation, children's friendships should be studied as processes of befriending in concrete contexts, rather than as fixed and stable entities. In the social landscape of the classroom, friendship groups are relatively stable contracts of mutual agreement between people, recognized by all as such, even though some members in various friendship groups change, especially among the popular girls who exchange best friendships quite frequently. The process around making friendship contracts serves the function of enlarging the self as visible and ahead of social time. When *in* a friendship, you *have* this friend. When discussing identities, this "being and having" of friends is important and a description corresponding to how the children themselves talk about their relationships with friends. Considering self as a multiplicity of internal *I* positions, and external *me* positions, William James was the first to formulate the gradual slippery between me and mine: "People and things in the environment belong to the self, as far as they are felt as mine" (James, cited in Hermans, 2001, p. 244). Friendships in the 6th class classroom function as enlargements of the self, and they are crucial for how social identities are practiced and recognized, just as the lack of friends and the lack of best friends, especially, places one in a belittled and marginal social position. Being someone with many best friends supports an influential and legitimate position in the 6th class classroom. Receiving many texts, messages on Arto profiles on the internet, and being invited to afterschool activities with friends are publicly announced and discussed among the popular girls. The more the merrier. Friends serve as enlargements of the self, due to this reference of ownership articulated when denoting someone: "*my* friend."

Chris' and Mickey's Marginal Social Identities in 6th Class

In the following, we are to meet two boys, Chris and Mickey, and follow them during their last months in 6th class and into their first months in the new school and classroom. Chris and Mickey are the most silent pupils in the 6th class classroom,[2] and only on rare occasions do they act in the role of speakers in classroom activities. They are chosen as cases because their social identities in 6th class are very much alike, and because one of them manages to integrate positively into the new classroom and the other one is denied a legitimate position, and thus they represent different developmental pathways in their transition. Both boys are frequently identified as childish, boring, gross, and stupid by the leading girls in the classroom, and they are not in a best-friend relationship with any of the other four boys in this 6th class. Chris does have friends among two of the other boys in the classroom, and they sometimes play computer at each other's houses, and form study groups, when asked to work in groups by their teachers. But he doesn't figure as part of their friendship group, and they talk about him as a mate, but are clear about their best-friendship as exclusive. Chris is also depicted as a lonely standing peer, just as Mickey is in all drawings made by their peers. Mickey never talks about seeing classmates outside of school, but he names all boys in the classroom as mates, although no one names him as a friend in interviews, and he is even forgotten about in one of the drawings, not figuring as part of the peer group. On that account, both boys would fall into the category of neglected social status, suggested by researchers working with peer group life in classrooms (Bee & Boyd, 2009). Both boys struggle with school, and both boys are oriented towards other spheres of life. Mickey's passion is farming, and his best friend is an old farmer, whom he helps two to three times a week. He takes care of the crops and the animals, driving the tractor, and assisting in seeding. Farming is also the topic of his solitary play. Chris is oriented towards free time, playing with his little brother and their dog, and spending time with his family. These activities are unsupported by their peers as these occupations are regarded as childish and deemed as lagging behind in social time. The only subject in school the boys enjoy is sports, and in other scholastic activities, they are recognized as poor achievers, so their teachers are also critical towards them and think that they ought to be more interested in school learning.

Anti-Activities as Manifestations of Youth

In this 6th class classroom, becoming recognized as a young person requires participating in what I call "anti-activities," as these activities refer to the childish activities that they are replacing. The anti-activity of *talking* replaces the activity of playing among the dominant girls in the classroom. Bringing and eating lunch, doing homework, and being cooperative with the teachers have become controversial activities among those defining what is hot and not in the classroom, and the ways the children are affiliated with these anti-activities are paramount to their social identities as marginal or legitimate in the stratified social system. Talking with friends, expressing opinions, making jokes, gossiping, and discussing relationships and how others dress, and so on, are ways of making oneself visible as someone young in the classroom, but also refraining from eating lunch, refraining from playing, and refusing to obeying teachers demands are important ways of showing that one is no longer a small child (see also Frosh, Phoenix, & Pattman, 2002).

Not bringing lunch is practiced by the popular girls in the classroom, but some girls and all boys bring lunch and eat it. I ask Mickey how he feels about eating in this environment.

> **Mickey:** When I am at my mum's house it is no problem, but when I am with my dad . . . I make my own lunch, because if he makes it there is dog hair on it, and it looks disgusting. Then they'll tease you, that's for sure. So I hide my food and eat it quickly hoping that no one will notice.

Clearly Mickey risks being ridiculed when eating his lunch, indicating that the anti-activities practiced by the popular girls travel around the classroom and affect all.

Also in relation to performing well in school activities, the anti-activities set in during the last months of 6th class. Stanton Wortham (2006) and others (Davies & Hunt, 2000) persuasively show how academic performance produces and is co-produced by social identification, power relations, and interpersonal struggles in this age group. There is an interesting paradox in performance towards scholastic activities in the 6th class classroom. No one wishes to be identified as *not being able* to perform well in school—but the popular pupils choose not to perform well and are lazy around their learning showing that they don't care about it. The popular girls and a few of the boys master this social identity as pupils who are able to but are not willing to perform well in school. By refusing to do their homework and not hand in assignments on time, they are engaging in anti-school work, and thus they are "practicing youth." Mickey and Chris are in the unfortunate position of actually having difficulties in meeting school demands, and this is strengthened by their shyness. Their shyness is not only interpreted as stupidity, but is also often confused with submission to the teacher's demands; Caty expresses this connection:

> **Caty:** "I talk a lot . . . I talk all the time, not like Mickey who never says a thing" . . . (he does not reply), "but in reality he can speak up for himself, in breaks and stuff. He is not a teacher's darling" . . . (Mickey frowns and turns red).

Caty is actually flattering Mickey, creating a possible identity for him as someone more cool in reality, and the above quote is the nicest description of him I detected in the 6th class, but when Mickey refuses to take the role of the speaker in the dialogue, Caty acts as his spokesperson. Friends often take the position of presenting one another, but that happens in dialogue, not as in this case, where Mickey does not verbally respond. By talking on his behalf and with him not responding, they are jointly creating and reproducing Mickey as a nonperson in the classroom (Aronsson, 1998; Goffman, 1959). Chris sometimes achieves moments of recognition by his peers when the teacher scolds him for handing in bad assignments, and he explains that he has been too lazy to work with his paper, but this recognition is not outweighed by the ridicule he mostly receives from not being able to solve his tasks.

> They are working on foreign words in a Danish lesson. Chris asks Maria, sitting next to him, about the word *nuance*. "Don't you know the word nuance?" she asks sceptically. "No," he replies. "Have you never heard about nuance?" (she rolls her eyes. He shakes his head). "How can you not have heard of nuance? Like a blue nuance and pink nuance... It's French," she says (with annoyance and turns her back to him).

Also in relation to the activity of playing, the two boys are regarded as childish and behind by the girls in the classroom, as they still enjoy playing football and other ball games as well as computer games and even pretend playing. They only engage in pretend playing at home, and Mickey only reveals that he still enjoys playing in interviews, not in the classroom surrounded by peers.

> **Researcher:** Are you still pretend playing sometimes?
> **Mickey:** Yes I enjoy playing, but only at home. I play farming and I drive the tractor and pretend to seed and plough in the barn. But I only play alone and I don't talk about it.

Mickey keeps his playing hidden by not talking about it, indicating that he knows that playing is controversial among dominant peers; Chris is more open about his continuation of playing in his free time and also talks about it in front of the class, when asked what he is looking mostly forward to doing in his summer holidays, he answers, "I look mostly forward to spend time in the garden, playing with my little brother and the dogs."

In the classroom anti-playing is practiced by literally refraining from participating in ball games and ridiculing those who want to play them. None of the boys behave in accordance with the social representation of how to behave as a young person, since they eat their lunch, they play and fool around, and they do not obstruct classroom learning activities or question the teachers' authority. This positions them in social identities as childish, stupid, boring, and gross, and thus in marginal social identities. These identities are difficult to battle, since the boys are reluctant to speak up and defend themselves, and they have no friends who speak on their behalf.

The two boys are doing a minimum of preparation regarding the school transition compared to their female counterparts, but in interviews, both boys tell me that they worry about their academic performance, and they fear that they cannot live up to the greater demands in lower secondary school, and they are also both overwhelmed by the thought of the big school and getting to know everyone. Both boys fear ridicule and social isolation more than their bad academic performance. Also, both boys say that they mostly think about these matters because I ask them to do so in my interviews. Chris does not look forward to the new school life, but Mickey regards the transition as a chance for breaking away from his neglected social identity, and he wants to fight his shyness. He sets a goal for himself when voicing a hoped-for possible self:

> **Researcher:** What do you fear about Greengrove?
> **Mickey:** If nobody wants to be with me . . . and show me around and stuff . . . and if I don't get any new friends.
> **Researcher:** What would be the best scenario?
> **Mickey:** To get new good friends right away.
> **Researcher:** What about your friends from Heatherfield?
> **Mickey:** I would mostly want some new friends.
> **Researcher:** Like starting over?
> **Mickey:** Yes, starting over. I would like that.
> **Researcher:** How is that going to be?
> **Mickey:** I think I could be different, less shy and that.
> **Researcher:** Because you all start anew in Greengrove?
> **Mickey:** Yes.
> **Researcher:** If you don't say much it is maybe harder for people to get to know you?
> **Mickey:** Yes, it is better to talk more. Hmm, but I never put my hand up. That I don't.
> **Researcher:** Why is that?
> **Mickey:** I just don't want to. I don't want to speak up in class. But I know now that it is not so good, people think, the teachers think, that I don't know anything. . . . So, that is not so smart. . . . If no one else put up their hands, then I'll put up mine; if I know the answer, and then I can say it.
> **Researcher:** Ok. It matters to you that the teachers do not think you are stupid?
> **Mickey:** Yes, and Beth (class teacher) knows that I just don't want to speak. It is because I don't feel like it. She says I should try. . . . I am going to try in Greengrove.

As Mickey formulates a developmental project for himself, he also identifies his main problem as shyness. It seems also that he feels caught in his social identity in 6th class and he cannot change his ways before starting in Greengrove. During the interview, as he formulates a hoped-for possible self,[3] he decides that he is going to be willing to raise his hand in Greengrove, which is a step in the direction towards becoming more outspoken. It is clear that he is encouraged by his teachers to participate, but mostly both Chris and Mickey are "left to themselves" with their shyness and not forced to take part in classroom debates and plenum discussions in 6th class.

STARTING 7TH CLASS: THE QUEST FOR SELF-PRESENTATION

At the new school, the teachers, from the first day, make reference to how important lower secondary school is for the pupils' prospects of a successful adult life. The constant reminder about their future success or failure along with increased demands on the pupils' self-dependence in relation to school work is the teachers' ways of trying to enhance work ethics in 7th class. "We are no longer reminding you all the time when you are to hand in assignments. On this calendar all dates are marked, when you are supposed to hand in papers in maths and Danish, and we expect you to remember and follow these deadlines," the teacher says during the first week. The teachers thus actively support a concern for one's school achievements and self-dependence, which answers back to the already existing motives towards youth-life among the dominant pupils. The class teacher along with the teacher team in 7th class do their best to make incentives for the children to engage in learning activities, and it becomes more legitimate to take one's own learning more seriously. There is still a group of boys (particularly) who obstruct classroom teaching and do whatever they can to be noisy and naughty, but this behavior becomes controversial, and some of the new popular kids in class find their attitude childish and problematical. In other words, one of the central "old" anti-activities, that of anti-school work, changes in status and is not regarded as a marker of youth any more, along also with anti-eating, which is not practiced in 7th class. Disobeying teacher's and school demands is not considered cool, and refraining from participating in learning activities is sanctioned by both teachers and peers. In addition to a higher awareness of academic demands in Greengrove, the class teacher initiates several activities that demand self-presentation from the pupils. Among other activities, she asks all pupils to bring a personal item and explain to everyone why that item means something to them. This self-presentation happens in plenum where the pupils each present themselves and their item. Mickey brings a medal from his team in American football, and even though he speaks in very low voice, the teacher manages to guide him through a self-presentation in which it is obvious that he is into sports and the occupation of farming. She openly declares that she respects this as a proper activity from which you can learn a lot and create a self-sustained adult life. Chris has forgotten to bring an item, and he refuses to talk about it anyway, when the teacher encourages him to do the presentation without item. The class teacher then asks him to bring it the next lesson, which he agrees to, but this presentation in the next lesson is never actualized.

Mickey's Self-Presentation and Integration

Several factors are influential for Mickey's successful transition. It turns out that the new class teacher is a neighbor of the farmer who is Mickey's friend. On their first day in school, she tells me, "I know Mickey—he is such a good boy. He is such a nice person helping Old Martin at the farm. And a good farmer, I believe." The positive relation to his new class teacher—and Mickey's own decision to speak up more—makes it easier for Mickey to actually perform in self-presentations. He speaks up more than he did in Heatherfield, and he participates much more readily, even sometimes raising his hand, resulting in approval of his perspective on things. Compared to his peers in this classroom, Mickey is still among the least noisy, and he is cautious not to put himself in the spotlight to attract attention. Looking at him from the outside, he has not radically changed his ways particularly, but his efforts of making a little more of himself pays off, and he manages to get a new friend (aside from Johnny and Chris, whom he both knew already). Mickey settles in, integrates, and grows due to the new circumstances and new relationships. This is how he sees it (two months into the new school year):

Researcher: Do you think you succeeded in being more open and talkative towards others in this new classroom?
Mickey: Yes, I think so, actually! (smiles).
Researcher: Do you still find it hard to raise your hand?
Mickey: Sometimes, but in maths, I participate and in Danish, she asks me and then I answer.
Researcher: So you are not forgotten about in this classroom?
Mickey: Certainly not.
Researcher: You were sometimes a little forgotten in Heatherfield?
Mickey: Yes.
Researcher: How is it academically here?
Mickey: It is good, I am not the worst. And I think if they can do it, then I can do it, too. I don't know why, I am just attending much more. I also get more help here, with homework, both at home and in school. I am just as good as Johnny, Joan, Martin, and Chris in solving tasks and in math and stuff.

Mickey is in a fortunate situation of integrating into a more legitimate, outspoken, and participating social identity. He compares his academic performance with other poor achievers, which encourages his participation in classroom learning activities.

Chris' Self-Presentation and Marginalization

From the outset Chris meets with difficulties in the new classroom environment. He is more than one head shorter than most of the boys in Greengrove, who also seem to care more about their physical appearance and clothing, and who act more in youth-style and speak in deeper voices. Instead of playing ball during breaks, the boys from Greengrove stand in circled crowds talking or yelling loudly, competing and showing off, laughing and making fun of each other. Chris doesn't find a room in such a circle. As another major new condition, his teachers are critical towards his silence, and they demand of him to speak up. His behavior is very much the same as in the classroom in Heatherfield, but in Greengrove he is ridiculed by his teachers.

Two situations are mentioned here, because they jointly underscore his social identity as stupid and childish. This incident takes place six weeks into the school year:

> "You are supposed to be able to calculate like this in 7th class," the teacher, Corben, says to Chris with annoyance. "Ok, let's try it in another way then. What do you get in pocket money a week Chris?" "Nothing," he says. "Well then, what do you get a month?" "Nothing" (even lower voice). "Don't you get money for clothes then?" Chris only shakes his head now. "Candy-money?" Corben tries. "No, I get candy from my Granny." Corben looks lost, as he would have used pocket money as an example for his teaching and Chris proved a wrong choice then. "So you are not even allowed to have your own money!" he concludes with dissatisfaction. Chris looks embarrassed and frowns. Two other boys are eager to be taken as examples, and both are bleating that they earn their own money. Corben chooses Christian and uses his wages for the scholarly example.

Clearly the math teacher is disappointed with Chris, firstly because he does not know how to calculate at the level he is supposed to, and secondly because the scholarly example the teacher planned to make fails with Chris as he is not managing his own money. In this episode, the teacher identifies Chris univocally as stupid and childish. A few weeks later, another incident in which Chris is belittled takes place, now in an English lesson.

The English teacher, Natalie, comes in. It is the last lesson of the day, and she is annoyed. She scolds Maja and Miranda for the mess on their tables as the first thing; then she says, "This is the 6th lesson for me too," and sighs. "Repeat months and seasons with me," she orders. Christian mentions the three months of winter. She asks Chris to name the three months of spring. He shakes his head. She says (in English), "Christian named the winter months; December, January, and February, then what do you say?" He shakes his head again. She points at Simone. "March," she replies. "Correct," Natalie says. "And then what? . . . What comes next, Chris?" He shakes his head. "Come on, Chris! Don't you know, or don't you want to tell?" There is a thick silence, and everyone looks at him. Chris turns red and places the book on his head. "Put the book down!" she yells angrily. She waits and waits, and he is not answering. She gets mad and yells, "Don't make such a show! You have to open your mouth to learn the words." Complete silence in the otherwise noisy classroom. "Don't make such a show—you are too big for this now." Now tears are rising in his eyes and she quickly turns towards another pupil. "Rehearse it at home, Chris," she says without looking at him, as she asks Simone to name all the months.

After the first few months, and this last particularly humiliating episode, Chris becomes even more univocally introverted, and he refrains from social as well as academic interaction. In other words, his self-presentations fail in persuading others of a legitimate social identity. I notice that his peers call him lazy, and he himself explains his own disengagement as laziness on a few occasions in peer interaction. But in the new classroom, laziness entails not being willing to work, and Chris quickly earns a reputation as someone you wouldn't want to work with in a group for this reason. In the last interview I make with Chris I ask him about these issues:

> **Researcher:** I have heard that some people call you lazy.
> **Chris:** (He instantly bends over the table) Yes, he yawns.
> **Researcher:** Is that new?
> **Chris:** No, I don't think so.
> **Researcher:** Are you lazy as well at home?
> **Chris:** Mostly in school.
> **Researcher:** What is this laziness about?
> **Chris:** (long pause) . . . It is like if you feel like something, then you don't feel like it anyway.
> **Researcher:** (Pause) Would you not rather feel like doing stuff?
> **Chris:** Well . . . Yes, and at home I can do more.
> **Researcher:** What for instance?
> **Chris:** Today I am going to Granny's house to play with my dog, and I play computer. (his voice is light and little and sounds like a small child's)
> **Researcher:** What do you prefer, being with your friends or playing computer?

> **Chris:** I would prefer my friends, but I am too lazy now … to call
> them …
> **Researcher:** Are you maybe a little shy also?
> **Chris:** I am just lazy.

Chris was also sometimes identified as lazy in 6th class, but in that context, he gained moments of recognition on that account by his peers, because laziness was a way of showing disobedience to the teacher's demands, and part of the anti-activity scheme. For different reasons, laziness as part of his social identity in the new school takes on a different meaning: firstly, because laziness is no longer a valued attitude among his peers in the classroom, and secondly, because his laziness is not only directed towards schoolwork, but also related to refraining from doing things he would actually want to be doing, like calling friends. I suggest that the social identity of laziness is another way of dealing with shyness and fear of rejection. He refuses this connection between laziness and shyness when he responds, "I am just lazy." Why is it that he chooses to self-identify as someone lazy rather than as someone shy? This I suggest is due to the situational imperative of the transition: the demand for vocal self-presentation, made not only by new peers, but certainly also by teachers who no longer accept shyness as excuse for not taking part in classroom discussions. The demand for verbal self-presentation in plenum among new peers at the new school is overwhelming to him and I suggest also beyond his own control. Laziness, despite its obvious social disposition in 7th class, at least connotes some level of choice on his part, and maybe Chris manages to maintain some personal sense of agency by self-identifying as lazy, rather than shy, stupid, and childish, which are his other alternatives. The identification of Chris as lazy in the new classroom is not just a category circulating in the group—rather it becomes a reified "truth" about him as he also self-identifies with it, appropriates it, and self-presents as such in the school context.

DISCUSSION

Processes of Legitimization and Marginalization

The cases of Mickey and Chris exemplify the mutual transactional process of identification in microgenesis, in which the person himself and others jointly create developmental possibilities embedded in a social order, answering to particular social and institutional values. The examples also illustrate how the values of the social order change when the institutional setting, group, and pedagogical environment change. Processes of legitimization and marginalization are taking place and unfolding in situated action, but they cannot be understood without reference to the structural features of social life, connected to the institutional values and goals framing the interaction—in this case the goals of lower secondary school as preparing grounds for success in adult life. Being lazy was cool in 6th class, but regarded childish in 7th class as this becomes associated with a lack of concern with one's future as an adult. Circulating identifications of Chris as someone who is lazy shows how a set of utterances can become reified as an established truth about someone, when these identifications are not battled or denied by the person identified.

Both boys travel from marginal social identities in 6th class, but Chris' marginal social identity in Heatherfield is turned into a mocked one in Greengrove. His teachers work at belittling him, and without any close friendships among peers ready to speak up for him, take his defense, and circulate counter-stories about him, his social identity is defined as lazy. The teachers encourage a new work ethic, which among other things implies that they do not accept shyness as an excuse for not participating in classroom discussions. Consequently, some of the pupils take their scholastic activities more seriously, and being ambitious with one's own learning is no longer merely recognized as boring and childish. A new representation on how to become legitimate is finding its way into the 7th class classroom, which diminishes the old rules of the social order (the anti-activities). Mickey is in a position in which he is ready to grow along with these new conditions and is served in the legitimization process by teachers and friends, and Chris is not.

CONCLUSION

In this chapter, I argue that social identity construction during a school transition is negotiated around a particular set of virtues and values connected to how "being young" is supposed to be practiced. The workings of these standards are consequential to processes of marginalization and legitimization among the children, as some are deemed appropriate and legitimate and others lag behind and are identified as childish. Regarding social identities as rooted in activities and dialogically negotiated in microgenetic encounters of the everyday, identifications are communicated with reference to a social order drawing on social representations of youth.

Within an ethnographic field study, a group of 6th class pupils were followed in their last months of primary school and into a new 7th class in lower secondary school. The popular and influential pupils define a particular way of behaving as a young person as opposed to behaving childishly. The popular pupils prepare their transition using friendships as enlargements of selves in that process. Instead of playing, they are talking and hanging out, engaging in anti-activities (of anti-eating, anti-schoolwork, and anti-playing). The actualization of the transition into 7th class involves a quest, a clear demand that the children readily and loudly present themselves in order to become known to everyone. The quest for verbal self-presentation in plenum is a particularly challenging imperative for the shy pupils, and those children who for various reasons are able to speak up and become recognized as young people survive the transition socially, whereas those who don't disintegrate. This is illustrated with case material on two boys both traveling from marginal and neglected identities in 6th grade: The one manages to become more legitimate in the new school, not least due to a class teacher identifying him systematically in positive and appreciative ways, whereas the other boy receives a systematic negative identification by both teachers and peers in the new school. The role of teachers and peers as people who support or deny support in relation to legitimization is crucial to integrating into the new environment. Identification processes are interwoven with the fluidity of social action and a social order, which is undergoing changes in regards to which virtues are recognized as legitimate ways of participating as a young person. These changes in the institutional environment directly influence processes of marginalization and legitimization, characterizing the social system of the classroom. How participation in this system is experienced and managed I suggest is only detectable with a methodology open to investigating the children's participation in situated action, and reflecting their perspectives and meaning making regarding this action. The close connection between academic abilities with positive social identities in the peer group places a responsibility on the teachers to take into consideration how their identification of students may serve as legitimizing ridicule of particular persons. Counteracting children's anti-school activities and making incentives for replacing those with a motivation for learning and participating is a legitimate project, but unfortunately, the way the teachers do this undermines the possibilities for the shy pupils to integrate positively. I argue that teachers should not underestimate their role in relation to identifying the children in ways that are consequential for their social lives among their peers.

NOTES

1. Denmark has a policy of nine years' compulsory education including a reception class at age 6, and a voluntary 10th class.
2. Their names and utterances rarely appear, as they are hardly ever called upon by others or even mentioned, and since they do not often speak—they are almost invisible in my material.
3. H. Markus and P. Nurius (1986) introduce a concept of a hoped-for possible self, as a way of comprehending how people create anticipated self-images.

REFERENCES

Abreu, G., & Cline, T. (2008). Schooled mathematics and cultural knowledge. In P. Murphy & R. McCormick (Eds.), *Knowledge and practice: Representations and identities* (pp.189–204). London, UK: Open University Press.

Adler, P., & Adler, P. (2003). *Peer Power: Preadolescent culture and identity*. New Brunswick, NJ: Rutgers University Press.

Aronsson. K. (1998). Identity-in-interaction and social choreography. *Research on Language & Social Interaction, 31*(1), 75–89.

Bang, J. (2009). An environmental affordance perspective on the study of development: Artefacts, social others and self. In M. Hedegaard, M. Fleer, & J. Tudge (Eds.), *World yearbook of education 2009: Childhood studies and the impact of globalization: Policies and practices at global and local levels* (pp. 161–181). London, UK: Routledge.

Bee, H., & Boyd, D. (2009). *The developing child* (12th ed.). Boston, MA: Allyn & Bacon/Pearson International.

Christensen, P., & James, A. (Eds.). (2003). *Research with children: Perspectives and practices*. London, UK: Routledge Falmer.

Davies, B., & Hunt, R. (2000). Classroom competencies and marginal positionings. In B. A. Davies (Ed.), *A body of writing, 1990–1999* (pp. 145–164). Walnut Creek, CA: AltaMira Press.

Duveen, G., & Lloyd, B. (1993). An ethnographic approach to social representations. In G. Breakwell & D. Canter (Eds.), *Empirical approaches to social representations* (pp. 90–109). Oxford, UK: Oxford University Press.

Duveen, G. (2002). Psychological development as a social process. In L. Smith, P. Tomlinson, & J. Dockerell (Eds.), *Piaget, Vygotsky and beyond* (pp. 67–90). London, UK: Routledge.

Eder, D. (1985). The cycle of popularity: Interpersonal relations among female adolescents. *Sociology of Education, 58*, 154–165.

Frosh, S., Phoenix, A., & Pattman, R. (2002). *Young masculinities: Understanding boys in contemporary society*. Basingstoke, UK: Palgrave.

Goffman, E. (1959). *The presentation of self in everyday life*. New York, NY: Anchor Books.

Goffman, E. (1982). The interaction order. *American Sociological Review, 48*(1), 1–17.

Goodwin, M. H. (2004). The relevance of ethnicity, class, and gender in children's peer negotiations. In J. Holmes & M. Meyerhoff (Eds.), *The handbook of language and gender* (pp.43–68). Oxford, UK: Blackwell Publishing.

Greene, S., & Hogan, D. (Eds.). (2005). *Researching children's experience: Methods and approaches*. London, UK: Sage.

Hammersley, M., & Atkinson, P. (2007). *Ethnography: principles in practice* (3rd ed.). London, UK: Routledge.

Hedegaard, M. (2009). Children's development from a cultural-historical approach: Children's activity in everyday local settings as foundation for their development. *Mind, Culture and Activity, 16*, 64–81.

Hedegaard, M., Fleer, M., Bang, J., & Hviid, P. (2008). *Studying children: A cultural-historical approach*. Berkshire, UK: Open University Press.

Hermans, H. (2001). The dialogical self: Toward a theory of personal and cultural positioning. *Culture and Psychology, 7(3),* 243–281.

Hughes, L. (1991). A conceptual framework for the study of children's gaming, *Play & Culture, 4,* 284–301.

Hughes, L. (1995). Children's games and gaming. In B. Sutton-Smith et al. (Eds), *Children's folklore: A source book* (pp. 93–119). New York, NY: Garland.

Hundeide, K. (2004). *Børns livsverden og sociokulturelle rammer.* Copenhagen, Denmark: Akademisk.

Hviid, P. (2008). "Next year we are small, right?" Different times in children's development. *European Journal of Psychology of Education, 23*(2), 183–198.

James, A., & Prout, A. (1997). *Constructing and reconstructing childhood.* London, UK: Falmer Press.

Kofoed, J. (2008). Muted transitions, *European Journal of Psychology of Education, 23*(2) 199–212.

Markus, H., & Nurius, P. (1986). Possible selves. *American Psychologist, 41*(9), 954–969.

Moscovici, S. (2000). *Social representations: Explorations in social psychology.* London, UK: Polity Press.

Osterman, K. (2000). Student's need for belonging in the school community. *Review of Educational research, 70*(3), 323–367.

Turner, V.W. (1979). Betwixt and between: The Liminal period in Rites de Passage. In W. A. Lessa & E. Z. Vogt (Eds.), *Reader in comparative religion: An anthropological approach* (pp. 234–242) New York, NY: Harper and Row. (Work originally published in 1964)

Valsiner, J. (1997). *Culture and the development of children's action.* Hoboken, NJ: Wiley.

Winterhoff, P. (1997). Sociocultural promotions constraining children's social activity: Comparisons and variability in the development of friendships. In J. Tudge, M. Shanahan, & J. Valsiner (Eds.), *Comparisons in human development: Understanding time and context* (pp. 222–252). New York, NY: Cambridge University Press.

Winther-Linqvist, D. (2009). Game playing: Negotiating rules and identities. *American Journal of Play, 2*(1), 60–84.

Wortham, S. (2006). *Learning identity: The mediation of social identification through academic learning.* New York, NY: Cambridge University Press.

Zittoun, T. (2008). Learning in transitions: The role of institutions. *Journal of Psychology of Education, 23*(2), 165–181.

CHAPTER 12

COMMUNITIES OF CHILDREN AND LEARNING IN SCHOOL

Children's Perspectives

Charlotte Højholt

INTRODUCTION

To support children in some kind of difficulties in their school lives—as well as to organize conditions for the living and learning of children—professionals need knowledge about how situations look from children's perspectives. How does a child experience this situation, what is the child engaged in, what seems to be important from the child's perspective? Professionals often work to organize things in relation to optimizing children's life conditions and personal learning processes, but they do not know in advance how things work in the life of the children in relation to their activities and their personal engagements. As a consequence of this lack of knowledge, professionals confront situations where they do not understand the behavior of a child. How can research contribute to ways of dealing with this dilemma?

This chapter will discuss how a search for "children's perspectives" has turned my investigation to the *social situations* where children take part and where children relate to what is at stake to them. Understand how children

Children, Childhood, and Everyday Life, pages 199–215
Copyright © 2012 by Information Age Publishing
All rights of reproduction in any form reserved.

in different and personal ways experience situations in their lives, we may as researchers analyze their personal reasons for action in relation to their position in situated interplay. "The perspectives of the children" is conceptualized as an analytical concept in relation to anchoring personal meanings in social practice.

Consequently, this is also a way of dealing with the dilemma about how to relate children's personal subjectivity to the social conditions that they face in their personal ways. As we stated in the introduction to this book, the question about children's perspectives points to theoretical dilemmas about conceptualizing the inner connection between the child as an acting subject and the social conditions for the personal activities. Many variations of contextual approaches deal with this challenge, but we have found that neither the deconstructionist approach (e.g., Burman, 1994) nor the childhood approach (e.g., James, Jenks, & Prout, 1998) has sufficiently caught the relation between the situated activity of children's everyday life in different institutional practices and children's own engagements and perspectives.[1]

This chapter takes its point of departure in an understanding of human subjectivity as anchored in social and historical practice. Development of subjectivity is seen as an aspect of participation in social practice (for an unfolding of this approach to subjectivity see, e.g., Axel, 2009; Dreier, 2008; Holzkamp, 1987, 2012; Schraube, in press; Tolman, 1994; and for my interpretation, Højholt, 1999). The concept of practice gives a possibility to focus on *the dynamic between collective activity and a subject's actions* (for a background of the understanding of social practice this chapter builds upon, see Dreier, 2003; Hedegaard, Chaiklin, & Jensen, 1999; Jensen, 1987, 1999; Lave, 2008; Lave & Wenger, 1991; McDermott, 1993—and for my interpretation, Højholt, 2011). In prolongation of this, the concept of "the children's perspectives" plays a central part as a possibility for investigating what is going on within structures of social practice *in its personal meanings* for concrete children taking part here. To understand the child as a living subject acting, creating, and engaging in her life we need knowledge developed in an analytical intention of identifying meanings, engagements, and personal reasons from situated studies of social practices.

In order to grasp these connections, this chapter will draw on the theoretical concept of *participation* as a main concept to understand the relation between human beings and their social possibilities (compare Hedegaard, 2008; Rogoff, 2003). *Participation* is rooted in notions of "action," but I also want to conceptualize "acting" as "taking part" in something (cf. Leontjev, 1978). Children learn and develop *through their participation* in social practice together with other persons, and they constitute important developmental possibilities for each other.

Understanding the relation between children and their social possibilities is not just meant as a theoretical question but is indeed challenged from practical dilemmas about how we societally may organize our professional institutions for children and aim our professional support at the social interplay where possibilities for taking part are to be found.

While doing research in the manifold professional arrangements for the learning and development of children, it is striking that these arrangements are structured as though the question of learning and development is a kind of solo project—a solo project of a single individual, where other persons are often seen as people who may disturb, help, support, or make up models, representations for quite an isolated individual process.

At the same time, observations of children—on playgrounds as well as in classrooms—reveal their intense engagements with each other and their continuous efforts of relating to possibilities of *becoming part* of relevant peer communities, contributing to and creating activities within these—or disputing about the same (Højholt, 2008). More than anything else, the children seem occupied about each other in the observed situations; they enter the new learning tasks together, and they are engaged in the question of belonging. But in social processes of conflicts, powerlessness and mutual "giving up on each other," some children participate from marginalized positions.

The chapter draws on empirical examples from children followed during a two-year period through their transition from kindergarten to school and their starting school and their after-school center lives. The children were followed though participant observations in the classroom, the school yard, the playgrounds, and the after-school center and by interviews with groups of children and with their parents and professionals (teachers, pedagogues, psychologists). Drawing on this empirical material, children's perspectives, engagements, and personal reasons for acting are discussed. The discussions start with an example from observations of a child in difficulties and the professional support in relation to this. Trying to understand the perspectives of the involved boy turns the discussions towards more general considerations about how to analyze the activities of children, and how their personal significations and reasons are connected to their common life and possibilities here. In relation to this, I draw on more general material from the trajectory of the children, and based on examples of children's interplay in the period of starting school, I will focus on children's perspectives, and discuss the *general dynamics* and social movements between the children.

The implication of the research is discussed in relation to how to organize school practice and social service. When children are in difficulties, special interventions seem to concentrate on compensatory education related to individual children and isolated functions—and oversee the general challenges in the everyday lives of children. The chapter will illustrate how working with children's perspectives points to the significations of "the other children" to a child's personal learning process. To support children's learning, educational settings have to work with communities of learning and more specifically with possibilities of taking part in learning communities.

METHODOLOGICAL CONSIDERATIONS

The very concept of "children's perspectives" has consequences in relation to how to work with knowledge. This point of departure implies that knowledge is anchored in different locations and positions in social practices—that persons develop their perspectives due to their particular engagement in the world (cf. Dreier, 2003; Hedegaard et al., 1999; Jensen, 1987; Stetsenko, 2008).

As human beings we engage in a shared social world and therefore our perspectives are at one and the same time *different* and *connected*. We engage ourselves and arrange our lives in relation to common dilemmas, and therefore specific and personal experiences and perspectives may tell us about the general in all its variations (cf. Axel, 2009; Dreier, 2008).

Acknowledging this plurality, we as researchers confront a challenge in relation to working analytically with quite different kinds of perspectives originating from different locations in social practice. We need theoretical possibilities for *anchoring* the differences in social practice and for analyzing the basis from which subjects form their perspectives. The aim of this kind of analytical work is creating *general* knowledge through the variation of experiences from locations in structures of social practice.

More concretely, I find different "sources" for gaining knowledge about the children's perspectives that must be combined. An important source is to follow groups of children over time, getting to know them, their interplay, and their personal positions, engagements and perspectives—achieving insights into the conduct of life, activities, and social movements of children (Dreier, 2008; Kousholt, 2008). But the way we as observers place ourselves, the design we make, and how we participate in children's lives must be planned in line with the knowledge we want to create. In the present research, I was occupied with how children lived their lives across different general contexts (kindergarten, school, institutions, playgrounds, and families) and combined observing what the children did in these places, listening to what children talked about and seemed engaged in and aimed at, talking to children and interviewing the grown-ups of the children (their parents, pedagogues, teachers, psychologist, etc.), and participating in their meetings and exchanging about the children. In this chapter I concentrate on observations from the school and the institutions for children's leisure time.

When conducting observations, I tried to position myself in ways that made it possible to watch the children's play, dialogues, and social movements. This implies being close and free to move at the same time. Sometimes just watching, other times chatting with the children about what they are doing, and so on—being available for their questions and curiosity. Experiences from participatory child observations indicate that children are quite open to accepting a position of a grown-up who wants to learn about their life (for a discussion see, e.g., Epstein, 1998; Mandell, 1991)—as a girl told some boys who talked about whether the observer would investigate how naughty they were: "No, she just wants to know about how it is to join first grade."

The material also involves small group interviews with the children, where they chat about their different places in life (home, kindergarten, preschool class, institutions for children's leisure time, etc.)—and easily come to talk about friends, what is a close friend, what do they like to do together, and so on. During my observations, if the situations allow it, I ask questions about the trajectory from kindergarten into school, what the changes mean to them, and how they experience the different places, or questions closely related to what the children are engaged into in the very moment. It became my experience that we as grown-ups gain more information about the children's perspectives by trying to join *their agendas* rather than asking them questions based on our own. Still, we must experiment and further develop our methods for participatory research with children.

DIFFERENT CONCEPTUALIZATIONS OF LEARNING

The professionals working with the children are working within institutions where responsibility is distributed between places and parties—parents, pedagogues, teachers, and psychologists have the responsibility for different parts of the learning and development of the children. Interviews with the different parties in general illustrate *different* understandings of learning and development and different standpoints about how to help children.

However, especially when special help is at stake, even more professionals become involved and with them a more complicated distribution of tasks, methods and procedures evolves. And the more extra support the children receive, the more they also lose—to receive the "extra" means to leave something else, and in relation to this, I think we pay too little attention to the resources of learning located within the children's communities (Morin, 2008).

The children seem to be creating their engagements in learning together—and this applies to the more explicit learning tasks they receive from their teachers as well (Morin, 2008). The children seem to have a different approach to some of the academic tasks from what grown ups do. Even (as seen from the perspective of the observer) quite a neutral matter such as a letter can be the object for debate and demonstration of preferences: In a line of lots of E's that a boy has just written, he tells me with satisfaction, "This is my favorite E." The paradox is that in school, learning is organized as an individualistic project, where others are seen as some kind of competitors—competing about resources as well as achievements—or as disturbers, destroying the possibility for individual concentration. Still, you may observe lots of interplay, cooperation, and common engagement in the classroom.

> In a math lesson, the children in first grade are given the task of creating figures with rubber bands and small plates with sticks on. The children talk a lot about this task, help each other, show their results to one another, and so on. However, Martin does not have access to this possibility, since an extra teacher enters to sit beside him to help him. It seems as though the two teachers have quite different approaches to the task as well as to helping Martin. The assistant teacher says that she and Martin will do it their way.

> It is difficult to know exactly what happens in the dialogue between the extra teacher and Martin, but again and again they disagree about the task. It looks as if Martin finds that the extra teacher is not following the rules and especially: that she does not believe in what he says (between the teachers and Martin's parents there are huge conflicts—among other things about whether Martin lies or not). He looks as if he feels cheated and he argues, he gets angry and sad, and he gives up—just sitting watching the other children.

> The other children are working with concentration and are engaged with their figures, and they shout loudly for more rubber bands and show figures to each other. Martin tries once more, but again the cooperation between him and the extra teacher becomes deadlocked. This time, Martin becomes quite miserable and desperate. It seems that the extra teacher gives up as well. Martin sits on his own and the math teacher turns to Martin and tries to help him. As I have seen on other occasions, she combines insisting, pressing, and praising him—but maybe the most important thing is that she believes his explanations about what happened, and that they follow the same method. Anyhow Martin goes on, on his own, and soon shouts about his results and shows his result to the other boys.

What struck me in this episode was the boy's energy to try again and again and that he succeeded in "coming back" after several episodes of feeling lost and giving up on everything. I am interested in the opposite of "giving up"—all the small moments you as an observer may watch when participants succeed in their interplay in spite of conflicts and problems. That is why I include the last part as well—it is not to praise one teacher at the expense of another. In my observations of the situated interplay between the participants, I have found lots of trials, lots of openings and possibilities, but as processes become deadlocked in conflicts and powerlessness, it seems that resignations lead into more resignations and the parties do not even notice the attempts of each other. This seems to be characteristic to this example as well: Between the professionals, there is an ongoing exploration about how to understand and handle the problems they have with Martin—but in connection with this example, the teachers pointed to the situation as just one more proof of how "impossible" Martin is—"you saw it, he had a mental block."

CONFLICTS AMONG THE ADULTS AND POSSIBILITIES OF PARTICIPATION AMONG THE CHILDREN

With this example, I want to discuss several matters. First, the underlying disagreement about the methods, the procedures and rules in relation to learning—it seems that there is a disagreement about what the children are taking part in; the social praxis is ambiguous. Second, what the children are supposed to learn is not just results, definitions, and facts—it is a way of taking part in school life; they learn procedures in social practices and "how to arrange things," to "manage" here. Furthermore, and as a third matter: In the school context, some of the methods and understandings of learning seem to locate the social conflicts in the personalities and individual competences of the children (McDermott, 1993; Mehan, 1993; Mehan, Hertweck, & Meihls, 1986; Varenne & McDermott, 1998). The child becomes the problem, and the problems that the child himself experiences disappear. This leaves us with the question about the perspectives of the children—what seems to be meaningful to Martin? What is he occupied about, and what is he trying to achieve?

In the distribution of responsibilities, tasks, and contributions, it seems that the responsibility for the learning of Martin is more or less relocated to another place and to other persons than those who have access to Martin's possibilities of participation (such as, for example, special teachers in special interventions). This may be seen in continuation of individualistic understandings of children's problems as well as in the way we have structured our support.

Returning to the question about the children's perspectives the actions of Martin are difficult to understand without studying what he is participating in. Neither researchers nor professionals can understand his strategies without knowing something about the social interplay he is occupied with, involving himself in and finding a way of dealing with. Children's perspectives must be explored in relation to their *conditions* for taking part different places.

Like other persons, Martin is participating in social practice, and his reasons for acting can be analyzed in relation to his possibilities for pursuing his engagement in his particular situations (see Schraube, in press). Personal reasons are connected to something in life, and in order to understand the actions of a child we must explore what kind of activity these actions are part of, what it is that the child is engaged in, and what kind of dilemmas are related to this.

Observing the movements of Martin—in the classroom, the school yard, and the institution for the children's leisure time—I realized how often he tries to join a group of boys and how he is increasingly rejected. In relation to these processes, I started to explore *the other children's reasons* for withdrawing from Martin and found that these reasons must be analyzed in relation to the community of children. In this case, the class seems to be a more or less insecure community with frequent fights about the power and influence and with an agenda of sharp differentiations between those who were in and those who were not. This should not be taken to unambiguously. Observing children over time, you find developments of solidarity, friendships, and care as well as rejection, conflicts, and exclusion—what is important to the present discussion is that the dilemmas in the children's communities never become object for investigation, discussion, or consideration among the professionals.

Still, adults are *part of the social conditions* for children, and maybe the reasons for rejecting Martin are related to the fact that the grown-ups have many conflicts with Martin and especially *about* Martin. At the same time, where he "belongs" becomes at stake in the process where special arrangements are aimed at him as a person. Under all circumstances, the children do not have the same access to the learning resources among themselves, and it seems as if some children participate from marginalized positions characterized by *social conflicts.*

Children have different *access* to the kind of resources among the children that this chapter points to. They have different conditions in relation to becoming involved in communities of learning and participating in the engagements, structures of meanings, and experiences gained from taking part in such interplay. It seems that especially when someone worries about a child, they focus on interventions aimed at special, individual, and isolated functions and *overlook* the general challenges in the ordinary life where children live together with each other across different places with different things at stake. The *common* aspects of organizing a child's life across different life contexts, different activities, contradictory demands, social conflicts, and possibilities of engagements, fall out of focus.

To follow up on this discussion I will turn to some more general considerations from the observed children's interplay in the period of starting school.

SCHOOL START

Concerning the start of school, professionals in Denmark are occupied with how to prepare, receive, and orient each child individually. In this research I have explored what the start of school *means* to different children and how and why some children seem to have difficulties starting in school, learning how to behave—and learning how to learn. Politically, the benefits of the educational system have been a hot question—especially in relation to *where to place the responsibility.*

It entails, for instance, discussions about who should teach children what, whether children should learn more "school-like-things" in kindergarten and how we may support children in difficulties in relation to school—and especially how to make their *parents* responsible for supporting school at home and for delivering ready and well-behaved children to the school. The field of children is characterized by quite substantial disagreements between adults about the children (Højholt, 1999, 2006). This may be between parents and professionals, between different groups of professionals, and between politicians.

In relation to the school start, I was quite struck by *the engagements of the children* when I conducted group interviews and participatory observation in school. They did not seem to be occupied with the same questions as the grown-ups. As mentioned, the children seemed directed towards each other. Already in the first days in school, the children organized games together—even though some of them did not know each other; they talked, asked questions, and had fun together.

When the children were insecure about how to behave in this new context—what is allowed here, what is forbidden, what are we supposed to do now (the timetable of the school is a difficult arrangement to orientate in)—the children asked each other: What kind of subject must we do now? Even though the teachers made a lot of efforts to inform the children, to help them in the new setting, to explain the academic tasks as well as the rules for behavior, the children seemed *to use each other* as social resources more than anything else in relation to learning how to participate.

And the children were not just acting in relation to entering the new learning challenges together—they also seemed occupied with precisely these communities and how to belong there (cf. Stanek, 2011). They seemed to be occupied with belonging and with the different communities in school life. This is an important aspect about school life that is often overlooked—or is seen as *separate* from the agenda of learning, or even as something in opposition to learning (cp. Lave, 2008). The present analyses show that this kind of occupation of the children is not in opposition to the tasks of the school. The children enter the school, the new tasks and their learning processes together—engaging, investigating and contributing to the communities of learning in the school. Their common orientation processes may appear as noise from the position of the teacher but often the chatting is about the school tasks.

The point here is to argue that learning is specifically connected to involvements in social practices, and to contributions to the ongoing—and contradictory—changes of social practices. This extends work on learning connected to the concept of participation (in continuation of clarifications by Lave & Wenger, 1991; Dreier, 2008; Hedegaard, 2008; Rogoff, 2003). It is a theoretical effort to anchor personal learning processes in participation in social practice, contribution to and thereby influence on social practices. Learning is not just a question of acquiring competences—it is also a question of taking part in a common development of competences in communities.

Returning to the observations of the children and their social engagements I will emphasize how the children in school negotiate their communities, and work continuously to maintain, develop and influence their communities. In the observations I often heard the children appeal to connectedness: 'You are going to sit here, aren't you?' '*We* are going to make this together, aren't we?' The way the children enter the new context together and in one and the same time relate to this kind of practice and to each other might be illustrated by a short example:

> In the preschool class, there are often different activities going on at the same time. William and Peter play a game together on the floor. Jasper asks if he can take part, and that is okay. But as soon as Jasper becomes part of the game, he notices some appealing playing in the room next door—"They are jumping on the pillows in the next room, look, look, that looks like fun." William tries to avoid the dissolution: "No, it does not look like fun—we don't want that!" But he cannot stop Jasper and soon after neither Peter. Then William uses another argument: Peter has to tidy up! In that way William maintains the community, and after tidying up the boys join the other game together.

William has an insecure family background, and the professionals were very worried about how he would handle school life. So far he has surprised everyone by doing quite well and through the observations, it seems that his strategy is to relate closely to the friends he has from kindergarten and in general to participate from a powerful position among the boys.

As can be seen, the children constitute fundamental learning conditions for each other, and this small illustration of their situated interplay is also meant to illuminate how they actively act in relation to the possibilities, rules, and challenges of the school. They do not just listen to directives about how to behave and learn, they investigate, involve themselves in, reproduce and in a way "capture" the new contexts of their common life. And in this process, they explore their situations of life together, they engage in different activities and develop personal preferences together—and they learn how to take part together. In this process the children have to develop strategies for dealing with quite contradictory demands and engagements in their life, as I will elaborate on in the following.

DEALING WITH CONFLICTING AGENDAS AND ENGAGEMENTS

The trajectories of the children illustrate how the learning process of children is connected to ways of dealing with a plurality of agendas, different matters going on at the same time, contradictory demands, as well as different possibilities for engaging in relevant activities.

In the classroom, the teaching is quite a dominating activity, but when you observe the classroom from one of the chairs among the children, a lot of other things are going on at the same time. This may, as mentioned, be related to the teaching, as for instance when helping each other with educational tasks or studying the material together, but there is no unambiguous demarcation between these different matters: When some children engage a little too much in pictures from the book it may be discussed whether this is aimed at the teacher's agenda. Still, there is no doubt that when some boys turn their attention towards getting the football first, the teacher is not satisfied.

Some of the boys in my observations developed strategies for dealing with the school work in a way that will optimize their chances to get the ball first and thereby the best position during the break. William organizes his best friends to get ready for the break in time while he controls the access to the ball, telling the teacher when Martin touches the ball: "You are not allowed to do that—is it not so?" Martin seems to come under stress due to the double agenda—or to the conflicts he has with the teachers as well as the other boys; he touches the ball too early, cannot concentrate on the schoolwork, and ultimately does not get the ball.

Exploring social situations in school life from the perspectives of Martin and his classmates brought the analyses into general challenges in relation to taking part in different—and sometimes contradictory—activities and developing ways of conducting a social life across different contexts. The empirical material illustrates that the children in general confront these challenges and that Martin's conditions for dealing with these are especially restricted and conflictual.

In the period of life course where I have followed these children (about two years, from the end of kindergarten into first grade), the children develop close and continuous relationships, developing their way of taking part in school life as well as in other places. Of course I also witnessed breaks and changes in relations and constellations of children. For some of the children, these processes may be characterized by expanding personal limitations and developing their participation in the direction of *contributions to and influence* on situations of their life (cf. Haavind, 2005). Among other things, they seem to develop strategies for operating within the contradictions. Together, the children have to investigate *possibilities for participation, for engaging and for influencing situations* in their daily life. A search for the children's perspectives has turned the investigation into the social situations where children relate to what is at stake to them.

CHILDREN'S PERSPECTIVES

In this last section, I will sum up some theoretical connections in relation to my empirical work on children's perspectives. What do we refer to when we talk about creating knowledge through the perspectives of children? Is it just to listen to what they say?

It seems quite obvious that different persons are localized differently in relation to the same—and from different angles develop different perspectives and standpoints about what is going on. But in this way, the concept of the perspectives of the children challenges an understanding of knowledge as universal, unambiguous, uninvolved, and best created from the outside and often about children's inner needs, cognitive structures, and so on. On the contrary, the concept of children's perspectives points at knowledge as situated and differentiated; it originates from various locations, in particular structures of practice, and therefore it must be acknowledged as open and not as something final (cp. Dreier, 2008; Jensen, 1987; Lave & Wenger, 1991). This may sound quite harmless, but it is in contrast to the knowledge that we use in, for instance, making decisions about children (e.g., Røn Larsen, this volume).

These considerations turn the discussion about children's perspectives into a more general discussion about knowledge. Anna Stetsenko (2008) has formulated some general characteristics about knowledge, relevant to the way knowledge is anchored in social practice: "There is, in other words, no knowledge and no human being that exists prior to and can be separated from transformative engagement with the world including, importantly, other people" (p. 484).

In the light of this, knowledge is connected to *different* perspectives and different kinds of engagements in the world; and instead of judging some perspectives as more true than others, we as researchers need to analyze perspectives in relation to the different positions in social practices from where they originate. In this way, personal perspectives may add knowledge about how a social practice is experienced and meaningful from different positions and localizations—as for instance the particular positions of individual children.

Following that, *in order to contextualize the research about children*, we have to investigate how children live their lives, what children *do*, what different social contexts *mean* to them, what concrete children are engaged in, and what this looks like from their perspectives. And in order to understand the subjectivity of a child, the child's personal engagements and perspectives, we have to look not only at the child itself but also "from the child"—at what the child is looking at, occupied with, taking part in. A child perspective may be seen as a personal perspective *at* something *from* a certain position in social practice.

To be concerned with the perspectives of children thus represents a methodological argument about searching for knowledge from certain perspectives in children's social practice. This has become relevant since knowledge about children typically refers to discussions between grown-ups about what they—from their quite different perspectives—think is best for children. In these often quite *principled* disagreements, the question about investigating what situations, conflicts, and so on *mean to the children* seems to disappear.

In that sense, the intention with the concept about the perspectives of children is not to find something more original, true, or private about how children really are or think. But in relation to involving children as acting *persons* in their life, it must be acknowledged that they, like other persons, are *directed at something*. They do not just repeat, react or adjust—they take part, they want things, they do things, and they want something with the things that they do—as I have tried to illustrate with the examples.

Children have intentions related to their life and what is important to them here, and this calls for *situating* and "decentering" research in order to explore their personal reasons related to their engagement in concrete social situations with different things at stake. What these things may mean to different children we cannot come to know from the 'outside' (Schraube, in press).

Reasons are at one and the same time personal and social – they are related to the different meanings that social situations may have to different participants – from their respective social positions. In this way, the children's perspectives do not just tell us about children but about their *relations* to social situations and therefore about the social situation as well. For instance about structures for helping children in difficulties: Exploring the perspectives of children and their interplay generate knowledge about how children in a life across arrangements of help and general institutions sometimes have complicated conditions of participation *in relation* to these structures (e.g., Kousholt, this volume; Røn Larsen, this volume; Morin, 2008). This gives possibilities of exploring the arrangements we societal make for children—our teaching, our special support, our pedagogical efforts—in the light of how it works in the daily lives of the children and in relation to the daily organization of the children themselves. We may obtain knowledge about some consequences of our support arrangements of which we have not been aware (Højholt, 2011).

The children's ways of taking part in these arrangements, their perspectives and experiences may tell us about the conditions in which we place them, not as something stable and unambiguous but as something that the children—together—are acting with and thereby telling us what kinds of meanings these social conditions may have for them. Meanings that may vary due to changes in the conditions in the life of the children—children's perspectives are changing, insecure, influenced, and transformed (Schwartz, 2011).

CONCLUSIONS

Exploring everyday life from the children's perspectives leads to knowledge about the challenges, contradictions, and social conflicts they are engaged in dealing with and insight into engagements, possibilities, and attempts to overcome difficulties.

Analyses of children's perspectives point to the great significance children attach to the lives and learning processes of each other. Children are occupied with other children, and children make up important conditions to one another. Supporting children's learning therefore implies working with communities of learning and with *conditions* for taking part in relevant communities of children.

In continuation of the findings in the presented research, children's specific difficulties must be seen in connection to *general* and social contradictions and conflicts in their lives. The examples illustrate that the social conditions of the individual children for dealing with these general challenges in their everyday life are indeed not the same. The children take part in the same classroom from different positions and have different possibilities for influencing what is going on.

Still, widespread understandings of children in difficulties and professional practice aimed at supporting children in difficulties often *isolate* problems and support from everyday dilemmas and everyday contexts (as illustrated by the situations with Martin). In this way, the institutional organizations do not take the perspectives of the children themselves nor their special conditions for acting and pursuing their engagements into account.

Endeavors to assist children in difficulties are impaired by lack of knowledge about how situations in their lives look from their perspective. The professionals reflect on questions of how situations are experienced by different children and what situations mean to children, but in their search for understanding connections in the children's lives, they often have little access to situations between the children. Furthermore, the professional vocabulary is characterized by closed categories about inner deficiencies. If the professionals want to explore children's perspectives, they have to cooperate in an interdisciplinary manner, and not just cooperate about supporting a child's individual solo project of learning, but about possibilities of taking part in learning communities and different places.

In future research, we need theoretical developments that can support and inspire the professionals' daily explorations of children's concrete situations. Research and theoretical concepts should strengthen a situated search for the moments of possibilities that the examples illustrate. Especially in relation to the children's perspectives, we need a continuous and situated investigation of the interplay between children and of their dilemmas and challenges related to taking part in learning communities.

NOTE

1. This is not to say that such questions are not taken up elsewhere—see, for example, Christensen and James (2000) and Mayall (1994)—but in the present approach, issues about the involvement of children in the research and their situated way of engaging in their life will be addressed in relation to a psychological search for understanding of subjects in social practice.

REFERENCES

Axel, E. (2009). What makes us talk about wing nuts? Critical psychology and subjects at work. *Theory and Psychology, 19*(2), 275–295.
Burman, E. (1994). *Deconstructing developmental psychology.* London, UK: Routledge.
Christensen, P., & James, A. (Eds.). (2000). *Research with children: Perspectives and practices.* London, UK: Falmer Press.
Dreier, O. (2003). *Subjectivity and social practice* (2nd ed.). Aarhus, Denmark: Centre for Health, Humanity, and Culture, University of Aarhus.
Dreier, O. (2008). *Psychotherapy in everyday life.* Cambridge, UK: Cambridge University Press.
Epstein, D. (1998). "Are you a girl or are you a teacher?" The "least adult" role in research about gender and sexuality in a primary school. In G. Walford (Ed.), *Doing research about education* (pp. 27–41). London, UK: Falmer.
Haavind, H. (2005). Towards a multifaceted understanding of children as social participants. *Childhood, 12,* 139–152
Holzkamp, K. (1987). Critical psychology and overcoming of scientific indeterminacy in psychological theorizing. *Perspectives in Personality, 2,* 93–123.

Holzkamp, K. (2012). Psychology: Social self-understanding on the eeasons for action in the conduct of everyday life. In E. Schraube & U. Osterkamp (Eds.), *Psychology from the standpoint of the subject: Selected writings of Klaus Holzkamp*. Basingstoke: Palgrave Macmillan.

Hedegaard, M. (2008). Children's learning through participation in institutional practice: A model from the perspective of cultural-historical psychology. In B. van Oers, E. Elbers, R. van der Veer, & W. Wardekker (Eds.), *The transformation of learning: Perspectives from activity theory* (pp. 294–318). Cambridge, UK: Cambridge University Press.

Hedegaard, M., Chaiklin, S., & Jensen, U.J. (1999). Activity theory and social practice: An introduction. In M. Hedegaard, S. Chaiklin, & U.J. Jensen (Eds.), *Acivity theory and social practice* (pp. 12–30). Aarhus, Denmark: Aarhus University Press.

Højholt, C. (1999). Child development in trajectories of social practice. In W. Maiers, B. Bayer, B. Duarte Esgalhado (Eds.), *Challenges to theoretical psychology* (pp. 278–285). North York, UK: Captus Press.

Højholt, C. (2006) Knowledge and professionalism: From the perspectives of children? *Journal of Critical Psychology, 18*, 81–106.

Højholt, C. (2008). Participation in communities: Living and learning across different contexts. *ARECE—Australian Research in Early Childhood Education, 15*(1), 1–12.

Højholt, C. (2011). Cooperation between professionals in educational psychology. In H. Daniels & M. Hedegaard (Eds.), *Vygotsky and special needs education: Rethinking support for children and schools* (pp. 67–86). London, UK: Continuum Press.

James, A., Jenks, C., & Prout, A. (1998). *Theorizing childhood*. Cambridge, UK: Polity Press.

Jensen, U.J. (1987). *Practice and progress: A theory for the modern health care system*. Oxford, UK: Blackwell.

Jensen, U.J. (1999). Categories in activity theory: Marx' philosophy just-in-time. In S. Chaiklin, M. Hedegaard, & U. J. Jensen (Eds.), *Activity theory and social practice: Cultural-historical approaches* (pp. 79–99). Aarhus, Denmark: Aarhus University Press.

Kousholt, D. (2008). The everyday life of children across early childhood institution and the family. *Australian Research in Early Childhood Education, 15*(1), 13–25.

Lave, J (2008). Situated learning and changing practice. In A. Amin & J. Roberts (Eds.), *Community, economic creativity and organization* (pp. 283–296). Oxford, UK: Oxford University Press.

Lave, J., &Wenger, E. (1991). *Situated learning: Legitimate peripheral participation*. New York, NY: Cambridge University Press.

Leontiev, A. N. (1978). *Activity, consciousness and personality*. Englewood Cliffs, NJ: Prentice-Hall.

McDermott, R.P. (1993). The acquisition of a child by a learning disability. In S. Chaiklin & J. Lave (Eds.), *Understanding practice: Perspectives on activity and context* (pp. 269–305). New York, NY: Cambridge University Press.

Mandell, N. (1991). The least-adult role in studying children. In F. C. Waksler (Ed.), *Studying the social worlds of children: Sociological readings* (pp. 38–59). London, UK: Falmer.

Mayall, B. (Ed.). (1994). *Children's childhoods: Observed and experienced.* London, UK: Falmer.

Mehan, H., Hertweck, A., & Meihls, J. L. (1986). *Handicapping the handicapped.* Stanford, CA: Stanford University Press.

Mehan, H. (1993). Beneath the skin and between the ears: A case study in the politic of representation. In S. Chaiklin & J. Lave (Eds.), *Understanding practice: Perspectives on activity and context* (pp. 241–268). New York, NY: Cambridge University Press.

Morin, A. (2008). Learning together: A child perspective on educational arrangements of special education. *ARECE—Australian Research in Early Childhood Education, 15,* 27–38.

Rogoff, B. (2003). Development as transformation of participation in cultural activities. In B. Rogoff (Ed.), *The cultural nature of human development* (pp. 37–62). New York, NY: Oxford University Press.

Schraube, E. (in press). First-person perspective in the study of subjectivity and technology. *Subjectivity, 6*(1).

Schwartz, I. (2011). Professionelles forståelser af børns særlige behov [Professional understandings of children in difficulties]. In T. Egelund & T. B. Jakobsen (Eds.), *Døgninstitutionen. Modsætninger og strategier når børn og unges anbringes.* København: Hans Reitzels Forlag.

Stanek, A. (2011). *Børnefællesskaber i overgangen fra at være store børnehavebørn til at blive små skolebørn* [Communities of Children in their Transition from being big kinder children into being small school children]. Unpublished doctoral dissertation, Roskilde University.

Stetsenko, A (2008). From a relational ontology to transformative activist stance on development and learning: expanding Vygotsky's (CHAT) project. *Cultural Studies of Science and Education 3,* 471–491.

Tolman, C.W. (1994). *Psychology, society, and subjectivity.* London, UK: Routledge.

Varenne, H., & McDermott, R. (1998). *Successful failure. The school America builds.* Oxford, UK: Westview Press.

Lightning Source UK Ltd.
Milton Keynes UK
UKOW04f0734150414

230001UK00001B/1/P

9 781617 357343